Venus on Wheels

Venus on Wheels

TWO DECADES OF DIALOGUE
ON DISABILITY, BIOGRAPHY,
AND BEING FEMALE IN AMERICA

GELYA FRANK

UNIVERSITY OF CALIFORNIA PRESS
Berkeley   Los Angeles   London

University of California Press
Berkeley and Los Angeles, California

University of California Press, Ltd.
London, England

© 2000 by the Regents of the University of California

Portions of this book appeared elsewhere in earlier versions:

"'Becoming the Other': Empathy and Biographical Interpretation," *Biography* 8:3 (Summer 1985): 189–210. © 1985 by the Biographical Research Center; used by permission.

"The Ethnographic Films of Barbara G. Myerhoff: Anthropology, Feminism, and the Politics of Jewish Identity," in *Women Writing Culture*, ed. R. Behar and D. A. Gordon (Berkeley: University of California Press, 1995), 207–32. Used by permission.

"Jews, Multiculturalism, and Boasian Anthropology," *American Anthropologist* 99:4 (December 1997): 731–45. Used by permission of the American Anthropological Association; not for further reproduction.

Library of Congress Cataloging-in-Publication Data

Frank, Gelya, 1948–.
  Venus on wheels : two decades of dialogue on disability, biography, and being female in America / Gelya Frank.
      p.   cm.
  Includes bibliographical references and index.
  ISBN 0-520-21715-2 (alk. paper).—ISBN 0-520-21716-0 (pbk. : alk paper)
  1. DeVries, Diane.   2. Physically handicapped women—United States—Social conditions.   3. Physically handicapped women—United States—Biography.   4. Handicapped women—United States—Biography.   5. Handicapped—United States—Psychology.   6. Sociology of disability—United States.   7. Discrimination against the handicapped—United States.   I. Title.
HV3021.W66F73   2000
362.4´3´092   98-50444
[b]—dc21   CIP r99

Manufactured in the United States of America

08   07   06   05   04   03   02   01   00
10 9 8 7 6 5 4 3 2 1

In memory of
Hilda Kuper

Ethnographer, novelist, playwright,
biographer, teacher, friend

Contents

Acknowledgments

I thank some of the people who helped to sustain this long project and enabled me to write this book:

L. L. Langness for his intellectual guidance and generous support of my professional development; senior colleagues in the Socio-Behavioral Group of the Mental Retardation Research Center, Neuropsychiatric Institute, University of California at Los Angeles, especially Robert B. Edgerton, Thomas S. Weisner, and Douglass Price-Williams; Michael Moerman, Allen W. Johnson, and the late Hilda Kuper, Department of Anthropology; Melvin Pollner, Department of Sociology; and James Goodwin, Department of English, UCLA.

Eiichi Shimomissé, professor and founding chair of the Department of Philosophy, California State University at Dominguez Hills, gave his kind friendship and mentoring in phenomenology. I await the published version of his phenomenology, fortuitously also called the "mirror phenomenon."

Elizabeth J. Yerxa, professor emerita and former chair, Department of Occupational Therapy, University of Southern California, offered me an ideal academic home for this project. I thank Florence A. Clark, professor and chair, Department of Occupational Science and Occupational Therapy, University of Southern California, for supporting the writing of this book with a generous gift of release time from teaching, and for introducing me to the literature on child development and her work on the influence of childhood occupations in later life. I thank Ruth Zemke for taking on the patient task of educating me to the perspectives of occupational therapy and sharing materials on the life adaptation of people with physical disabilities.

Jeanne Jackson and Mary Lawlor offered helpful and timely comments on a draft of this book. Diane Kellegrew lent perspectives on resilience of children at risk. Diane Parham, Linda Fazio, Ann Neville-Jan, Anne Dunlea, Cynthia Hedricks, and Cheryl Mattingly provided collegial support for the project as it developed over time. John Wolcott gave gracious assistance with computer applications. Robin Turner, Janis Wise, Linda Wright, Stacy Payne DeArmand, Bill Ortiz, and Sarai Villagran assisted with many small but necessary tasks over the years.

I thank Carol Stein, presently Clinical Education Coordinator for Rehabilitation Medicine, West Los Angeles Veterans Administration Hospital, for countless stimulating and supportive conversations essential to this project through its many phases. I am forever grateful for her humor, sharp insights, and friendship.

I have also learned a great deal from graduate students in occupational therapy and occupational science, too many to mention. I especially thank Margaret McCuaig, Melinda Suto, Esther Huecker, Nancy Bagatell, Ruth Segal, John White, Heidi Pendleton, and Rebecca Chiu for their contributions to this book. I also thank undergraduate students Elizabeth Collins, Ericka Gutierrez, Edith Garcia, Keri Garcia, Melissa Herrera, Oralia Corral, Elsa Ramirez, and Corinne DeLuigi for their thoughtful and helpful comments on a draft of this book.

The late Barbara Myerhoff, professor and chair, Department of Anthropology, University of Southern California, encouraged me and led the way in combining ethnographic and life history methods, and opening the realms of narrative and reflexivity. G. Alexander Moore, chair of the Department of Anthropology, University of Southern California—as well as J. Stephen Lansing, former chair, and Paul Bohannan, former dean of Social Sciences—offered welcome support through a joint appointment and other kind accommodations.

Janet Hoskins and Nancy Lutkehaus have offered close friendship and many contributions to my thinking. Nancy Lutkehaus shared reflections on her fieldwork in Papua New Guinea, was an enthusiastic sounding board for changes in the scope and organization of this book, and inspired me to make the cultural dimensions of biographical image-making an explicit part of my definition of cultural biography. Janet Hoskins has been a constant source of helpful advice and encouragement especially in the final phases of the project. Her careful reading of drafts and revisions, her stimulating reflections on her own work with life histories and life stories, and the example of her admirable scholarship and elegant writing have been an invaluable gift.

As a fellow writer working with the interplay between life history and life story, Soo-Young Chin generously read and commented insightfully on an earlier draft. Patsy Asch, formerly at the Department of Anthropology, Australian National University, made valuable contributions through innumerable helpful conversations. Joan Weibel-Orlando, Eugene Cooper, and Andrei Simić supported me in various ways in my work on life history, including our shared guidance of graduate students. Arianne Gaetano, Gillian Goslinga, Erica Angert, Barbara Malcolm, and Carolyn Rouse provided helpful critical perspectives and lent their expertise in ethnographic film. Steven Lael Kurzman shared his fresh insights into disability studies from an anthropological perspective and also offered useful comments on a draft of this book.

I thank Harlan Hahn, Department of Political Science, University of Southern California, for offering a privileged view of the emerging disability rights movement through his guest lectures and conversations, publications on disability rights and disability culture, shared syllabi and reading lists, and thoughtful comments on a draft of this book.

For helpful conversations about disability rights, disability culture, and rehabilitation policies, I am grateful to Paul Longmore, director, Disability Studies Program, San Francisco State University; Carol Gill, director, Chicago Center for Disability Research; June Isaacson Kailes, former executive director, Westside Center for Independent Living; and Douglas A. Martin, former executive director, Westside Center for Independent Living, and present coordinator, Americans with Disabilities Act Compliance Office, University of California at Los Angeles. Mary B. Culbert, director, Disability Mediation Center, Loyola Law School and Western Law Center for Disability Rights, provided helpful advice concerning tenant law.

Adrienne Asch and Michelle Fine helped my work find its way to readers of the interface between feminism and disability consciousness, and Adrienne especially has been a source of continuing advice and inspiration. Conversations with Barbara Faye Waxman, Jenine Meltzer, Bonnie Sherr Klein, and Marissa Shaw helped move forward my thinking about women and disability.

Joan Ablon, professor emerita, Medical Anthropology Program, University of California at San Francisco, offered encouragement and mentoring in the anthropological study of disability. Sharon Kaufman has been a constant source of ideas and encouragement through our shared interests in life history and medical anthropology and loving friendship over many years. Gay Becker has given me generous collegial support at all times, including helpful comments on a draft of this book.

Arthur Kleinman, Judith Greenwood, the late Robert Murphy, Louise Duval, Joseph Kaufert, Jessica Scheer, Ronald Frankenberg, and Gerald Gold, colleagues and occasional editors, have helped to frame and support my approach to disability within the fields of anthropology and disability studies.

Yoshio Setoguchi, medical director, Child Amputee Prosthetics Project, University of California at Los Angeles, and the late Milo B. Brooks, founding medical director, gave helpful interviews about their first cohort of patients with multiple limb deficiencies. I appreciate Dr. Setoguchi's forbearance of criticisms of CAPP that are unavoidably part of this book and remind readers that the experiences of Diane DeVries and her cohort are only a small part of the CAPP story. Susan D. Clarke, occupational therapist at CAPP, provided valuable advice in accessing and interpreting the medical records and life experiences of Diane DeVries.

Craig Vick and Charles Jumps generously shared their insights and experiences as former patients at CAPP.

Robert Hahn, medical anthropologist with the Centers for Disease Control and Prevention, facilitated my contact with epidemiologists concerning the incidence of limb reduction defects. Richard S. Olney, formerly at the National Center for Environmental Health, Birth Defects and Genetic Diseases Branch, Centers for Disease Control, and now at the School of Medicine, Stanford University, generously shared and helped me interpret the literature on limb reduction defects.

Ruth Behar has offered unfailing encouragement and helped to midwife an earlier version of this book; I am grateful for her beautiful writing and courageous example as a "vulnerable observer." Faye Ginsburg helped sustain me with her confidence in this book over its long gestation and her many constructive comments and creative suggestions through its publication. Charlotte Linde, Tristine Rainer, Don Brenneis, and Meira Weiss shared friendship and offered useful references at just the right moment. Mary Catherine Bateson, whose creativity has been inspiring in the study of lives as a process of cultural adaptation, has given helpful criticism and warm personal support, not least reminding me that "one has to end a life history sometime."

Marianne Gullestad, James Olney, Sidney W. Mintz, Birgitta Holm, and Charlotte Heinritz contributed significantly to this book through enriching conversations at the conference "Constructions of Childhood in Autobiographical Accounts," held in Voss, Norway, May 10–12, 1992. I thank the Norwegian Center for Child Research, University of Trondheim, for its kind invitation and generous hospitality. With Fred Dallmayr I had a brief but very helpful conversation concerning empathy and *Dasein* at a conference on Heidegger, held in 1989 at the University of California, Berkeley. E. M. Broner provided loving support at an early stage in the project and offers continuing inspiration as a writer. I also thank Savina Teubal, Marcia Cohn Spiegel, Janet Carnay, Jane Littman, and Sue Levi Elwell for the warmth and buoyancy of our *mikveh* group as this book made its way into being.

Jim DeVries and Irene Fields generously shared their life stories so that Diane's could be told more completely, and Irene entrusted me with the family scrapbook for the duration of the project.

Naomi Schneider, executive editor, University of California Press, has offered enthusiastic editorial support. My thanks to project editor Jean McAneny for her patience and care, and also to Erika Büky for copyediting. Deborah Chasman at Beacon Press and Barbara Lowenberg also offered helpful editorial and publishing advice.

Laurel Anderson graciously researched the rights to reproduce the photograph of Frieda Pushnik. I thank Frieda Pushnik for her permission to use the photograph and Fred Dallinger, collections director, Circus World Museum, and James E. Foster of *The White Tops Magazine* for helping me find her. For their assistance with permissions that were particularly difficult to obtain, I also thank Julie Shaperman, formerly of CAPP; Shari Faris, Legal Affairs Department, UCLA; Gina Lubrano, *San Diego Union-Tribune*; and Bob Andrew, chief librarian, Bernice Romo, and Rich Archbold, *Long Beach Press-Telegram*.

Lois Halpern offered loving family support and lent her skills as a copy editor. Betty Macías, Eric Eisenberg, Laurie Levin and Peter Butterfield, Leslie J. Blackhall, R. Ruth Linden, Laura Larson, Robert Gottlieb and Marjorie L. Pearson, Marjorie K. Toomim, Robert E. Brooks, Haim Dov Beliak, and Richard Frank all listened, cared, and gave good advice.

Finally, I thank those to whom I owe the very most:

My parents, Betty and the late Charles Frank, for their love and devotion, especially their support for my education and their wish for me to have opportunities surpassing their own. I hope this book finds its place among the spy novels and Westerns on my father's night table in heaven.

Marita Giovanni and my daughter, Rebecca S'manga Frank, for a very happy family life, freeing my energies for the final push. I thank Marita also for her excellent editorial advice and other contributions to the pleasant completion of this project.

George Vilakazi and Kim Thomas for sharing the responsibilities of raising "the girl" and building a harmonious extended family.

Most of all, I thank Diane DeVries, with admiration and affection, for our long and productive collaboration. Now that I am through copying down everything you say, I look forward to our discovering "eachother" in new ways.

The dissertation phase of my research was sponsored by a University of California Regents Fellowship and by grants from the Department of

Anthropology, UCLA. Portions of this book were written with the support of a three-year grant to the Department of Occupational Science and Occupational Therapy from the American Occupational Therapy Foundation, establishing a Center for Scholarship and Research in Occupational Therapy at the University of Southern California.

1 My Introduction to Diane

In 1976 I began writing about the life of Diane DeVries, a woman born with all the physical and mental equipment she would need to live in our society—except arms and legs. I was then twenty-eight years old and a graduate student in anthropology at the University of California, Los Angeles. Diane was twenty-six and an undergraduate major in sociology. It was the spring quarter, and Diane was enrolled in the large introductory lecture course on cultural anthropology, for which I was a teaching assistant. From my vantage in the back of the lecture hall I watched a blond woman enter the classroom in an electric wheelchair. She looked to be in the fullness of womanhood, wearing a sleeveless white top with narrow straps. Her tapered arm stumps seemed daringly exposed, and the mysterious configuration of her hips was encased in tight blue jeans that ended where her legs should have begun. She maneuvered her wheelchair with a lever control mounted on one side to face the lectern. Leaning on a wood and Plexiglas desk fitted over her chair, she took notes holding her pen between arm and cheek.

As I observed this woman, I imagined that she lived at home with her parents in a sheltered and socially isolated household. I supposed that she would never marry or have sex. I guessed that she couldn't even masturbate. In short time I was proved wrong on all these counts, and perhaps I should not have been surprised. There was something of the sexual rebel in Diane's appearance, a touch of the "bad girl" that may have engaged my voyeurism and sexual fantasies at the same time that I tried to suppress and ignore them. My preoccupation with Diane's ability to marry and have sex revealed much more about me than about Diane. I hadn't met her. I didn't even know her name.

This book records the relationship that developed between Diane and me over the next twenty years. It is an experiment I call cultural biography, which combines the genres of ethnography and life history. Ethnography is the cultural anthropologist's stock-in-trade, a firsthand description of a people's way of life.[1] Unlike the early anthropologists, whose published works often consist of cultural inventories and static generalizations about the people they studied, contemporary anthropologists tend to write narrative ethnographies.[2] These are stories based on events we have experienced—more as observing participants than as participant observers— through which we try to convey how people within a particular group or tradition create meaningful solutions to life's challenges. Here I tell a story based on my observations while participating in Diane's life for more than two decades. Reflexivity, which has important precedents in ethnography, has been defined as "the capacity of any system of signification to turn back upon itself, to make itself its own object by referring to itself."[3] This narrative ethnography experiments with putting the emphasis on reflexive issues: how I came to understand Diane, how working with her transformed my understanding of her life, and how our collaboration may have influenced the life story Diane has to tell.

The life history is a related anthropological genre that traces how a culture influences the experiences of a specific individual.[4] Most life histories consist of autobiographies or life stories in the oral tradition. My research about Diane, which has been published in numerous journal articles and book chapters over the years, includes her life story as told to me in formal interviews.[5] My data also include documents, such as letters written by Diane, her unpublished autobiography, and her clinical records; interviews with key people in her life; informal conversations; and my firsthand observations. I focus equally on retrospective and contemporaneous materials, deliberately moving back and forth between Diane's narrated recollections and her observed actions.[6]

Cultural biography, then, is a synthesis of ethnographic and life history methods by which I have enhanced my understanding of both Diane DeVries and the culture to which she belongs. Diane's life is a powerful exemplar of changes in mainstream American culture during the second half of the twentieth century. I will argue that she offers a *perfect* example of an American woman of her era, especially regarding the position of people with disabilities. Diane's early life trajectory, starting with her birth in 1950, coincided with the peak of the American medical profession's cultural authority to define normalcy and deviance.[7] The technical approach of biomedicine to biological, social, and moral problems coalesced into the new specialty of rehabilitation that was founded at the end of World War II.[8] Much of Diane's childhood was dominated by surgeries and therapeutic regimens prescribed by physician-led rehabilitation teams. At the same time, Diane experienced a life fairly typical for a child raised in Long Beach, in a trim grid of single-family tract houses that was the prototypical American suburb. By the time Diane finished high school in 1968, she had effectively resisted being defined by the heavy impress of institutionalized medicine and had abandoned the artificial arms and cosmetic legs with which she had been supplied. Such antiauthoritarian attitudes and behaviors were becoming increasingly common among young adults with disabilities. Influenced by the gains of the women's and civil rights movements, a full-fledged movement for independent living and disability rights was emerging that was to have a profound effect on Diane's life and on American culture.

My reflections on reconstructing Diane's life provide the basis for a theory of biographical interpretation in daily life that I call the mirror phenomenon. When I first noticed Diane, I had no special interest in studying disability. But I was attracted to phenomenology, a branch of philosophy that deals with the problem of intersubjectivity—that is, how people understand one another. My fascination with Diane prompted me at once to explore the sources in myself that made the image of a woman without limbs so intriguing. Through systematic self-reflection I probed my identification and empathy with her situation, uncovering my own invisible disabilities and then disentangling them from the way Diane sees herself.

Impressions of others' lives have an important element of empathy or mirroring that needs to be identified so that understanding (in philosophy, *Verstehen*) can take place. The *Verstehen* approach rests on three principles:

1. All human manifestations are part of a historical process and should be explained in historical terms. The state, the family, even man himself cannot be adequately defined abstractly because they have different characteristics in different ages.

2. Different ages and differing individuals can only be understood by entering imaginatively into their specific point of view; what the age or the individual thought relevant must be taken into account by the historian.

3. The historian himself is bound by the horizons of his own age. How the past presents itself to him in the perspectives of his own concerns becomes a legitimate aspect of the meaning of that past.[9]

Empathy has been central to the *Verstehen* tradition in modern American anthropology since its inception by Franz Boas, its popularization by Ruth Benedict and Margaret Mead, and the "interpretive turn" in the discipline in recent decades, led by Clifford Geertz. Attempts to clarify empathy, or the mirror phenomenon, can help to undermine oppressive practices that turn diversity into alienating "difference." Paradoxically, they also help in respecting the "difference" of disability—difference that must be recognized so that people like Diane who need accommodations can continue to gain independence through social and political action.

My first decade of getting to know Diane DeVries, from 1976 to 1987, was a period marked by her marriage and her college graduation. Diane had met her husband-to-be, Jim DeVries, a good-looking Vietnam War veteran, just after finishing high school in 1968. Having lived together and then apart, they reunited, moved to Oakland, and married in 1978. Diane attended the University of California at Berkeley, the mecca of the independent living and disability rights movements and a vortex of feminist activity. Jim's problems with alcohol and his abusiveness when drunk led Diane to return alone to Southern California. Rebuilding her life in the Long Beach area, Diane was forced to reside in a convalescent home. Although Jim soon followed her to Southern California, he was still drinking. In 1980, Diane filed for divorce. She began attending services at a fundamentalist church and was "born again." I remember standing with the congregation to witness Diane's baptism by total immersion in the swimming pool of an apartment complex with a steep red roof like an IHOP restaurant. At Diane's urging Jim began attending church, and the following year he was saved and delivered of alcohol. Diane left the convalescent home to resume married life with him.

Thus began a long, stable, and rewarding phase of marriage for Diane and Jim: "seven good years," as Diane later described it. They participated energetically in their church community, attending Bible school daily, and planned to enter the ministry. But they became disillusioned with the church leadership—in fact, furious at its hypocrisy when their pastor denied Diane membership in the choir because having Diane on stage "wouldn't look good." Diane returned to UCLA with Jim as her driver and attendant, a job he supplemented by driving a cab. They took holidays together, including a great vacation in Hawaii. In June 1987 Diane graduated with a bachelor's degree in sociology.

In the next decade Diane completed graduate school and began her professional career. In 1988 she entered the master's program in clinical social work at the University of Southern California (where I was by then a faculty member in the departments of occupational therapy and anthropology). She and Jim lived near the ocean in Redondo Beach. They had stopped attending regular church services and instead considered themselves members of a TV ministry. While Diane focused on clearing the next hurdle toward a professional career, however, Jim began to drift. He now usually drank a glass or two of wine with dinner, discounting his history of alcoholism. One night in May 1988 he failed to come home from work, leaving Diane stranded without an attendant. When he finally called, he said he wanted to split up. They had nothing in common anymore, he said. He was "burned out" from caring for Diane and felt he had no life of his own. Jim's problems with alcohol worsened, and, as he later revealed, he was also feeding a cocaine habit. He lost his driver's license and his job. Diane moved to a campus apartment that was adapted with wide doorways for wheelchair users.

Fighting fears of ruining her credibility as a serious student, Diane talked to a supportive adviser at the School of Social Work about her situation. The adviser arranged for Diane to receive a scholarship and encouraged her to switch temporarily to part-time student status. Jim lived in their van until he sold it to buy drugs. Then he dropped by, stole the keys to the new van that the Department of Vocational Rehabilitation had provided Diane for doing fieldwork, and left town. As Diane grieved for their marriage, she was overwhelmed by the logistical challenges of finding attendants and drivers, attending classes, writing papers, attending therapy and doctors' appointments, and dealing with wheelchair breakdowns. Within weeks she landed in the hospital with an asthma attack. Back at home, she found herself crying uncontrollably and contemplating suicide. Following her therapist's advice, she wisely let herself be treated for depression over the next two months at Parkside West, a locked psychiatric unit, in the outlying city of Covina.

Diane and Jim eventually reconciled and even moved to Utah to make a fresh start, but by the end of 1989 their marriage was over. Diane returned to Long Beach with a sizable loan from a wealthy friend who was also a local community leader in disability affairs. Through another friend at UCLA, Diane found work as a hospital discharge planner, but she was almost immediately fired, in a flagrantly discriminatory manner, because of her disability. She filed suit under California law and received a settlement. In 1991, Diane established herself in an apartment with an attendant near the newly built Metro Blue Line between Long Beach and downtown Los Angeles, which ran close to USC. She returned to graduate school and began a research project on the self-esteem and sexuality of adolescents with disabilities.

In June 1992, Diane met and fell in love with a handsome accountant and musician introduced by a coworker during fieldwork at an agency serving African Americans with AIDS. Her summer was very happy. I knew little else about Diane's life that year; my contact with her was devoted to resolving our disagreement over interpretations of her life that I had presented in a conference paper (described in a later chapter). In May 1993, Diane was awarded her master's degree in clinical social work from USC. Among the dozen or more celebrants at her "Emancipation!" party later that day at the Ports O' Call restaurant, Diane's boyfriend was notably absent. Things had not worked out, although Diane was having a hard time shaking him.

Straight out of graduate school, Diane was offered a job as a clinical social worker at Partners, a city-funded agency in West Hollywood that assisted senior citizens and gay men with AIDS. Diane loved the work and was rewarded with the esteem of clients and colleagues. In 1994, however, Partners lost its funding. She moved back to Long Beach. A series of crises kept Diane in hospitals and out of the labor market. When she needed to face down her landlord over an eviction notice in the summer of 1996, I became Diane's publicist. The story, broadcast on radio and TV, emphasized "how far Diane had come" and her need, not for charity, but for an appropriate job. Perhaps I was naive not to expect the gifts of cash that poured in, but what pleased me most was Diane was indeed offered a job, which she accepted, as a professional social worker.

In the early months of my relationship with Diane, before these and many other events unfolded, I was busy grinding my academic lenses, focusing my fantasies and projections about Diane into questions suitable for Ph.D. research. What were Diane's experiences of her body and self? What kind of life could she have in our society? More urgently, I wanted to know what it would mean to understand just one other person, a question of basic sanity that I needed to explore and answer.

Professionally, such a topic still seemed risky in the 1970s. As Sherry Ortner has written, "When I was in graduate school in the sixties, it was virtually unheard of to get the blessings of the department (not to mention a grant) to do American fieldwork."[10] Writing about Diane obliged me on numerous occasions to account for my choices not only to remain in the United States but also to study only one individual. Such accounting enabled me, however, to explore and make visible my own painful experiences and hidden disabilities. Without performing that groundwork, I saw little point in traveling to any of the remote places to which my teachers and fellow students had chosen to go. With what sense of myself could I do that? And with what illusion of helping whom?[11]

The image of a graduate student in anthropology letting her gaze fall upon (and penetrate) Diane from a seat high in a lecture hall calls up a colonial (and patriarchal) era in the profession. A static snapshot of the past can be distorting, however. Just as there is no timeless "ethnographic present" for the people anthropologists study, anthropologists and their work are also products of history.[12] This book and its strategies for representation depend on processes of understanding over time. In the mid-1970s, Diane and I were women in our twenties influenced by the rising "second wave" of feminism. We were also engaged, respectively, with the disability rights movement and a movement in anthropology to recognize more fully the interests and voices of the often disempowered people whose lives were studied.

One anthropologist who attempted to give a voice to others and preserve their stories was Barbara Myerhoff, whose book *Number Our Days* is a remarkably life-affirming ethnography about a dwindling community of elderly Jews in Venice, California. One of the people Myerhoff interviewed was Shmuel, who had come to the United States from Eastern Europe early in the century, when pogroms against Jews were commonplace but before the Holocaust. He reminisced with Myerhoff about life in his childhood town in Poland before it was "wiped out like you would erase a line of writing":

> As long as my eyes are still open, I'll see those beloved people, the
> young, the old, the crazy ones, the fools, the wise, and the good ones. I'll
> see the little crooked streets, the hills and animals, the Vistula like a sil-
> ver shake winding in its beauty, and then I fall into a dream. It's a dream
> you can feel, but you cannot touch it. . . . All is ended. So in my life, I
> carry with me everything—all those people, all those places, I carry
> them around until my shoulders bend. I can see the old rabbi, the work-
> ers pulling their wagons, the man carrying his baby tied to his back,
> walking up from the Vistula, no money, no house, nothing to feed his

child. His greatest dream is to have a horse of his own and in this he will never succeed. So I carry him.

And he explained: "It is not the worst thing that can happen for a man to grow old and die. But if my life goes, with my memories, and all that is lost, that is something else to bear."[13]

Marjorie Shostak, author of the exemplary life history *Nisa: The Life and Words of a !Kung Woman,* further articulated the goals of promoting tolerance and understanding cultural differences that guided Myerhoff's work and her own. In reflections written eighteen years after her relationship had begun in 1969 with Nisa, a tribeswoman of the Kalahari Desert, Shostak urged:

> It is for Shmuel, Nisa, and the silent others they represent, as well as for ourselves, that we should continue to record these lives and memories. The ethical and methodological problems may be formidable, but they are small compared to the goal. Indeed, the most important ethical message regarding life histories is not a restriction but an obligation: we should make every effort to overcome obstacles, to go out and record the memories of people whose ways of life often are preserved only in those memories. And we should do it urgently, before they disappear. . . . As we cast our net ever wider, searching for those close as well as those far away, the spectrum of voices from otherwise obscure individuals helps us learn tolerance for differences as well as similarities. What better place to begin our dialogue about human nature and the nature of human possibilities?[14]

The life history method, through which individuals tell their own stories, is more than a tool for salvaging memories, however. Unlike most reports by social scientists or those found in commercial media, first-person narratives have the power to "liberate the subject" of history to express and represent herself in her own terms.[15] I first knew the excitement and power in gaining a voice when L. L. Langness, my thesis adviser, invited me to collaborate in revising one of his books, a standard reference on the life history method.[16] Lew made it a general practice not to edit what I had to say, although sometimes we disagreed hotly. On one such occasion, I remember striving to convince Lew, then editor of *Ethos,* a journal of psychological anthropology for which I was editorial assistant, to implement the policy of using nonsexist language adopted in a 1974 resolution by the American Anthropological Association.

"Everyone who speaks English knows that *he* includes women," Lew objected.

"Women don't see themselves when they read *he*," I insisted. "Growing up, when I read *he*, I pictured a boy."

Lew had done his field research in Papua New Guinea. "Look, Lew," I said. "You went halfway around the world to listen to the natives. Why won't you believe what women tell you here?"

The policy was adopted and I carried it out with a certain fervor—striking sexist usage in manuscripts, demanding that authors clarify their meaning concerning women, triumphantly inserting "people" everywhere that "Man" had been.

In the introduction to our jointly authored book, *Lives: An Anthropological Approach to Biography*, I wrote:

> In finding ways to give voice to persons in a range of societies—many of them members of subgroups shuffled about in the continual struggle of class interests and shifting national alliances—anthropologists who use the life-history method convey directly the *reality* that people other than themselves experience. But we do not want to dwell exclusively on the idea that other worlds are miles away or in some enclave—religious, geographical, or ethnic. Getting to know any person in depth is a major experience because we have to admit that another way of structuring the world truly exists.[17]

Now, two decades later, my claims about the life history method may be put to the test. First, at the outset I suggested that as an anthropologist I could "give voice" to Diane. In retrospect, I ask myself, Didn't she have a voice already? Did she need my help to be heard? And, if I have helped Diane to reach certain audiences, what has been their reaction? Has Diane's voice changed in the course of our long conversation? Has she been merely an informant, passive and compliant, recounting her experiences to me? Or an agent who has actively constructed her life in the telling? What uses has Diane made of the opportunity to tell and retell the story of her life?

Second, I claimed that a life history could convey the reality of experiences such as Diane's better than other kinds of reporting. Many critical and feminist anthropologists now argue that the use of life histories and life stories, compared to other kinds of ethnographic texts, is the most effective way to challenge stereotypes and correct misrepresentations of others' lives. Some go further and reject the life history approach in favor of the seemingly more egalitarian life story. They define a *life history* as an account constructed by an ethnographer that consists of data about the subject's life, whereas a *life story* is the subject's own self-construction.[18] Could I portray the reality of Diane's experience "directly"? Since I acted as interviewer and editor, wasn't Diane's story mediated, perhaps even tainted, by my reporting?

Finally, I claimed that studying the life of any individual raises the possibility of encountering new ways of structuring the world. But this statement is problematic from the standpoint of anthropology. Doesn't a focus on one individual's uniqueness undercut the greater significance of a shared or common culture? Is Diane's world really so different from mine? What cultural influences have shaped her life, and what permits me to understand them? Is there a separate culture of disability? Is Diane interesting only because of her physical difference? Is she a different kind of woman because she lacks arms and legs? What exactly is different about Diane, compared to what or to whom?

2 The Crisis of Representation

WHY IT IS TIME FOR CULTURAL BIOGRAPHY

As I was choosing to study and write about Diane's life in the 1970s, a major shift was occurring in American anthropology. Many researchers were turning to the study of communities and issues in the United States. This movement in the discipline responded, in part, to calls for social relevance and activism in the 1960s.[1] It was also influenced by economics, as federal grants for research abroad were drying up. Many studies during this period were written from a critical viewpoint to help unmask and transform forces of political, economic, and social oppression.

Barbara Myerhoff's research for her celebrated book and ethnographic film, *Number Our Days*, was conceived in this critical climate, even if it was not primarily motivated by its ideals.[2] Myerhoff claimed that she undertook her study about the aging community of Yiddish-speaking Jews of the Israel Levin Center, in Venice, California, because she expected someday to be a "little old Jewish lady."[3] But there was more to the story. As a doctoral student, Myerhoff had conducted research in Mexico among the Huichol Indians. Her book *Peyote Hunt: The Sacred Journey of the Huichol Indians* received a National Book Award nomination. Later, in her forties, married and raising children, Myerhoff turned to the cultural study of aging. She approached members of the Chicano community in Los Angeles, where she hoped to put her fluency in Spanish to good use. She was met, however, with a challenging response: "Why don't you study your own people?"[4] Myerhoff's acceptance of this challenge eased the entrance of anthropologists into American studies. Perhaps more important, it helped to legitimate an emerging style of research known as "native anthropology," in which researchers studied the familiar with methods designed to make sense of the strange.[5]

By the mid-1980s, in a mood of heightened self-consciousness, a handful of scholars were leading the discipline in using methods and theories of literary criticism to cast ethnography less as an empirical science than as a form of cultural criticism.[6] Their questioning of ethnographic authority has made it impossible to read or write critically without considering whose voices and interests are being constructed, and whose suppressed, within the text. The success of this approach has resulted in a frenzy in the social sciences that threatens to invalidate every possible strategy of ethnographic narration.

Some hardliners in the crisis of representation—mainly non-anthropologists, of course—argue that no one but the natives, those whose lives are at stake in ethnographic descriptions, should have the right to speak authoritatively.[7] Ethnographic fieldwork, the prime contribution of modern anthropology, is founded nevertheless on the idea that natives are the experts. Most contemporary anthropologists are sympathetic and responsive to the right of oppressed and decolonized groups to represent themselves. Some anthropologists are members of such groups.

Native ethnography does not entirely solve the crisis of representation, however. For one thing, as Marshall McLuhan noted in the 1960s, international markets and mass media have made the world a "global village." The easy dichotomy between native and nonnative has begun to blur because cultures can no longer be conceived as neatly contained by geographic boundaries or the lines of race and class.[8] Further, the narrative authority even of native ethnographers remains vulnerable to challenge. Although Barbara Myerhoff was Jewish, she was not really a native of the Venice community because she did not speak Yiddish. It was impossible for her ever to do fieldwork in the Eastern European shtetls; they vanished after their inhabitants were exterminated by the Nazis. Moreover, as Marc Kaminsky suggests in his introduction to Myerhoff's collected essays, her perspectives reflected the wrong class (the middle).[9] Her professional interest in myth and ritual led Myerhoff afield from the fiercely held political commitments of the secular working-class Jews whose life histories she recorded. Most were socialists to whom religion was no less an enemy than the czar and capitalist bosses.

But Barbara Myerhoff's methods were *supposed* to take her on a course that negotiated sameness and difference. Describing her approach, which involves the disciplined use of self-reflection, Myerhoff emphasized a basic premise of the American anthropological tradition: "You study what is happening to others by understanding what is going on in yourself. And you yourself become the data gathering instrument. So that you come from a culture and step into a new one and how you respond to the new one tells you about them and about the one you came from."[10]

A search for evidence of appropriation, co-optation, exploitation, or erasure of the Other is insufficient for judging the full merit of an ethnography. But the importance of these epistemological and ethical concerns can be a flash point for critics. The question: "Whose voice?" has a primacy that must not be ignored. The editors of a book on feminist theory and personal narratives, for example, write: "Working with personal narratives raises questions about authorship: Whose story is to be told? Whose voice is to be heard? This section [of our book] addresses the complex power and authority involved in the production and ultimate use of personal narrative texts. None of the authors represented here is comfortable with the traditional scholar's assumption of the voice of authority in the creation or interpretation of life stories."[11]

Whether writing about informants constitutes exploitation, a debate that began among feminist scholars in the mid-1980s, is particularly pertinent to my research about the life of Diane DeVries. Some scholars question the propriety of an anthropologist claiming to be the author, or sole author, of a life history. They focus on a definition published in 1965 that was undoubtedly meant to be descriptive rather than prescriptive, but which contemporary readers find problematic: "A life history is actually defined by anthropologists as 'an extensive record of a person's life told to and recorded by another, who then edits and writes the life as though it were an autobiography.'"[12] Daphne Patai, whose work includes interviews with very poor women in Brazil, has warned that the research practices of even well-meaning feminists have the potential to perpetuate and reproduce structures of inequality and domination in the Third World. Patai writes: "The dilemma of feminist researchers working on groups less privileged than themselves can be succinctly stated as follows: is it possible—not in theory, but in the actual conditions of the real world today—to write about the oppressed without becoming one of the oppressors?"[13]

Judith Stacey, a sociologist of family life in the United States, has argued similarly that the potential for betrayal and exploitation is inherent in any ethnographic fieldwork because "the lives, loves, and tragedies that fieldwork informants share with a researcher are ultimately data—grist for the ethnographic mill." There is often a conflict of interest and emotion between the ethnographer as "authentic, related person (i.e., participant)" and the ethnographer "as exploiting researcher (i.e., observer)."[14]

To avoid such methodological and ethical quandaries, some ethnographers interested in studying individual lives focus their research on life stories rather than life histories.[15] By highlighting the subject's own narrative, they attempt to diminish the power of the ethnographer as author and as authority. A "new ethnography" also has been proclaimed that treats subjects biographically, not as mere components of social worlds but as "active interpreters who construct their realities through talk and interaction, stories, and narratives."[16] The use of dialogues or "multivocality" is a key strategy for the new ethnography, "centering on the question of how to deal with participants' own representation of their worlds, with objectivity being only one of several related issues."[17]

Ironically, however, full-length life histories were introduced in the 1930s and 1940s precisely to counteract the depersonalization and lack of historical perspective in traditional ethnographies.[18]

A rich literature of life histories, including a number of truly great works, has been published by anthropologists—including, for example, *Son of Old Man Hat: A Navaho Autobiography Recorded by Walter Dyk* (1938); *Sun Chief: The Autobiography of a Hopi Indian* by Leo Simmons (1942); and George Devereux's meticulous and compassionate record of therapeutic dialogues in *Reality and Dream: Psychotherapy of a Plains Indian* (1951). These works set standards of respect for narrative self-representation that are rarely met even in contemporary research.[19]

In practice, even life story research involves a great deal of eliciting, selecting, and interpreting of informants' accounts. Conversely, many of the life histories produced by anthropologists are essentially life stories. The distinction between life histories and life stories—and anxiety about the potential to violate the interests of informants—is an issue with which the profession continues to wrestle.[20]

Oscar Lewis's *Children of Sánchez: Autobiography of a Mexican Family* is composed entirely of life stories. It is a montage of interviews with a working-class father and his four adult children in a poor neighborhood in Mexico City during the 1950s. The book documents each family member's responses to economic deprivation, their desires for love and security, their efforts and aspirations to improve their lives, and the children's sibling rivalry. With its appearance in 1961 and wide popular readership, Lewis's book became the gold standard for the life history genre.

The book offers few clues, however, about what Lewis may have edited out of the interview transcripts or how his relationships with the various members of the Sánchez family may have affected what they told him. With regard to these issues, Ruth Behar's book *Translated Woman: Crossing the Border with Esperanza's Story*, published in 1993, introduced a number of creative modifications to the genre.[21] *Translated Woman* is the life story of a feisty street vendor in a town in Central Mexico. Esperanza, who has suffered severe domestic abuse, is suspected by her community of being a witch because of her independent attitude and is a devotee of a cult dedicated to Pancho Villa. Behar pieced together

Esperanza's vivid, emotionally powerful narrative from transcripts of taped interviews that she recorded and translated over many months of research, just as Lewis did. But Behar also describes her ongoing relationship with Esperanza, especially the rituals of gift-giving after Behar agreed to be godmother to Esperanza's daughter and their effect on Esperanza's self-disclosure. Behar's trenchant observations, self-reflections, and interpretations add important layers of meaning, including a courageous, if controversial, autobiographical conclusion.[22]

Given the complex, collaborative nature of works such as these, the contrast between "life history" and "life story" research may be overblown. The view that life stories are better and more true than life histories is simplistic. Its corollary, that one person's experience can never be approached or described adequately by another, is dangerous. At the imaginable endpoint will be several billion people on the planet all telling our life stories. It will be empowering. But maybe we should pay some attention to the question of how to listen.

A more sophisticated analysis of power must be brought into the debate about life histories and life stories, as anthropologist Aihwa Ong argues.[23] Ong, whose research focuses on Malay women laborers and the Chinese diaspora, acknowledges that serious risks to informants are posed by their inequality with more powerful researchers. But she feels that greater recognition is needed of the complex and unexpected ways in which power works, and of what is actually exchanged in life history collaborations.[24] Perhaps we have become too pessimistic, suggests Ong, about the possibility that the life history will benefit both sides in the exchange.

Critics tend to consider informants' power to be totally defined by the ethnographer and their words given little weight because they are represented and rescripted. Ong challenges this view: "If one considers power as a decentralized, shifting and productive force, animated in networks of relations rather than possessed by individuals, then ethnographic subjects can exercise power in the production of ethnographic knowledges. . . . While we do not deny our use of informants' stories for our own purposes, we can also choose to introduce their perspectives into rarefied realms of theory-making." The greater betrayal, Ong suggests, "lies in refusing to recognize informants in their own right, whose voices insist on being heard and can make a difference in the way we think about their lives." The point is less that scholars may reap material and social benefits from informants' stories than that, more important, "we help to disseminate their views and that we do so without betraying their political interests as narrators of their own lives."[25]

From the moment I met Diane, she inverted and subverted the predictable dynamics of power implied by our relative social positions. My earlier work as an ethnohistorian on a California Indian reservation, in the early 1970s, had resulted in my recording several life histories of women. Some of these were private accounts, conversations that I documented in field notes. But I learned by experience that I could not always use the material I had collected. Several days after showing my closest friend on the reservation what I had written about her, we were driving down the long, winding reservation road when she turned to me and said, "I read the shit you wrote about me." I was crushed.

"I wrote down what you told me," I said. "Isn't it true?"

"Yes, it's true."

"I tried to make it sound like you."

"Sounds just like me."

"So what's the problem?"

"You can't publish it. I told you things I don't want everyone to know."

But, a few years later, when I approached Diane with the idea of working together to document her life, she agreed without a moment's hesitation. "I've always wanted to write my life story," she said.

I suggested the following terms: Diane would read drafts of everything I wrote before publication. Nothing would appear in print without our discussing and working out any concerns she might have. If a book was developed from my dissertation, I would appear as the author.

As I began writing the final version of this book, I invited Diane to be my coauthor. She declined, saying, "No. It's *your* book." However, when I discussed including Diane's unpublished autobiography in its entirety, perhaps as one of a series of three volumes, something I believed I had earlier proposed and which I thought Diane had found acceptable, she replied, "I never gave you permission to publish that. That's *my* work."[26]

In our original negotiations, Diane also asked what would happen to the royalties. I proposed splitting any royalties fifty-fifty, to which she agreed. This remains our arrangement.

I did not expect what followed. Diane began giving me assignments.

First she suggested that I look at a recent article on people with disabilities in UCLA's student newspaper, *The Daily Bruin,* which had featured an interview with her.[27] Then she suggested that I talk with a couple of graduate students in the cinema school who were filming a docudrama based on Diane's life.[28] She was growing impatient with the filmmakers, who were dwelling on the most sensational and painful aspects of her life. In choosing to work with me, I came to realize, Diane was exerting competitive pressure on the filmmakers that might give her more control over how she was being represented. I duly ran to the office of the *Daily Bruin* to get a copy of the article Diane thought I should see.

Diane continues to subvert structures of power and expectations that might tend to put her in a subordinate position because of her limb deficiencies. When she returned to UCLA in 1985 to finish her undergraduate degree, after an absence of several years, she enrolled in a course taught by Edwin Schneidman, a well-known sociologist and an expert on suicide and suicide prevention. Professor Schneidman asked if Diane would be willing to speak to a class about the experience of living with her disability. She agreed to do so.

"Have you ever addressed a group before?" he asked. Diane and I once had made a presentation to a class taught by Barbara Myerhoff across town at the University of Southern California. Diane told Schneidman about that event and her research collaboration with me. She collegially offered to let him read some articles I had written about her.

Professor Schneidman may well have been taken off guard by Diane's sophisticated self-presentation. And if he was, my comment is, "Join the club!"

When I attended UCLA's commencement ceremonies in 1987, Diane received a huge bouquet and award for her achievement at the sociology department's precommencement breakfast. A network TV crew was there to film the event; it was broadcast as far away as Texas, where some of Diane's estranged relatives saw it and phoned her in California to reestablish contact. Diane was not at all camera-shy. She basked in the attention.

Diane's perceptions and presentation of her relationship with me were evident during a trip to the mountains in July 1989. With my eighteen-month-old daughter, Rebecca, I joined Diane and Jim DeVries for a weekend reunion at Camp Paivika, a retreat for children with disabilities where Diane had spent her happiest summers. Her blond hair freshly colored, sporting a terrific tan and long dangling earrings, Diane looked marvelous. She wore a strapless dress made from fabric printed with a chic Army camouflage design. By far the most glamorous person at the event, Diane greeted former friends and counselors warmly. She introduced her companions: "My husband, Jim DeVries," and "my biographer, Gelya Frank."

Much as I might have been thinking of Diane as "my" subject, her casting me in a supporting role in her life suggests that a more embracing approach to the study of lives is needed than the current terms *life history* and *life story* provide. Such an approach must bring out the dynamics of power as the process of understanding takes place, not simply as an afterthought.[29] The authors of an ethnohistory of the lesbian community in Buffalo write:

> In order for the dialogue between narrators and ourselves to be effective, it was not enough just to intersperse extended quotations with our analysis. We also tried to include the development of our thought processes as we progressed with the research. What did it mean to make working-class lesbians central in our thinking? How were we blocked and in what ways did we move ahead? How were we affected by the feminist sexuality debates? This kind of self-consciousness seemed necessary in order for us to negotiate the power difference of class and race and think creatively about the past.[30]

Informants are rarely passive, and they are unlikely to accept a position in which they perceive themselves as victims.[31] When I expressed to Diane my fear that critics might condemn this book as exploitative, she chided, "What kind of person would I be to let you exploit me for twenty years?"

Life story research focuses on how people tell stories about themselves under specific circumstances and for particular purposes. Life story researchers often assume that individuals maintain a metaphor of the self or, as Gabriele Rosenthal describes it, a "comprehensive, general pattern of orientation" to past and future that links the individual's biographically relevant experiences.[32] Consequently, life stories should be analyzed without adding any supplementary content, theories, or interpretations.[33]

A life story is integrally and necessarily related, however, to a reconstruction of events or life history, regardless of whether the life history is created by the subject or by another person. As Rosenthal remarks, "Life story and life history always come together. They are continuously dialectically linked and produce each other; this is the reason why we must reconstruct both levels no matter whether our main target is the life history or the life story."[34]

Rosenthal defines life history as nothing more than a chronology of the events embedded in a life story narrative. Psychological and cultural insights emerge from a strict, formal analysis of the way a narrator constructs her life story in relation to her life history, which is the crux of Rosenthal's approach. Such an analysis would explore what kinds of events a narrator includes in or omits from her life story and whether events are reported as facts or elaborated through argumentation. For Rosenthal, the layers of interpretation supplied by the listener or interlocutor are extraneous.

In a cultural biography, however, the relationship between the life story told by a narrator and its reception is precisely what is interesting and must be examined. This book draws on diverse sources: my ethnographic observations; first-person narratives (life story interviews, Diane's unpublished autobiography, field notes of conversations in person and on the telephone, and Diane's letters); interviews with other people in Diane's life; other primary data (Diane's clinical records and newspaper and television reports about her); and secondary data (films, ethnographies, and other studies, including statistical surveys) with which to reconstruct the context of Diane's life. Much of my approach belongs to conventional historiography, the method by which biographies are usually written. But cultural biography differs by including ethnographic materials—based on prolonged, disciplined firsthand observations while participating in the subject's life—and by putting methodological reflexivity in the forefront. That is, a cultural biography considers how specific biographical images arise and goes on to interpret them in terms of cultural processes.

A cultural biography need not be written by a professional anthropologist, but its methods and theory distinguish it from conventional literary and historical biographies. Although written by a journalist, Anne Fadiman's book *The Spirit Catches You and You Fall Down* fits my definition of a cultural biography. Fadiman's report, based on firsthand observations begun in 1988 with a refugee family from Laos living in Merced, California, uses a naturalistic approach that is common to ethnography and journalism. Published in 1997, the book reflects on negative images of the Lee family that arise through their resistance to the agendas of powerful agents of American society with whom they must deal as a result of their infant daughter's seizure disorder. It contributes explicitly to a reader's understanding of the cultures of Hmong refugees, mainstream America, and biomedicine. Karen McCarthy Brown's book *Mama Lola: A Vodou Priestess in Brooklyn*, published in 1991, also fits this definition of a cultural biography. It is a study of the voodoo religion of Haiti through ethnographic fieldwork and life history interviews over a dozen years focused primarily on one individual, a voodoo priestess in New York.

I define cultural biography as a cultural analysis focusing on a biographical subject that makes use of ethnographic methods, along with life history and life story, and that critically reflects on its methodology in action as a source of primary data, including the effects of power and personal factors such as the mirror phenomenon. The purpose of a cultural biography is to examine not only how an individual's experiences and consciousness are shaped in a particular cultural milieu over time but also how the biographical self contributes to cultural processes and transformations. I refer to the biographical self rather than the individual because it may be that *images* of the individual, more than the concrete person, have the more profound cultural significance.[35]

Much of the American anthropological tradition has been concerned precisely with relationships between images of the self and action. As Gene Weltfish, a student of Franz Boas, characterized the discipline,

"Human action is organized around man's image of himself; his directions and his goals must find expression in the form of symbols of man's own making, which extends to the creation of scientific symbols as well. . . . Our task will be first of all to understand the image-making process of the human mind."[36]

A cultural biography examines such image-making processes. Responses to images of others, including life stories, are the critical link by which cultural meaning is established beyond the intentions of a given biographical subject. In listening and responding to a life story, a cultural biographer offers her experience as a proxy for future readers. When readers engage with the life story and its various interpretations, new meanings are created that will reverberate in the readers' own local cultures and sometimes in the dominant culture as well.

The influence of Diane DeVries on the culture of disability, and that of other women with disabilities whose lives have been highly publicized, is described in the next chapter. Later in the book, I consider the effect of Diane's image on people in other settings: a group of university students to whom she spoke, donors at a fund-raiser for children with disabilities, a television viewer who saw her as a child on a local show, and, with a closer analysis over time, myself. In each of these circumstances, Diane's image—not only her physical image but also the image conveyed by the story she tells about her life—challenged those who encountered it, often forcing them to adjust their perspectives. Her life is consequently a study not only in disability culture but also in American culture and its transformations.

3 "There's Nothing about the Disabled Woman and the Disabled Culture"

— DIANE DEVRIES, 1976

As I sat in that consciousness-raising group, I
realized that disabled women have a long and
arduous fight ahead. Somehow we must learn to
perceive ourselves as attractive and desirable. Our
struggle is not unlike the striving for self-
acceptance of the millions of nonhandicapped
who also fall short of the Beautiful People image.
Our liberation will be a victory for everyone.

Debra Kent, "In Search of Liberation," 1987

There is always an underground. Notes get passed
among survivors. And the notes we are passing
these days say, "there's power in difference.
Power. Pass the word." Culture. It's about passing
the word. And disability culture is passing the
word that there's a new definition of disability
and it includes *power.*

Cheryl Marie Wade, "Disability Culture Rap," 1994

When we were interviewed together for a short ethnographic video
piece in 1995, Diane's recollection of our first meeting was much different from mine.[1] Should it surprise anyone that in Diane's version, *she* is
the principal actor, the agent who initiates our contact and makes things

happen? In her account, Diane confronted and challenged me, an anthropologist in training, to turn the attention of my profession to the culture of disability.

"I just remember that she was my TA in my cultural anthropology class," Diane said, responding to an off-camera question. "And I remember her sitting behind me, either a row or two behind me. And I could always see her kind of looking at me. Of course later I found out what she was thinking. . . ." Diane laughed and turned to me. "Shall I tell her what you were thinking?"

"Sure," I said, laughing nervously.

"She kept thinking: I wonder if she could have sex?"

Diane's imitation of me was droll. Now we were all laughing.

"So, then, I remember going to her one day because, I think, we were going to have an exam, and so I had to go to her office with some questions, or whatever. And, I went in and I remember . . . I remember her eyes. She had the greenest eyes in the world. Now . . . I found out . . . they were contact lenses. But I told her, You know, you got the nicest, greenest eyes. They just blew me away.

"And that was, like, the first meeting. It was basically just, you know, talking about the class, or whatever. Anyway, I think—if I remember right, I'm not sure, she can correct me on this—but it was either that meeting or sometime, another one, I mentioned something like:

"You're always in these classes and you hear about these different types of women. Black women, lesbian women, whatever. And different cultures. But there's nothing about the disabled woman or the disabled culture.

"And then she said something like: Do you really think there's a separate disabled culture? As we define culture?

"And I said, Yeah."

It is less daunting now to take up Diane's challenge to write about the disabled woman than it was in the mid-1970s, when the independent living and disability rights movements were still very young.[2] Disability culture thrives in politics, film, dance, theater, photography, and literature. The interdisciplinary field of disability studies is also flourishing.[3] Feminist reflections on disability are now an established genre.[4] But when Diane and I began our collaboration, her agenda was on the cutting edge.

Collections of first-person narratives by women with disabilities in the English-speaking world began appearing in the early 1980s.[5] And plenty of first-person narrative accounts have been published before and since then describing experiences of women and girls with chronic illnesses and disabilities. But in Diane's comment that there was "nothing about the disabled woman" I took her to mean work at the intersection of the emerging feminist and disability rights movements. The intersection was, and remains, a volatile spot where pleasing commonalities and distressing contradictions could be found. Bonnie Sherr Klein, a documentary filmmaker and radio journalist, has commented, "Disability, like feminism, offers new perspectives—sometimes unsettling ways of looking at questions to which we thought we had the answers."[6]

A meeting of able-bodied feminists and feminists with disabilities can be doubly unsettling. At the First National Conference on Disabled Women and Girls, held in Baltimore in 1982, a sharp retort to Letty Cottin Pogrebin by her fellow keynote speaker, Judy Heumann, underscored differences between their positions and assumptions. Pogrebin was then editor of *Ms.*, the well-known feminist magazine, and Heumann a leading disability rights activist whose public career began in 1970 when she filed a successful civil suit to safeguard her right to teach in the New York City public schools.[7] Two years later, Heumann cofounded the World Institute on Disability in Oakland, California. An issue of *Ms.* in the late 1970s named Heumann one of eighty women to watch in the coming decade. In 1993 she became the assistant secretary for special education and rehabilitation services in the Clinton administration.[8]

"The concerns about sexual harassment affect all women," claimed Pogrebin.

"You know, I use a wheelchair," Judy Heumann replied, "and when I go down the street I do not get to be sexually harassed. I hear nondisabled women complaining about it, but I don't ever get treated as a sexual object."

Pogrebin asserted, "You would hate it."[9]

The book *Women with Disabilities: Essays in Culture, Psychology, and Politics*, in which this story was recounted, sparked more conversation about such issues.[10] The collection, which appeared in 1988, included work by feminist scholars and activists with and without disabilities. Importantly, the editors—a woman with a disability, Adrienne Asch, and one without, Michelle Fine—mirrored the conversation through their own negotiations. In a chapter that I contributed to the volume, Diane's account of her experiences and attitudes concerning her body was introduced to a broader audience. Her story helped to frame a challenge to many prevailing views. The image of her body that Diane had developed was remarkably positive. As she reported, "The only thing that's wrong with me is just that I don't have any arms and legs."[11]

How did Diane come to see herself this way? The answer lies in her occupational history—her approach to everyday activities, the doing of ordinary things since infancy—which I reconstruct from interviews with Diane's mother, Irene Fields, against a baseline of normal infant development.[12] The first year of life is the one in which the most remarkable developmental gains are made.[13] Diane's earliest development might be imagined against these milestones. By about six weeks, most babies gain neck control of their disproportionately large heads. By two to four months, they are able to look up and around. By six weeks, a baby locates her hands by feeling one against the other. By ten to twelve weeks, she can find her hands by sight, bring them to her mouth to suck, and begin to bat at toys. By the time three months have passed, she does quite a bit of kicking, a skill that prepares her for creeping, crawling, and walking. All we need is to think of a typical three-month-old lying on her back in a crib, sucking a thumb in one hand, twiddling her ear with the other hand, and bicycling her feet in the air, to grasp Diane's earliest physical impulses.

In the following months, an infant becomes mobile, gaining trunk control, the ability to twist and roll over, and sitting balance. She learns to reach for toys, hold a ball with both hands, and transfer a block from one hand to the other. She learns to crawl, creep, and pull herself from kneeling to standing. Then she begins to cruise, holding onto furniture at first as she practices stepping and then walking. Around age one, the

infant can stack cubes, retrieve a ball, hold a crayon and scribble, ham-
mer, and string large beads. By eighteen months she can climb stairs, use
a tricycle, pivot, walk sideways and backward, and climb over obstacles.
She can build with blocks, put pegs into holes, pull apart pop-it beads,
put together snap-it toys, tear pages from a book, and play catch with a
ball. By the age of three, she can wash and dress herself, feed herself, use
the toilet, and play simple games with other children, as well as engage
in complicated fantasy play.

Two of Diane's developmental milestones stand out for her mother,
Irene.[14] The first was Diane's discovery that she could pick up an object.
She was in her wooden high chair, tied in so that she wouldn't "scoot out
the bottom." Diane had some large round plastic pop-it beads in front of
her when she discovered that she could pick one up and drop it. Diane
laughed to see that she could move something like that by herself, and
they called her father, Kenny, to show him. The family began to give
Diane plastic dishes with a wooden spoon to stir and let her make mud
pies. Pouring the contents of one bowl to another, hitting the bowl with
her spoon, and splashing made Diane "really excited," to the point of
falling asleep in her high chair. Irene thought Diane was about a year old
when this occurred.[15]

Diane's mother also recalled Diane's first steps. Diane had learned to
sit up by herself by age one or two. They used to prop her up on pillows,
and she learned to right her own position. One day Irene and Kenny
were sitting in the living room with Diane's Aunt Hazel and Uncle Burt
when they noticed Diane walk across the room. She was concentrating
very seriously, looking down, and moving with a rocking motion from
side to side. She was two or three years old.

As a baby Diane hadn't moved her toys around very much. She had a
teddy bear and pink stuffed cow that she snuggled against to sleep. Later
she used her arm and cheek to cuddle dolls.[16] When her baby sister Debbie was on the floor, Diane would put her cheek against her. Irene surmised that touching things with her cheek "must have had a warmer
feel." Diane's favorite toys were Little Red Riding Hood, a bride, and a
soft squeaky toy bought by her father, "a red Indian with a feather." She
loved to hit the feather with her arm to make it squeak.

These recollections capture Diane busily accomplishing some of the main work of childhood: the acquisition of competence in daily occupations.[17] She used the intact resources of her body to strive to do the things she saw others do.

Language acquisition for Diane was especially enabling. When Diane mused on what might have happened if she had no arms whatsoever, she realized it would most have affected her pleasure in expressing herself verbally.

"I would have had to learn to write with my mouth, but since I enjoy talking too much," Diane said, "I would have had to cut down quite a bit on my favorite pastime, writing."[18]

Irene recalled that Diane's first word was "Mama." Kenny swore she wasn't saying "Mama." Later Diane looked up and said, "Dada." By age two, Diane was putting together sentences. The family owned a dive-bombing parakeet that would run down the couch, pull Diane's hair, and run back. Diane got irritated and slapped the couch. Once, when he pecked her, she turned and said, "Damn bird!"

Like most children between the ages of two and three, Diane had an imaginary playmate. She called her Martha. According to psychoanalysts, children create imaginary playmates when they are learning to control their socially unacceptable impulses in order to earn the love and approval of their parents.[19] Attributing such impulses to an imaginary companion allows the child to maintain a good opinion of herself.

Diane used to play with a certain little girl from across the street. Irene remembers looking out the window and hearing Diane say, "Martha can't go!"

No one was there but Diane and the other girl.

Diane gave the order, "Martha, you go in the house now! It's your nap time!"

From then on, Diane had tea parties with Martha. When it was Diane's bedtime, Martha had to go, too.

Diane's temper tantrums were normal. If she was made to take a nap or eat something she didn't like, she would bang her arm on the table, cry, and insist, "I'm not going to do it! I'm not!"

Irene still made Diane eat or take her nap.

Although Diane was "a good baby" and an obedient child, she was punished occasionally. Once she was spanked for biting her sister. "I knew it was Diane's only defense," Irene acknowledged sympathetically. "But I punished her anyway."

Kenny, who worked as a carpenter and form-fitter, was Diane's link to the outdoors. He built ramps and poured a cement area in the backyard where Diane could get around. He later built a playhouse for Diane and her younger sister, Debbie, in which they spent hours at a time. It had a toy stove that plugged in, a refrigerator, a table and chairs. The side of the playhouse lifted entirely so that Diane could ride in on her three-wheeled scooter, opening the door herself.

As she grew up, Diane was a member of a neighborhood pack consisting mainly of the Fields girls and their neighbors, the Helmses. It rounded things out nicely that the parents of the Fields and Helms children were also close friends. Diane was the oldest of the group. Gene Helms appointed himself Diane's protector. Once when Diane was in her wagon at a trailer park, a boy approached her with a little knife. "You ain't got no arms, you ain't got no legs," he threatened, "and now you're not gonna have no head." He held Diane by the neck. She didn't need to say much because Gene was there and started beating him up. "It was one of those bratty kids that did weird things," was Diane's unruffled appraisal of the encounter, looking back.

When Diane was old enough to go to school, she took with her a background of accomplishment in everyday occupations. Many children with disabilities face demoralization from having their competence continually challenged, "not because one actually is incompetent but because the able-bodied think one is."[20] Diane had been fitted with her first lower prosthesis at the age of three and artificial arms at five, but she entered kindergarten expecting to be able to participate in the usual activities in her own way. Why shouldn't she be able to fingerpaint, for example?

> When the time to fingerpaint arrived, my well-meaning teacher placed a paint brush within my hooks. Even though I did not like this, and my picture looked like something done by an angry Etch-A-Sketch, I tried. I wanted to get paint all over my "fingers" and slap it all over the butcher

paper like my friend Kathy was doing. Mrs. Lipton tried to explain to me that the paint might not be good for artificial hands, and that I could have just as much fun and paint just as well as the other children with a brush. What she actually was trying to say was that fingerpainting is very difficult to do without fingers. That really upset me, and I said, "I want to paint with 'my fingers' too. I want to feel the paint. I have fingers too. Just take these dumb arms off me and I'll show you." Somehow, Mrs. Lipton understood the truth of what I was saying, and how important it was for me to fingerpaint as freely as her other children. She had my prostheses removed. Not only did I bring home a dress very dissimilar in color to the one I was sent off in, but I also—and not too humbly—presented my parents with a very colorful masterpiece of my first "stumppainting."[21]

Diane's memories of Camp Paivika, where she spent two weeks every year between the ages of eight and eighteen, were those of a perennially happy camper. High in the San Bernardino mountains, Paivika was the first resident camp in the United States built especially for children with physical disabilities.[22] It offered swimming, archery, horseback riding, arts and crafts, sing-alongs around the campfire—in short, all the activities that a child from the city or the suburbs could want at a sleep-away camp.

Diane began her first session at Paivika looking somewhat withdrawn. But by the second week she was folk dancing and square dancing on her wooden rocker legs. She became fast friends with the caretaker's daughter, who, it was noted by a counselor, was not disabled. Diane impressed her fellow campers and staff by "her amazing abilities," which included feeding herself and going on overnight trips.[23]

Four summers later, when Diane was eleven years old, she was praised by her counselor as "the most delightful camper in our cabin, and perhaps the whole camp."[24] Diane was described as agreeable, enthusiastic, and popular—if special, even among children with handicaps, because quadrilateral limb deficiencies were so rare.[25] Diane loved crafts, swimming, and horseback riding. She moved around the camp using her three-wheeled tripod and a crutch. Diane was always coming up with clever remarks and constructive suggestions for cabin activities (she originated the idea for her cabin's flag) and could be depended on for articles for the camp newspaper and ideas for skits. Her attitude toward her disability was self-accepting and compensatory: "She would talk freely about her disability and seemed to want to show everyone that she could do things as well as anyone. The first day, as I was carrying her, Diane remarked, 'You know, I'm not very heavy because I don't have arms and legs and stuff like that.' Carrying articles under her chin from the table after meals was a favorite task, and she could dust bed tops in the cabin very well."[26]

It turns out that Diane's orientation toward *doing* without arms and legs, which originated in her childhood, is common among children with congenital limb deficiencies. A study conducted in the early 1960s found that "contrary to expectations, congenitally malformed children of normal and superior intelligence develop an early and gratifying curiosity about their environment; they manage to explore outside reality almost as adequately as non-handicapped children."[27]

Diane entered the stormy years of her adolescence with a fair amount of experience and confidence with the opposite sex. At Camp Paivika she had had a series of "summer loves." Although the best-looking boys at camp were already spoken for, Diane's affections for male staff were usually reciprocated, within the limitations of relationships between camper and counselor. The first of her crushes was Mike, with whom she exchanged vows of love at a tourist attraction near the camp:

> When that gorgeous blond first flashed his warm smile and fixed his sky blue eyes my way, my knees would have given out, if I had had knees. Instead, I settled for a sweaty upper lip and heart palpitations! Immediately we formed a very close bond of loving and devoted friendship. This was sealed oddly enough at Santa's Village. They had an ice pole which people used to carve their names on. Mike carved "Mike & Diane" above his hand print and my stump print.[28]

Mike brought Diane special dessert creations (not always entirely edible) and affectionately teased her, once leaving her behind when he picked up a group of campers in his truck, then returning to let her sit in the cab with him. Diane knew that her "summer loves" were only for the mountains, but they were no less satisfying for that reason. She understood that a crush was not the same as a boyfriend. And by the time

Diane was twelve she had her first steady boyfriend, a classmate at the Tucker School for Handicapped Children.

In January 1964 Diane, soon to turn fourteen, was admitted to Ward 502 at Rancho Los Amigos Hospital, where she lived for most of the time until she finished high school. At one time a county poor farm, Rancho became a major rehabilitation facility with support from the Easter Seals Society during the polio epidemic of the mid-1950s. Rancho was again a major center for rehabilitation at the height of the Vietnam War, when Diane lived there. Many of the patients were young men wounded in service. In fact, for about a year in 1965 and 1966, because of the high volume of patients with war injuries, there were no beds for Diane and several other long-term residents from her ward. They were transferred to convalescent homes.

Rancho was no Camp Paivika. During one stay at a home for the elderly, Diane watched three young friends from Rancho die within a two-week period.

"It was as if I stepped off the movie set of *State Fair* and onto that of *West Side Story*," Diane later wrote.[29]

Of the eight young women on Ward 502, Diane's closest friend was Christie, a vivacious eighteen-year-old who acquired paraplegia in a car accident.

> After the dinner trays were picked up, I took off with Christie and others as far away from the 500 area as possible. We usually ended up at the "fish pond" or the 700 area where all the good-looking spinal cord injured men were. The equivalent of our parents stepping out onto the porch yelling their child's name in order to bring them inside was hearing our names being blasted over the paging system: "Diane Fields, return to your ward. You have visitors." After they finally realized the purpose for my timely escapes, and found themselves making this announcement too frequently, the pages went something like this: "Diane, return to your ward . . . now." . . . A few times I failed to send out a "scout" and almost missed a visit with my father. However, unlike Irene, he would go looking for me. Fortunately, he never found me in any compromising situations.[30]

Officially, Diane was admitted to Rancho to provide her with functional lower prostheses so that she could walk. For Diane, the real reason was her mother's rejection of the burden of caring for her teenage daughter and the constant friction between them. Diane's experiences at Rancho toughened her and introduced a cynical dimension to her outlook:

> When I entered Rancho, I could not independently dress or undress all of me, fix my hair, put on or remove my jewelry, clean myself after using the toilet, put all of my makeup on myself, cook, make my own bed, or do the bossa nova! I could do the twist and the shimmy, though. And when I left in 1968 I still could not do those things. However, I did learn how to properly handle a cigarette, how to dress in order to please, and which drugs mixed together would provide the desired—but not fatal—"high."[31]

The youngest on her ward, Diane quickly absorbed all that was offered by Rancho's distinctive underground culture of disability. Among the "crips" at the Ranch of Friends, Diane consciously adopted a set of strategies to manage the impression she made on others. These strategies meshed with Diane's outgoing and adventurous personality. She abandoned the use of artificial arms and her tripod scooter, preferring the appearance and function of her unencumbered arms and an electric wheelchair fitted with a lever control. Although she did use a pair of cumbersome cosmetic legs for a while, eventually she abandoned them also. In cultivating an appearance that she called "looking together," it was important to Diane and her friends to resist the stereotypic image of a cripple. Diane later articulated these choices in an interview with me that appeared in *Women with Disabilities:*

GELYA: What are some of the things that people do when they don't look "together?"

DIANE: It depends on your handicap. Like me, I would never wear a skirt, a long skirt, like they used to. I've even seen some people with no arms wearing long sleeves pinned up or rolled up clumsily so they're *this* fat. You can find a lot of clothes that fit you. It's not hard. If they have someone take care of them, they won't tell them: "No. I want my hair this way." They'll just let them do it. That's dumb. It's *your* body. They're helping *you* out. And just the way you sit, too.

G: What do you mean?

D: You can sit so that they really notice your wheelchair—mold your-self to the chair—that's bad. Or you could just sit in it like you sit in any chair. And when you talk, talk. Don't just sit there stiff so they can still notice just your chair. You got to let them see *you*. I mean they're going to look at you anyway, so you might as well give them something to look at. That's how my best friend, Christie, was. I think I just molded myself a little bit after her, 'cause she was that way. She figured, "Hell, if they're going to look, they can have something to look *at*." She knew her good points, and she used them. And that's what I did.[32]

Diane's positive attitude toward her body was evident to me in such comments as "I've always been really in tune with my body."[33] When I asked whether she *felt* crippled or handicapped, Diane replied, "Yeah. Lately." Her back had been giving her trouble. She was aware that her scoliosis was worsening, partly a consequence of her posture when writing and accomplishing other tasks without prostheses. She felt lucky that her arms were still strong enough to pull her up when she transferred from place to place. But she did not see herself as inherently limited and flawed. Being handicapped was a condition that could happen by degrees—and was happening to her only lately.[34]

When I asked Diane how she thought she looked best, she laughed, then answered frankly:

> I don't know. Shorts, or body shirt and shorts. Because you've got to show off what's best. My best thing is my boobs, you know, 'cause that's big and they look nice. That's all I got that looks real good. And when I'm thin, my shape's all right, for someone with no legs. You know, looks like a time thing—whatever that thing's called.

G: An hourglass.

D: So you shouldn't cover up what you got. But if you're shy, that's a problem.[35]

For scholars in the new field of disability studies, Diane's forthright self-acceptance in this interview helped to demonstrate that women with severe disabilities can have high self-esteem. Asserting their abilities and desires, they can experience their own beauty, find lovers and life partners, and enjoy the full spectrum of life's activities. As reviewer Barbara Hillyer noted in the *Women's Review of Books:*

> Body concept and the objectification of our bodies are perennial topics in the disability and women's movements. Gelya Frank's article on the concept of embodiment is based on a detailed study of interviews with Diane Fields DeVries, a woman born with quadrilateral limb deficiencies. The interviews themselves are quoted extensively to demonstrate DeVries' persistent acceptance of her body as "natural and fundamentally normal" despite enormous social pressure to the contrary.[36]

Another reviewer, anthropologist Nora Groce, wrote in 1994 that the chapter "continues to represent a major challenge to the enormous literature in social psychology by able-bodied researchers debating the various 'adjustment problems' individuals with disabilities face."[37] Oral historian Karen Hirsch wrote in 1995 that the chapter exemplifies "an approach to understanding of disability experiences that promises to reveal complexities generally lost in behavioral research based on cultural constructs and statistical averages."[38]

Disability rights activist James I. Charlton wrote in 1998 that the chapter was among several explorations of embodiment and disability worth noting:

> These range from the disability rights activist Jean Stewart's novel *The Body's Memory* to the anthropologist Robert Murphy's historiography *The Body Silent* to Gelya Frank's ethnography "On Embodiment." . . . Frank takes an observational approach in her treatment of the disabled body. Her examination of Diane DeVries's growing self-consciousness is an important contribution to understanding how women with disabilities develop positive self-images in spite of an array of reactionary, body-centered ideas.[39]

Hillyer's own book *Feminism and Disability,* published in 1993, focused on issues of dependence and independence.[40] Although independence is a tenet of both the feminist and disability rights movements, Hillyer argued that its implications are unique for women with disabilities. All women who are feminists must struggle at some time against being treated as inferior, regarded as dependent on men, and kept on the margins of power. But the self-esteem of women with disabilities is put at special risk when they cannot achieve the degree of independence demanded by feminist ideals in America. Many women with disabilities fail despite their best efforts to achieve independence and make unnecessarily harsh and heroic efforts to avoid dependence on others.

Diane has worked hard to achieve the ideals that Hillyer cites: to support herself financially, live as an adult in her own home, cultivate a rich social life, and engage in activities that she chooses for personal fulfillment. Because Diane must rely on various kinds of helping systems to achieve her goals, the line between independence and dependence is not clear-cut.

I find it useful to think in terms of factors that promote stability and instability in Diane's lifestyle as a complex balance of resources, a kind of adaptive system.[41] Diane's supplemental security income (SSI), which she receives from the federal government as a consequence of having a permanent disability, is the bedrock of her independent lifestyle.[42] In spring 1997, Diane received $560 a month from SSI. The rent for her one-bedroom apartment in Long Beach was $470 (discounted because of her disability).[43] Diane also received $1,132 per month from the State of California program for In-Home Supportive Services (IHSS) to pay for a personal assistant.[44] She was enrolled in Medicaid, the federal and state program to subsidize health care for low-income residents of California. Diane's base resources gave her adequate housing and a personal assistant but allowed little or nothing for food, utilities, transportation, and other expenses. She could have benefited from the ability to shift the allocation of her combined resources if it were permitted in California as in certain other states.[45]

Once Diane qualified as a professional, she would have preferred to work for a living and reduce her dependence on SSI. She would also rather have had private health insurance. But she has had to retain her eligibility for SSI and related benefits because even a master's degree in clinical social work hasn't guaranteed her a job. Even when she is employed, certain expenses, such as paying a reliable and competent full-time assistant, remain very high.

In the 1980s Diane's marriage to Jim DeVries was a primary source of stability. He was both her partner and her personal assistant. Diane's definition of independence at the time was not feminist. But her lifestyle worked to meet her needs:

> Independence is being able to function in society without having to rely on a whole stream of people and places. I see myself as independent because I don't have to depend on my family anymore, on Mom, or on hospital care, always running to the emergency room. I'm independent of Rancho and my family, and even of attendants, because I'm married. I'm dependent on Jim basically, but most women are dependent on their husbands. Even in a convalescent home, I was still independent. I didn't need a lot of help from the nurses. But I *am* dependent on the government, financially, for what I can get and can't get.[46]

At that time, Diane and Jim were active in their church and lived within walking distance of it. Diane was at the church most weekdays, three nights a week for Bible college, and on Sundays. During the day she helped out in the office and replaced the receptionist when needed, typing envelopes, correcting catechism tests, running the post office, and doing "things people don't have the time to do." She and Jim ran the hospital ministry and visited sick members of the congregation. The circumstances were right for her:

> Where we are now, it is perfect. I don't have to have the fear of what am I going to do if Jim's not around. The people I know now are different. I know I can call and they'll come over no matter what they're doing. The Lord brought me to this point. If Jim's not around, people pitch in. It's like a big family. No one is embarrassed about helping me. I've been here three years now and they all know me. It's real easy, real nice. If anything happened to me, I'd just pick up the phone. They'd be there to help me. If I got real sick with asthma, or had to go to the bathroom, or couldn't get off the couch, they'd be over.[47]

When she became disillusioned with the church, Diane returned to school to finish her bachelor's degree. The change occasionally thrust her into situations in which she needed to depend on strangers for help:

> It is not easy to get someone you have only known as, say, a fellow student, for approximately two weeks, to assist you in going to the bath-

room without making either of you so uncomfortable that you pray you never run into each other again! But if you have to go to the bathroom bad enough and the person who usually assists you is not available, you will put on your most congenial personality, don your most understanding and compassionate countenance, call forth all your courage, and remind yourself that you have given up your right to personal privacy long ago, and ask for help from anyone you hold any semblance of a relationship with.[48]

If dependence involves powerlessness, as Hillyer points out, it can lead to manipulation, coercion, and playing on others' feelings of pity, guilt, and shame. It can also result in efforts to bend the rules of the entitlement system. These may be considered acts of political resistance and self-help within a radically unfair, skewed system of resources.[49] But they can also be morally damaging and physically dangerous. *When Billy Broke His Head . . . and Other Tales of Wonder,* a documentary that won the Freedom of Expression award at the 1995 Sundance Film Festival, exposes how people with disabilities often become ensnared by government-sponsored "helping systems" that produce greater dependency than freedom.

Two California women with disabilities not much younger than Diane drew widespread publicity for their acts of desperation during the period of my research. In 1979, the television program *60 Minutes* devoted a segment to the suicide of Lynn Thompson, a twenty-seven-year-old San Fernando Valley woman.[50] Thompson, who had muscular dystrophy, received SSI in the amount of $390 a month and lived in an apartment with her full-time attendant. Her rent alone was $379. Thompson wanted to work so badly that she accepted a part-time job as a telephone dispatcher for a health-care service provider, working nights from her home, although she knew her earned income might violate SSI guidelines. She was an exemplary employee, who worked three years for the same company, eventually earning $490 a month. She reported her income to the Internal Revenue Service but not to the Social Security Administration.

Thompson took her life after receiving a computer-generated letter saying that her SSI payments were being terminated because of her failure to report her earnings. Agency policy held that anyone who worked

for at least nine consecutive months, or who earned at least $200 a
month, was self-supporting and no longer eligible for SSI. Termination
also meant loss of IHSS for Thompson's attendant and her MediCal
health care coverage. The letter ordered her to pay back $10,000 for past
benefits. About two months later, Thompson took an overdose of drugs
combined with alcohol. She dictated a final message to her father on her
tape recorder:

> I don't want you to think of this as suicide. Think of it as R & R for-
> ever. . . . It's just a matter of time before the county catches up with me
> anyway so they'll cut me off, too. Then I *would* be in trouble, without the
> attendant money. I realize the system's here to help people but it needs
> some going over. It'd be great if I could work or support myself and still
> receive the full attendant benefits and, of course, some kind of medical
> benefits. . . . If I got to the point where I can make, you know, $1,200 or
> $1,500 a month, fine, they can keep their money and their medical insur-
> ance. I wouldn't need it then. But I'm on $492 salary . . . it's just not
> enough.[51]

She had a special message for the administrators who sent the letter:
"Thanks for being the straw that broke the camel's back."[52]

Lynn Thompson did not know that a new state law, A.B. 922, had just
been passed that allowed the State of California to cover the medical
costs of people with disabilities who were returning to work. The law
already protected Thompson, but even the local office of the Social Security Administration was ignorant of the policy change, and no one had
informed her about it.

The *60 Minutes* segment, "Help Wanted," allowed disability rights
activists to convince the public that people like Lynn Thompson who
wanted to retain their benefits while also working were not cheaters,
malingerers, or frauds.[53] Her needless death activated members of Congress to amend the Social Security Act in 1980 by introducing a work
incentive provision, Section 1619, modeled on the new California law.
Although some work disincentives remain in Social Security Administration policies, Section 1619 stands as Lynn Thompson's memorial.
Because of the amendment, thousands of people with disabilities are
working who previously could not. The federal government is also sav-

ing about $12 million a year as a result of reduced entitlements and increased tax revenues.[54]

In 1984, the case of Elizabeth Bouvia, a twenty-six-year-old woman with paralysis from birth due to cerebral palsy, made national headlines. Bouvia petitioned a court in Riverside, California, to help her starve in a hospital because, she said, "I choose no longer to be dependent on others."[55] Bouvia asked to be provided with pain killers and not force-fed. A handful of disability rights activists dissented, surging forward to save Bouvia from herself and the American Civil Liberties Union lawyers who had unquestioningly supported her desperate request.

Disability activists such as political scientist Harlan Hahn, historian Paul Longmore, and psychologist Carol Gill—who at the time were attempting to establish a center for disability studies at the University of Southern California—filed a friend of the court brief opposing Bouvia's petition. They argued that it was not Bouvia's dependency that was intolerable, but rather society's failure to provide adequate resources.[56] Bouvia had recently been estranged from her husband and had also encountered obstacles related to her university education and future employment, as well as increasing limitations in coping physically with the demands of daily living. Under the circumstances, they pointed out, it was only reasonable for Bouvia to be depressed. Any nondisabled person would have been offered therapy and urged to live rather than commit suicide. The Riverside court turned down Bouvia's request for assistance to starve herself and, when she refused solid food, ordered her to be force-fed through a feeding tube.[57] In the aftermath of her turbulent court case, Bouvia eventually retracted her wish to die.[58]

Too many women with disabilities struggling under conditions of inadequate financial and social support have been worn down by their fight. Discouraged by negative stereotypes, institutionalized discrimination, and lack of sustainable opportunities, some have considered suicide their best option. Despite her remarkable success in meeting the challenges posed by the dominant able-bodied culture, Diane DeVries too has sometimes felt that life's demands are too heavy to bear. At those times, she has talked about suicide. While she and Jim were in Bible school, however, Diane wrote: "I was created and formed by God the

Father, to demonstrate His glory and His power in a person's life . . . by living an abundant life, filled with purpose and direction."[59]

If God helps those who help themselves, then Diane's successes are due to her ability to manage a complex set of resources to maintain a stable lifestyle. When an essential element is missing or destabilized, I have seen Diane's adaptive system teeter and fold like a house of cards. Otherwise, Diane is pretty much like anyone else going about her daily occupations: pursuing her career as a social worker, browsing shops in her neighborhood, painting ceramic masks with acrylic colors, attending a birthday party in the park for her goddaughter, or serving as a volunteer in an agency for AIDS patients.

Diane's conviction that she can and should be able to make it in the community is a legacy from three sources in American culture. First, her family maintained an adaptable, "can-do" approach to Diane's early strivings with her disability. Second, institutions of rehabilitation had the unintended effect of sponsoring Diane's participation in a distinct peer culture of disability as she grew up in the 1950s and 1960s. Finally, since the early 1970s, she has been empowered by the burgeoning independent living and disability rights movements.

Kenneth and Irene Fields hold their two-week-old baby, Teresa Diane. She was born on March 29, 1950, weighed 5 lbs. 3 oz., and was 14½ inches long, with red curly hair and blue eyes.

(Opposite, above) Here is Diane in her Easter bonnet, probably one year old. (Opposite, below) Diane held by her mother, with her father and his brother Johnnie.
(Above) Diane using a cart she acquired at about age three, in which she could get around by herself using crutches.

This signed publicity photograph of Frieda Pushnik was sent to Irene Fields by a well-wisher who, after seeing Diane on a local TV show, thought she should meet the Barnum and Bailey circus performer. Born in Johnstown, Pennsylvania, in 1923, Pushnik briefly tells her "Life Story" on the reverse side: "Although I have no arms or legs, I was born of perfectly normal parents. I have one brother and sister both normal. I attended public school, my mother carried me to and from. I can sew, crochet, feed myself, apply my own makeup, write and operate a standard typewriter. I can do almost everything any normal person can do."

A KIWANIS STORY

Pair of Red Shoes Tiny Girl's Dream

By DON HARRIS

This is the story of a brave little girl and her dream of a pair of red shoes.

She's a pretty little girl with golden blonde hair and her name is Diane.

You might even call her Cinderella.

For some day, she's sure, her fairy godmother will come along with a magic wand and brush all the tears away.

It's a story, too, of heartache, of love, and of the courage and devotion of a mother and father, Mr. and Mrs. Kenneth Fields.

You see, Diane was born without arms or legs.

Each Day Another Episode

And every day in a home at 1305 Emerald St., Pacific Beach, another episode in a drama unfolds.

It's a drama of life, of struggle, and of learning — and it's full of tears.

It starts in the morning when Diane's mother, I r e n e, bounces her on her crib until the sand man is chased away and mother and daughter are smiling and laughing and ready for a new day.

Can Feed Herself

Then she fits an artificial arm to Diane's right shoulder and picks her up and puts her in a high-chair at the breakfast table.

Diane is 4 and she has been using the arm for about two years. And she does pretty well. She can feed herself now.

After breakfast, it's time for a romp with baby sister, Debra, 16 months, and time to dress her dolly, Marie.

Diane can do that, too — with her artificial hand.

And now, mother takes off the arm and fits two little crutches to Diane's shoulders and she's off for an excursion on her scooter.

She pumps away with the crutches and goes scooting down the sidewalk. And tags along with mother on a shopping trip.

Later, perhaps, other little girls and boys gather at the house and mother gets out the crayons and color books.

Can Hold Crayon

They all sit around drawing elephants, tigers and lions.

Diane likes that and she can hold a piece of crayon in her hand pretty well.

But she looked at the other little girls for a long time and wondered why she couldn't walk. She cried a little:

"I want some pretty red shoes like the other little girls.

"And when I get big—I want to learn to dance!"

So about two weeks ago I ane got her first pair of sho, — and along with the shoes he st legs.

red. She's proud of them just the same. But the next pair will be red!

And the legs are short— but she's learning how to walk. And they will be lengthened— inch by inch—as she grows up.

'Walk to Mommie'

Every day now Mrs. Fields stretches out her arms to her daughter:

"Come, Diane, walk to Mommie!"

And she does. She swings her little shoulders and the legs, fastened to a bucket seat, move her across the floor.

There's a proud smile hiding the tears in her mother's eyes and Diane smiles back.

"Pretty soon now I can go to s c h o o l — can't I Mommie? They'll like my new shoes."

"That's a promise, honey," smiles her mother. And when the Fields find a permanent place to live and Diane gets a little older she will go to school — just like the other little girls.

Right now Mrs. Fields and her two children are living with a friend, Mrs. L. E. Rainwater, on Emerald Street.

'Maybe We'll Get Settled'

They came here from Denison, Texas, about two years ago. Diane's father, Kenneth, worked here for a while, but now he's on a temporary carpenter's job in Long Beach.

"Soon," said Mrs. Ferguson, "maybe we'll get settled here."

That's the story of a brave little girl and her dream of a pair of red shoes.

But it's also the story of a lot of other little boys and girls like Diane and the story of the Kiwanis Club p r o g r a m for handicapped children.

The North Park Kiwanis Club gave D i a n e her arm, the scooter and the legs. And she'll get a left arm when she gets a little older and stronger.

And tomorrow at 9 p.m., the North Park club is sponsoring a dance along with other Kiwanis units at Mission Beach Ballroom.

It will be another benefit in a series started in 1947 to aid physically handicapped youngsters.

You can dance to the music of Lawrence Welk and to the singing of Alice Lon and Lar ry Hooper.

And Diane will be with her new pair of shoes.

She's the guest of honor.

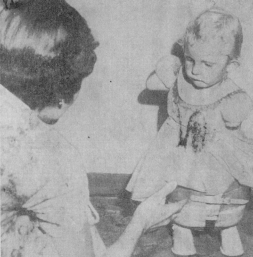

SHOES FOR DIANE—"Come to Mommie," smiles Mrs. Irene Fields, of 1305 Emerald St., Pacific Beach. And 4-year-old Diane twists her shoulders and her little artificial legs move her across the floor. She's proud of her legs and her first pair of shoes.—Evening Tribune Staff Photo

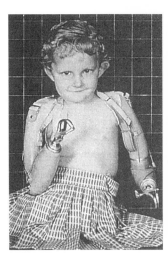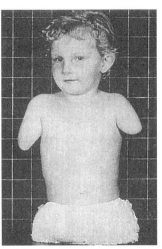

(Opposite, above) "You got your nerve, Diane. No clothes, but you got your jewelry on."—Diane's comment on seeing this 1956 photograph of herself. Diane loves this image: "I'd think I was cute, even if it wasn't me." (Opposite, below left and right) Diane became a patient at UCLA's Child Amputee Prosthetics Project in 1955, at age five.
(Above) Diane's sixth birthday party with her sister Debbie, at left, and the three Humes sisters from down the block. Diane loved to be cool and unencumbered by prosthetic arms and legs.

Publicity photograph of Diane for a Christmas event. Note her wooden rocker legs propped up on the wheelchair; these were provided by the Child Amputee Prosthetics Project from 1957 to 1960, when she graduated to a more conventional lower prosthesis with flexible locking knees and regular shoes. Diane hated wearing skirts or long sleeves, or having things put on her chair that "made me look like a clown."

Armless, Legless Swimmer Stars in Handicapped Children's Aqua Show

By VERA WILLIAMS

A pretty blue-eyed blonde with a happy smile, in a deep blue bathing suit, pauses at the end of the diving board.

She catapults into the water, a beautiful dive, either front or back. She swims the length of the pool. She swims on her face, and flips over on her back to get her breath.

She is Diane Fields, 12, born without arms or legs, and she will be the star of the Handicapped Children's Water Show, next Tuesday before the Shrine Club at the Lafayette hotel pool.

* * * *

CHILDREN with severe birth defects; children who have suffered polio, cerebral palsy and rheumatoid arthritis; children who are mongoloids; children who have defective vision and children who are deaf will participate.

Diane, daughter of Mr. and Mrs. K. L. Fields, 178 W. Plymouth St., was born in Texas — before anyone even had heard of the drug Thalidomide. Doctors attributed her condition to the fact that her mother had German measles in the second month of her pregnancy.

Diane has no legs; a rudimentary three-inch stump of a right arm; a rudimentary 1½-inch stump of a left arm. She is bright and well-mannered. She will be in the seventh grade this fall at the B. F. Tucker school.

She has a sister, Debra, 9, and a baby brother, Chris, 7 weeks, both normal.

* * * *

CHILDREN in the Water Show will include Garth Gersten, Tom Pillsbury, Carri Alba, Joey Bell, Yvonne Nelson, Doug Calhoun, Robby Scott, Michael duPont, Victor Lindsey, Kathy Daniels, Linda Sanders, Cindy Garver, Ryan Peterson.

The show's director is Evelyn Dempsey duPont, former Olympic swimmer and three times the winner of the Mississippi River national swim. She swam 54 miles in the Mississippi meet. Polio struck her nine years ago and her left foot still is paralyzed.

Non-handicapped swimmers in the show will be Bob Bittick and Art Overman who will do comedy diving; Joe and Don Sheridan, who will demonstrate life saving; Carol duPont, Deb and Miles Idom, Susan Scott, Joey Malarkey, Martha Williams, Laura Merk, Sheryl Kent. And the "baby" of the show, Brian Finch, 5-months-old swimmer.

The water show will follow the luncheon of the shrine club in Lafayette. A special guest will be Ralph E. Barnes, potentate of El Bekal Shrine Temple. Frank C. Finch (no relation to Brian) will be program chairman. Roy Wright, president of the Shrine Club, will preside.

(Opposite, above) Diane, age 13 or 14, playing pool at home, with baby brother Chris in the background. (Opposite, below) Diane's comment: "The Gang—aren't we gorgeous?" At a wedding party for Diane and Jim DeVries, August 1978, with filmmaker Michael Farkas, at left, and the author.
(Above) Diane and her good friend and role model from her days at Rancho Los Amigos Hospital, Christie St. Gean, reunited in 1985.

'I really believe I have a
purpose in life—to
use my disability to
encourage other people
to live their lives out
as best as they can.'

—Diane DeVries

Graduating From UCLA the Hard Way

By STEPHEN BRAUN, *Times Staff Writer*

When the moment of graduation came and UCLA's class of 1987 was asked to stand, Diane DeVries sat anchored to the wheelchair that has been her means of transportation since childhood.

But for a legless, armless woman who has spent her life extending herself to overcome obstacles, standing with her classmates hardly seemed necessary.

Along with 5,000 other undergraduates and 2,500 graduate students, DeVries celebrated her new status as a college-educated woman Sunday at UCLA's Drake Stadium. Surrounded by students who topped their black mortarboards with pink flamingos, winking lights and moose antlers, DeVries steered a more traditional course, flipping the white tassel of her mortarboard with the help of a fellow sociology major.

"This is real," she marveled. "I can't believe it's finally over."

DeVries, 37, handicapped since birth, took seven years to obtain her bachelor's degree and plans to spend another two pursuing a master's degree in sociology. Her ultimate goal is to work with the terminally ill.

"I really believe I have a purpose in life—to use my disability to encourage other people to live their lives out as best as they can," she said.

It has not always been easy to maintain that attitude. She was forced to drop out of college because of painful operations that required long months of recovery. When she did attend, DeVries often found herself hampered by the lack of facilities for the handicapped. Friends sometimes had to carry her up several flights of stairs to get her to class.

"What she's accomplished is just above and beyond what any of us have to go through," said Stacy Bunnage, 22, a fellow sociology major. "When she wanted attention, I would raise my hand for her in class. And when I wanted attention, she would yell, 'Yo,' until she got the professor's attention. If you help her out, she wants to do the same for you."

Born in 1950 in Denison, Tex., DeVries was later told by her mother that the doctor in the delivery room fainted when he saw her emerge. Three years later, the family moved to Los Angeles, where doctors at UCLA pioneered in work with children afflicted with

Please see UCLA, Page 21

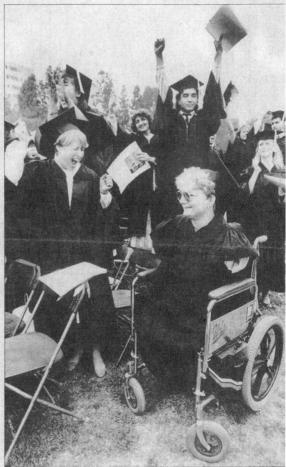

ALAN LESSIG / Los Angeles Times

Diane DeVries and fellow graduates at the end of ceremonies at UCLA Sunday

Diane and Jim vacationing in Hawaii in 1987, after she received her B.A. from UCLA—"Real good times. Jim wasn't drinking. We had fun." They stayed at the Hilton Hawaiian on Oahu, "the Home of Don Ho."

"Right after this photo, my wheelchair died. Jim insisted it could drive on the sand. It did and then it died." They spent the next day searching all over Oahu for a replacement fuse.

Diane taking a swim on Oahu.

Disabled woman fired, comes back fighting

Files complaint against hospital

By Robin Hinch
Staff writer

Bruce Chambers/Press-Telegram

Diane DeVries, fired from her new job as a hospital official, finds her optimism wearing thin.

When working as a counselor of disabled people in Paramount, Diane DeVries, born without arms or legs, always found words of encouragement. "I told my clients: 'It's OK; it's part of being disabled. Tomorrow will be better.'"

Now it's her own tomorrow she's worried about, and she's finding her characteristic optimism wearing a little thin.

After only four days on a new job as director of social services at Long Beach Doctors Hospital, DeVries, 40, says she was asked not to return to work because she turned pages with her lips.

"I was shocked and hurt," she said during an interview in her small, tidy Lakewood apartment. "What little discrimination I've experienced has been for being female, not for being disabled."

A Long Beach native and recent graduate of UCLA, DeVries, who's used an electric wheelchair all her life, said she was hired for the Doctors Hospital job on June 28 by Associated Social Resources Inc., a Los Angeles company that supplies hospitals with social workers. She understood it to be a permanent position, starting at $12 an hour. The hospital staff elevated a desk for her use and installed wall-mounted brackets to store her lap board when she wasn't using it.

Then on July 4, she says, she received a phone call from Meryl Stern, director of Associated Social Resources, saying hospital Administrator Thomas Olson didn't want her because she'd turned pages with her lips.

DeVries has now filed a complaint with the state Department of Fair Employment and Housing to get her job back, and says she may also file a lawsuit.

Olson, who's headed the 43-bed hospital on Pacific Avenue for nearly two years, refused to comment Thursday, referring calls to Los Angeles attorney Marta Fernandez. But in previous newspaper accounts of DeVries' job termination, he said it was "an infection control situation. We can't permit that. I feel sorry for the lady, but I just don't think that behavior could be allowed here."

Fernandez didn't deny that DeVries' problem was the way she turned pages.

"It wasn't just a page," Fernandez said. "It was medical records."

"What difference does that make?" retorted DeVries, who added she often turns pages with an arm stump. "It wasn't like I was out there licking the patients. You see nurses lick a finger before turning a page."

Fernandez did deny that DeVries had been hired permanently.

"We don't know what representation was made to her by the agency,

> ## What little discrimination I've experienced has been for being female, not for being disabled.
> —Diane DeVries

but we were not hiring her on a permanent basis," she said.

Meryl Stern of the placement agency would not comment.

In the meantime, DeVries fears she will soon lose her now-tentative hold on independent living — one of the things people with disabilities covet most and find hardest to achieve.

An energetic job search has turned up nothing.

The $615 she receives in monthly Supplemental Security Income will not pay her $550-a-month rent, plus utilities and food. She's afraid that by next month she'll end up in a nursing home.

But the fight hasn't been knocked out of her yet.

"I want the hospital to pay for what they did," DeVries fumed. "Those people just messed with the wrong person."

Diane at the end of her internship in social work at Long Beach V.A. Hospital, in 1993. "They don't usually give parties for their students going away, but they did for me. They all told me I was going to be a great social worker." Diane worked in oncology and with AIDS patients.

Diane and the author interviewed in 1995 for a short video piece.

4 Disability in American Culture

The independent living and disability rights movements began with protests by Vietnam War veterans, parents of children with disabilities, and feisty individuals fed up with the discrimination they faced in workplaces, schools, and other institutions.[1] The provocative imagery of people in wheelchairs gathering in public protests and obstructing traffic in Berkeley, Los Angeles, Denver, New York, and Boston was a magnet for television news cameras. The movements soon produced radical alternatives to the dominant ways people talked and treated people with disabilities in mainstream American culture.

Until the early 1970s, disability was viewed in America mainly as the private problem of unfortunate families and their individual members who suffered because of having an abnormal appearance or limitation in function. But a growing, vocal network of activists and scholars began redefining disability as a property not of people with physical and mental impairments but of their interface with their environments.[2] These activists argued that the degree of a person's ability or disability is determined by access to public facilities, social support, protection against discrimination, and cultural acceptance. Exclusionary conditions, not impairments, are the root cause of disability.

The independent living movement arose in resistance to rehabilitation, an area of medical specialization sponsored by the federal government near the end of World War II.[3] Antibiotics, advances in surgery, and other technological innovations began saving the lives of military personnel with severe injuries, such as spinal cord injuries, who in previous wars would have died. The medical breakthroughs that made it possible for them to survive were perceived by a few forward-looking physicians as creating a new medical challenge: restoring the ability of such patients to function in the community at their highest possible level. A new medical specialist, the physiatrist, was to lead teams of orthopedic surgeons, psychiatrists, and other professionals to assess and treat injured patients in all areas of function: medical, psychological, social, and vocational.

Through the 1950s and 1960s, this comprehensive approach to rehabilitation became the standard of care in civilian hospitals for adults and children with polio, injuries, chronic illnesses, and congenital anomalies. While countless patients benefited from the services offered, rehabilitation also had an insidious downside for those whose disabilities were permanent or incurable. Physicians reigned supreme over psychologists, social workers, nurses, physical therapists, occupational therapists, speech therapists, recreational counselors, art and music therapists, and vocational rehabilitation counselors. Lowest in the hierarchy came the person with the disability, imprisoned in the paradoxical role of patient for life.

Organized around a philosophy of self-help and skepticism toward expert authority, the independent living movement gained inspiration from the civil rights, feminist, and consumer movements. It offered an entirely new paradigm aimed at restoring autonomy to people with severe disabilities by "demedicalizing" their condition.[4] Although a physician's certification was still needed to authorize needed services, whether through private insurance or the public sector, activists encouraged people with disabilities to think of themselves not as patients but as consumers. As when purchasing other goods and services, the ultimate choice of treatments and services should lie with the consumer, not the physician. Most important, people with severe disabilities should have the opportunity, with its attendant risks, to live in the community like anyone else, rather than to live as a permanent ward of the family or in an institution. Eliminating architectural and social barriers in public places became a matter of civil rights. The point was for people with severe disabilities to get out of restrictive environments and move into the mainstream, with the resources and accommodations necessary to live meaningful, productive, self-directed lives.[5] These tenets of the independent living movement became federal policy with the passage of the Rehabilitation Act of 1973.

Such radical challenges to the status quo prompt the question: What is the meaning of disability in American culture? To answer it requires turning to the actual experiences of people with disabilities, beyond the language of laws and social policies. For an anthropologist, the first step in discerning what it means to have a disability in America is to look for contrasts with the experiences of people in other societies. The classic comparative approach reveals that behaviors and attitudes that seem natural and inevitable in one's own society are, in fact, culturally constructed.[6] Studies of disability by anthropologists highlight what it means to be a "person," a socially valued, fully participating member of the group on the basis of the questions: Is the individual included or excluded from desirable life roles and daily occupations in their society? Which ones, and why?

Robert B. Edgerton's book *The Cloak of Competence,* which appeared in 1967, was probably the first full-length ethnographic study of the everyday lives of people with a disability anywhere in the world.[7] Through participant observation, following a sample of recently deinstitutionalized inmates from a state mental hospital in California, Edgerton documented their ingenious attempts to cover up evidence of their mental retardation. The former inmates avoided all contact with their old associates from the hospital and tried to melt into the general population, terrified that one day someone would identify them as "retards" or "low-grade." One man who couldn't tell time, for example, wore a watch but pretended it was broken, giving him a pretext for asking others what time it was. One woman bought portrait frames for her home and displayed the commercial photographs that came with them to show that she belonged to a normal family. The picture of American culture refracted in Edgerton's study is one of almost unrelenting rejection and exclusion—the denial of personhood—to individuals with low intelligence, despite their sometimes impressive cleverness and adaptability.[8]

A contrasting picture of disability in a traditional society, the Punan Bah of Central Borneo, is presented by Ida Nicolaisen, who lived there three years:

> The very layout of a Punan Bah longhouse with its public space in the common verandah, from which a door leads to the room occupied by each family, contributes to the Punan Bah form of personhood. . . . The physically and mentally impaired live as members of their extended families. They stay in their family room and eat and sleep with their relatives. Leisure is spent in the company of fellow longhouse inhabitants, and they partake to the extent of their ability in social events and rituals. Depending on their handicap, they do their share of the daily household work in accordance with their age and sex, demonstrating more or less diligence, as any other member of the family. The disabled women I have known, be they crippled, mentally retarded, or incapacitated by old age, look after small children, do part of the cooking, chase chickens away from rice laid out on mats for drying, mend clothes, make sun hats, cut tobacco, and weave baskets and mats for household use or to generate cash income. . . . As far as I could observe, the Punan Bah treat their physically and mentally impaired children as they do their other children, but there may be subtleties I did not discern. The disabled were not singled out by nicknames connoting their impairment, nor were they referred to in terms of their disability. This is so, as far as I can discern, because they are recognized fundamentally both as humans and as persons.[9]

Such comparisons tend to show up most strikingly between Western and non-Western cultures and especially between technologically advanced cultures and those with traditional modes of production. In small-scale, village-based societies whose members are in frequent, direct contact, the identity of an impaired person tends to depend mainly on his ascribed place within family and clan, not his abilities or appearance.[10] These markers of status cannot be eroded by impairment as long as an individual can marry, have children, and participate in the community—and it is up to the family to make sure that these things happen, through adaptations such as surrogate reproduction. It is true that there are links between disability, gender, and poverty that place women—particularly poorer women—at greater risk for disability everywhere in the world.[11] But in societies where the status of an individual derives primarily from how well he or she performs a specific task in a competitive labor market—the situation in advanced capitalist societies—an individual with an impairment is *most* likely to be devalued and excluded from the mainstream, as is the tendency in the United States.

At first glance, assertions about the meaning of disability in American culture are likely to provoke debate. It is easily argued that the society is too large and complex to be characterized as having only one way of doing things, that change is constantly being introduced through factors such as the influx of new populations, and that individuals have unique personalities and life experiences that result in diverse attitudes about the proper way to act. This diversity is illustrated by Anne Fadiman's remarkable book *The Spirit Catches You and You Fall Down*, which examines a Hmong family's way of caring for an infant daughter with a severe seizure disorder in the Laotian refugee community in Merced, California. Fadiman documents a fascinating array of motives and responses among American doctors and other health care providers involved in the child's treatment.[12] Despite the diversity of individual responses, however, most of the doctors in Merced insisted on strict compliance with conventional biomedical practices. Only one physician—who was little respected by his peers—deviated from the dominant viewpoint and felt that the Hmong should be allowed to decide what treatments are best for them.[13]

Contemporary anthropologists no longer necessarily define and study cultures as coherent traditions passed from generation to generation.[14] Instead, culture is now viewed by many to consist of sets of competing discourses and practices, within situations characterized by the unequal distribution of power.[15] From this inherently political point of view, cultures involve conflicting ways of thinking about and doing things, even when people seem to exhibit a high degree of consensus and conformity. It has been argued that the more unified and stable a culture appears, the more power has been deployed to reinforce elite views and suppress alternatives. Also, the more likely it seems to members of the society that their cultural order is natural and inevitable. Sherry Ortner explains this theory of culture in a manner particularly appropriate to the study of Diane DeVries's life: "The emphasis has shifted from what culture allows and enables people to see, feel, and do, to what it restricts and inhibits them from seeing, feeling, and doing. Further, although it is agreed that culture powerfully constitutes the reality that actors live in, this reality is looked upon with critical eyes: why this one and not some other? And what sorts of alternatives are people being dis-abled from seeing?"[16] The struggle of disability activists to topple the authority of the rehabilitation approach amply illustrates that the meaning of disability in American culture is not stable and unified but contested.

It is necessary, then, to identify the specific institutions, social situations, and other sites of discourses and practices related to disability—and to analyze which discourses and practices are dominant and why. Dominant views of disability are most commonly found in ordinary face-to-face interactions between strangers. Such interactions tend overwhelmingly to stigmatize the person with a disability.[17] My observation of Diane in the lecture hall at UCLA provides a clear example: I stared at her, and I assumed that she was dependent on her parents and couldn't have sex. Later, when I began to read the literature on attitudes toward people with disabilities, I discovered that my tendency to assume sexlessness and childlike dependency was hardly unique.[18] Denying the sexuality of people with disabilities may be the most common form of repression of people with disabilities in Western industrialized societies, and it is linked to institutional barriers that prevent them from reproducing.[19]

Negative views about the marginalized and disempowered are especially pernicious when they become internalized and perpetuated by the people they oppress. To challenge such "ablist" discourses and practices therefore requires a highly disciplined critical perspective, because such claims can be unintentionally reinforced by recirculating them, even if to refute them. In a landmark article, "Uncle Tom and Tiny Tim: Some Reflections on the Cripple as Negro," the literary critic Leonard Kriegel called for people with disabilities to realize, like black people in America, that they must liberate themselves from limiting stereotypes and practices. Kriegel wrote: "The task of the cripple is to re-create a self, or rather to create a true self, one dependent upon neither fantasy nor false objectivity. . . . To embrace one's braces and crutches would be an act of the grotesque; but to permit one's humanity to be defined by others because of those braces and crutches is even more grotesque."[20]

Kriegel's argument was radical at the time, in 1969, but he still imagined "embracing" disability as grotesque. The cultural view that disability is essentially undesirable was still so deeply ingrained as to seem self-evident. It took another twenty years before Harlan Hahn, a political scientist and a leading theorist of the disability rights movement, deployed the tactic logically implied by the example of the black power movement to ask, "Can disability be beautiful?"[21]

The rhetorical distance between Kriegel and Hahn shows the difficulty, even for critics, in shaking off hegemonic views about disability. Works of cultural criticism like these have helped pave the way, however, for activists like photographer David Hevey and performance artist Jo Spence to mount alternative images of people with disabilities based on a politics of empowerment rather than conventional aesthetics. Braces, crutches, and other evidence of "the grotesque" figure prominently in their work in defiant, energetic, and life-affirming ways.[22] Diane once described her image in the mirror with appreciative humor: "What I see when I peer into that reflective sheet of glass trimmed in sea shells . . . is a 2'3" woman who J. R. R. Tolkien may have found appealing, with thick, light blonde hair; and a set of hazel-colored eyes enhanced by long lashes."[23]

Diane's ability to see herself as different, yet attractive and able to do most things, has arisen from specific experiences in precise settings: in her family, various residential neighborhoods, acute-care and rehabilitation hospitals, charity-sponsored events, a public primary school and a private camp for children with disabilities, her local high school, university campuses, peer-run centers for independent living, churches, and projects such as writing her autobiography, participating in a docudrama about her life, and collaborating in a life history research project with me. These settings, or sites, provided countless opportunities for Diane to assert and hear competing discourses about the meaning of her disability and also to cultivate her own distinctive practices for engaging in valued occupations.

Diane was born in 1950 in East Texas, arriving at the local hospital without arms and legs.[24] Long before Diane herself could speak or even recognize her name, her family was forced to ask, "Why?" Diane fashioned her own account of her disability from among competing explanations available in her family, community, and the wider culture. Her maternal grandmother, a member of a charismatic Christian sect, claimed that Diane's limb deficiencies were Satan's work. She accused Diane's mother, Irene, of fornicating with Satan and producing "the Devil's daughter." When Irene and the baby paid their first visit to Diane's grandmother, members of the Nazarene church were waiting there to perform an exorcism. Diane later narrated these events: "Carrying me in her arms, my mother had not even crossed the threshold when it began. Grandma snatched me from her daughter's arms and placed me in the midst of a circle of people. Some were shouting commands, some were wailing, and some were speaking in unknown tongues. But they all shared one common goal—casting Satan from this baby."[25] Not long after, Diane's parents fled to California with their firstborn child to seek their prospects in a sunnier climate.

Diane's grandmother saw freaks and oddities of nature as the result of traffic between the divine and the demonic, a view advanced during the Renaissance, which goes to show how tenacious cultural discourses can be.[26] Against the horrific implications of her grandmother's view, Diane hunted for a more naturalistic explanation. As a young adult, Diane finally summoned the nerve to ask her father point-blank the hard questions on her mind. Diane's key concern was to know more about her mother's behavior during the pregnancy: Had she been ill? Had she taken any drugs? The well-publicized cases of children born with multiple limb deficiencies caused by the drug thalidomide had occurred over ten years after Diane was born.[27] But an enduring effect of the media attention was to reinforce a tendency within the culture to look first to the mother for the cause of congenital abnormalities.[28]

"All I can tell you is what *I* know," Diane's father, Kenny, told her. "*I* know that when I saw your mother, she wasn't taking anything. And there's never been anything else like this in the rest of the family, going back."

Diane decided to adopt her father's uncomplicated and relieving explanation: "It's just something that happened."[29]

Cultures begin to change when people succeed in asserting alternative discourses and practices. Diane asserted her fundamental normalcy. She did so within a shifting cultural landscape in which children with congenital abnormalities were not as likely as before to be treated as "freaks," but rather as having a condition that medical intervention could mitigate even if it could not explain it. This message certainly reached the Fields family, as evidenced by newspaper clippings Diane's mother pasted in her scrapbook about the rehabilitation careers of children born without arms and legs, including three with quadrilateral limb deficiencies within a two-hundred-mile radius of Denison, Texas, Diane's birthplace.[30]

When playing with her younger sister and the neighborhood kids, Diane participated in most of the typical activities of childhood, but with certain modifications and adaptations.[31] When Diane's family camped at a lake and went swimming, her father rigged up an inner tube with a burlap bottom for Diane to sit in. When, unsupervised, the neighborhood children slid down the concrete embankment of a dry riverbed on tamped-down cardboard boxes, Diane managed to participate, despite the danger, by bossing and threatening her younger sister. Diane's memories of her childhood and family are far from perfectly happy, but she was exposed to and included in nearly the full range of occupations typical for her gender, age, region, and class. Within such experiences, Diane developed the sense that she could—and would—do all the things done by the people around her.

At the same time, Diane was exposed to surgeries, visits to the prosthetist, regimes of physical therapy and occupational therapy, special education, fund-raising events, and recreational activities sponsored by a host of disability-centered institutions and charities. With her sunny personality and blond curls, she did a stint as a local poster child for the March of Dimes, just as she had appeared while still a toddler as a disabled mascot for the San Diego Padres baseball team. Diane participated in an aquatics program for handicapped children in the Long Beach–Lakewood area founded by a former champion swimmer, Evelyn DuPont, and was the star of gala fund-raisers reported in the local press.[32] She was a student at the Benjamin F. Tucker School for Handicapped Children; an outpatient in the rehabilitation program at the Child Amputee Prosthetics Project at UCLA; a long-term resident at Rancho Los Amigos Hospital; and a camper at Camp Paivika. Each of these institutions had an official interest in defining Diane's disability. And, within such institutions, conflicts arose over what the proper definition should be.

The Child Amputee Prosthetics Project (CAPP), to which Diane's parents brought her for rehabilitation services at age five, became a key site for such conflicts of interpretation.[33] CAPP was newly established in 1955 by a contract with Crippled Children's Services of the California Department of Public Health, with funds from the United States Children's Bureau, and it later received support from other federal agencies.[34] In an interview with her parents in 1959, the rehabilitation team at CAPP envisioned Diane's future as a choice between being a "dependent person" requiring institutional care or an "independent person" with limited but attainable employment skills and the capacity to take care of herself. The rehabilitation team believed that Diane's future independence involved the use of artificial limbs. But they were proved wrong.

Diane worked diligently with both upper- and lower-extremity prostheses for many years. But she did not like using her artificial arms, for reasons both practical and aesthetic. Practically, it was impossible for Diane to be completely independent with artificial arms because someone else had to position the terminal hook devices for each specific activity. Since earliest childhood, Diane had been manipulating objects independently with her stumps. She could write and draw by holding a pencil or crayon between her stump and her cheek.

Aesthetically, Diane felt that the artificial arms were disfiguring and made her look like a "little Frankie" (a Frankenstein monster). They were also heavy and uncomfortable. Having a very low ratio of skin surface to body mass, Diane suffered frequently from bouts of heat prostration and preferred to wear as few clothes as possible. She sweated profusely, which made her stump socks damp and smelly. Also, because of painful overgrowth and bone spurs in her arms, Diane underwent numerous surgeries, sometimes more than once a year, to revise the ends of her stumps.[35] Diane's arms were tender before and after such surgeries, which complicated attempts to establish a regular pattern of wearing and use of prostheses.

All these factors contributed to Diane's preference for wearing sleeveless dresses and tops and for avoiding the encumbrance of artificial arms. This proclivity provoked debate among members of her rehabilitation team at CAPP when Diane approached puberty. Some members of the team felt that she was an "exhibitionist." They argued that it was offensive for her to appear in public with her stumps uncovered and that she should cover them up with artificial arms or bolero jackets. Others recognized that Diane was "happiest and most free" when unencumbered and felt that she should not be forced.[36]

Eventually Diane stopped using artificial arms and continued to dress as she pleased. As a result of treating patients like Diane, CAPP enlarged its focus from the design and application of innovative technology to one that also addressed social and emotional needs. By 1971, CAPP's statement of purpose indicated that prostheses were only one possible resource in providing "limb deficient or amputee children with the means and motivation to lead as nearly normal, productive and satisfying lives as possible."[37] But when CAPP began, prosthesis use was not presented to parents as optional.[38]

The moral of this story for an anthropologist is that official discourses and practices are subject to conflicting interpretations that can result in change.[39] The team at CAPP eventually learned from Diane and others in that first cohort of patients that, given the choice, most children with multiple limb deficiencies would abandon using prostheses in adolescence and adulthood.[40] They would decide for themselves what felt right, looked right, and worked best for them. Their resistance to rehabilitation would later be the theme of their life story.

Charles Jumps, for example, is two years older than Diane. When I met and interviewed him in 1985, he was manager of customer relations for a cable television network. Having been born with a complete absence of arms and hands, and with one leg about fifteen inches shorter than the other, he had been a patient at the Child Amputee Prosthetics Project for over a decade. Charles is a part-time actor who has had roles in film and television. In his spare time he is a photographer. He has equipped his cameras with cable releases; he operates them with his feet and, if alone, pulls them out of the car and carries them to the spot where he wishes to set them up. With his feet he can feed himself, type, write, and drive his adapted car. The only thing he has not figured out how to handle without assistance is what he calls "the physicalities": dressing and using the toilet. He has no use for the artificial arms with which he was trained. His story about CAPP is, like Diane's, based on a realization that he could do things better in his own way:

> I think maybe it was a myth, but they thought that by wearing the artificial arms all of a sudden everything was going to just fall into place, not taking into consideration that since I don't have any appendages off my shoulders, there were no muscles to tie into. . . . I remember having them [the prostheses] forced down my throat by the good people at the [Child] Amputee Prosthetics Project at UCLA. And I remember all the double-talk about being socially unacceptable without arms, etc., etc. And I tried. I went their way. I wore the arms for ten years. . . . About the time I was getting ready to get a driver's license I remember the Department of Motor Vehicles saying there was no way they were ever going to give me a license to drive with the artificial arms 'cause I didn't have control over them. And I said, "Well, what about my feet?" And they said, "Well, you show us that you can drive a car." And finally I did.[41]

Diane DeVries and Charles Jumps have worked the events of their lives into a type of narrative that is increasingly common in American culture, while also adding something new. The first requirement of the

American life story is that it be *personal.* Attempts by anthropologists to record the life stories of non-Westerners help to illustrate this tendency. When Janet Hoskins asked people "to tell her their lives" in Kodi, on the Indonesian island of Sumba, they responded with narratives about objects: a betel pouch, a hollow drum, a funeral shroud. Hoskins was frustrated until she realized that these were devices through which narrators did reveal their personal history and sense of self, but obliquely.[42]

Renato Rosaldo's experience of trying to elicit the life story of a man belonging to the Ilongot tribe, in a remote part of the Philippines, offers another sharp contrast with assumptions about the self in American culture. The man, Tukbaw, seemed an ideal life history informant. He was perceptive in human affairs, persuasive as an orator, charismatic, introspective. Rosaldo thought that Tukbaw's narrative would reveal a person whose inner life is intricate and deep, but he was mistaken. Tukbaw's narrative was concerned instead with things more on the surface of daily life: establishing his part in key events and his reputation among his peers. Tukbaw often told the story of a hunt, a raid, or a fishing trip. "What was not familiar," writes Rosaldo, "was that he himself should be the subject of the narrative."[43] Rosaldo's search for psychological depth in Tukbaw's account was an inappropriate expectation in Ilongot culture. Confessions of one's intimate or inner self are by no means natural or universal. They result in American society from a particular history of discourses and practices about "the self."

The expectation that people have a life story that they can readily narrate frames countless social scenarios in American life: filling out application forms, answering a physician's questions while being examined, preparing a resume, conversing with a new acquaintance, joining a support group, and talking to strangers on buses or airplanes. The kind of self-narration practiced in such situations makes possible some of the most interesting studies of American culture, such as the widely read book *Habits of the Heart: Individualism and Commitment in American Life.*[44] In interviews conducted from 1979 to 1984, a team of sociologists and philosophers in various parts of the country sought answers to questions about American character: "How ought we to live? How do we think about how to live? Who are we, as Americans?"[45] A propensity to display the self through narrative is a cultural practice that the authors counted on and hoped to encourage:

> We engaged them in conversations about their lives and about what matters most to them, talked about their families and communities, their doubts and uncertainties, and their hopes and fears with respect to the larger society. We found them eager to discuss the right way to live, what to teach our children, and what our public and private responsibilities should be, but also a little dismayed by these subjects. These are important matters to those to whom we talked, and yet concern about moral questions is often relegated to the realm of private anxiety, as if it would be awkward or embarrassing to make it public.[46]

The root of these narrative practices lies in the Protestant sects, with their emphasis on personal prayer and public testimony, fundamental American traditions that construct "the self" as we know it. The tradition reaches back to the seventeenth century with the landing of the first English colonists and was adopted—and "signified upon"—by generations of Africans brought by force and immigrants from other cultural backgrounds.[47] Another source, newer but no less powerful, is the exploration of the unconscious through psychoanalysis, which has given rise to countless forms of counseling and therapy through which millions of Americans become more and more skilled at self-narration every day.[48] These discourses and practices of the self feed into a vast market for life stories in books, periodicals, films, and electronic media.[49] For the sponsors of top-rated TV talk shows hosted by the likes of Phil Donahue, Oprah Winfrey, and Jerry Springer, can there ever be too many narrators willing to tell personal stories of adversity, struggle, and transformation?

The American life story is a moral tale about changing one's life and acquiring a new consciousness.[50] It is a conversion story dealing with the search for meaning in personal suffering and the redemption that comes with finding it. As Faye Ginsburg indicates in her study of abortion activists in a Midwestern town, life stories are continually reviewed and revised, but especially in the wake of disruptions and life crises.[51] People recognize that the plot line of their life has deviated from the normal or typical, and they hunt for a way to make sense of their difference. Gay Becker, who has studied disruptions in the lives of people resulting from

stroke, infertility, aging, and chronic illness, comments, "I did not foresee
the force with which certain tenets concerning normalcy in the United
States would dominate people's stories or the great extent to which they
would be used by people to make sense of disruption."[52] Yet many
people who experience life crises or disruptions will never be fully "normal," no matter how they define it. The crisis that prompts them to narrate their lives often signals that their story is missing or devalued in the
dominant culture.[53]

Diane's strong motivation to narrate her life story is evidenced by her
willingness, back at UCLA in the 1970s, to collaborate simultaneously
with a graduate student in cinema and one in anthropology on projects
to document her life. She has also written several versions of her life
story, including an autobiography of about 150 typewritten pages. An
episode that captures the heroic thrust of Diane's life story and her resistance to dominant views of disability occurs early in the manuscript, after
an account of her birth in Madonna Hospital, an institution staffed by
Catholic nuns.

As the story goes, when Diane was born, the nurse had to finish her
delivery because the doctor fainted. Diane says she heard much later,
from a friend of the family, that her parents, Kenneth and Irene, considered accepting an offer by nuns to keep their severely disabled baby or
place her for adoption. Diane writes:

> I hesitate to refer to this incident as a "memory" because I am not sure
> how far back one is capable of remembering, or just what is an infant
> capable of storing within its memory banks. However, I also have diffi-
> culty in referring to it as a dream because of its clarity and the fact that it
> has always been with me. But, since I have shared this with both my
> parents and their relatives—none of which recall such an event—or have
> chosen not to, I concede that it could possibly be just a dream of old:
> There is a very long and dark corridor. The darkness is due not only to
> the lack of light—for there is a slight ray coming through a small stained
> glass window hidden high up at the end of the corridor near the door—
> but also to the darkness and heaviness of the surroundings. The walls
> and hardwood floors are of a dark mahogany. Neither are there rugs on
> the floor or lighting fixtures upon the walls. Kenneth, and Irene with me
> in her arms, are uncomfortably sitting upon a very hard and dark

mahogany straight-backed bench. At the end of the corridor, near the small window is a dark heavy door which holds the attention of the two on the bench. The surrounding atmosphere is just as heavy, dark, and grave as the physical surrounding. Neither utter a word. They merely watch for the opening of the door at the end of the dimly lit corridor. After what appears to be a short but tiring wait, a nun steps out from the opening door and beckons to my parents. They proceed toward the door, and enter. This is where my "memory" ends. Because I recall being held as an infant, and since we left Texas three months after my birth, one must assume I was anywhere from eight days old to three months old. Since I have had problems discarding this event as a dream, my creative imagination has interpreted it in this fashion: My parents discuss the obstacles awaiting them and expenses involved in raising a severely disabled child, and, being newlyweds with a low income, feel it would be best to hand me over to the sisters. However, when Irene hands me over to my dad to hand over to the nuns (she, washing her hands of it so to speak), I nestle my curly red locks up against his heart, sigh that cute baby coo, and melt his heart for good. Being the traditional "head of all things" male that he was, Kenneth announces to all that they will be taking care of their baby. It will not be easy, but they will manage.[54]

A well-formed story can be written or oral, long or short, as long as it includes certain elements. According to sociolinguists William Labov and Joshua Waletzky, the structure of stories ordinarily told in conversations by English-speaking Americans includes a setting, complication, resolution, point or evaluation, and an added bit of narrative or "coda" to signal that the story is over.[55] Expanding on their work, Charlotte Linde defines a life story as all the stories a narrator ever tells of which the point or evaluation is about himself or herself.[56] It is an open-ended or discontinuous unit of discourse composed of many different stories told in conversations across a lifetime.[57]

When life stories are written as autobiography, they display the same episodic narrative structure as in an oral life story. But they are likely also to have an overall dramatic structure that for contemporary Americans is anchored in literature and film. Autobiography expert Tristine Rainer parses the elements of the dramatic story to include a beginning (an initiating incident; a problem that sets up the narrator's desire or quest), middle (a struggle with an adversary; interim pivotal events; an unexpected event that precipitates the narrator to act to resolve the problem), and end (a crisis; a climax in which the narrator acts to resolve the problem; a realization through which the problem is transformed or finally accepted).[58]

Diane's autobiography has this dramatic arc. The setting and problem she sets up with her description of waiting on the dark mahogany bench is whether she will be accepted or rejected by her family. Her desire, like any child's, is to be loved, not abandoned. Her mother especially fears that Diane will be a burden, as helpless as a newborn all her life. Then comes the critical moment in which baby Diane secures her father's love. Just as Diane's father hands her over to the nuns, she acts: "I nestle my curly red locks up against his heart, sigh that cute baby coo, and melt his heart for good." The climax of the story, her father's decision to take her home, satisfies the narrator's desire and resolves the problem.

What is the narrator Diane's dramatic realization? And what evaluation or point about herself does the narrator imply? In keeping with a long tradition of American autobiography, Diane casts her autobiography as a Christian testimony about her experience of God's salvation. She writes, alluding to the exorcism incident: "My mother did not screw Satan. I 'screwed' him by defeating his purpose of death, theft, and destruction by living an abundant life, filled with purpose and direction; and all this I do through his immortal enemy—Jesus Christ."[59] Even as a newborn, Diane does not wait passively for God to make things right, however. She uses all of her resources to assert herself. Giving herself a voice ("that cute baby coo"), she is transformed from a helpless object to an active subject—from a victim to an agent. Making use of her feminine charms, she wins her father over "for good," deciding her own fate.

Diane's narrative challenges dominant American discourses and practices that treat people with disabilities as damaged, defective, and undesirable.[60] Equally important, it transforms a set of family stories about the way the world is (people have bizarre reactions to a baby with disabilities) into a life story about the kind of person Diane is. The personal myth by which Diane lives fosters her self-assertion and resourcefulness as an American woman.

5 How Typical or Representative (and of What) Is the Life of Diane DeVries?

In a provocative argument, and quite ahead of her time, Margaret Mead asserted in the early 1950s that the study of American national character need not be limited to able-bodied descendants of the Mayflower. American culture could be perfectly well represented by its diversity, if careful attention were given to local and historical detail. "Any member of a group," Mead wrote,

> provided that his position within that group is properly specified, . . . is a perfect sample of the group-wide pattern on which he is acting as an informant. So a twenty-one-year old boy born of Chinese-American parents in a small upstate New York town who has just graduated *summa cum laude* from Harvard and a tenth-generation Boston-born deaf mute of United Kingdom stock are equally perfect examples of American

national character, *provided that their individual position and individual characteristics are taken fully into account.*[1]

Mead's inclusion of an individual with a congenital disability (the "deaf mute") in her roster of the types of people who could represent American culture was radical, when compared with other views held by social scientists and the lay public. Sociologist Erving Goffman claimed that the perspective below, written in his characteristically ironic style, not only was held by every American male, but that it constituted the one sense in which there was a common American culture. "In an important sense there is only one complete unblushing male in America," Goffman wrote. "A young, married, white, urban, northern, heterosexual Protestant father of college education, fully employed, of good complexion, weight, and height, and a recent record in sports."[2]

While Goffman viewed disability as a matter of deviance from the able-bodied American norm, Mead saw it as merely one variation within a broad range of possibilities. Who was right? The sociologist Goffman or the anthropologist Mead?

At the time of the passage of the Americans with Disabilities Act of 1990, about 43 million Americans—or 15 percent of the population—were estimated to have a disability.[3] Diane's impairment, known to epidemiologists as a limb reduction defect and, in her case, tetra-amelia (absence of all four limbs), is extremely rare: one international study reported only four cases of infants born with absence of all four limbs in almost 10 million births.[4] Should the life of a woman born with such a rare condition be understood as deviance from the American norm or, rather, in terms of diversity within an overall American pattern?

Following Mead, I regard Diane DeVries as a perfect example of an American woman coming of age in the second half of the twentieth century, while carefully noting her passage through specific social institutions designed to influence her health, education, and welfare. Her parents, teachers, and caregivers within the rehabilitation and social service systems were guided by their own visions of Diane's possibilities in life. Like most people, they were rarely able to see beyond the horizon of their own generation's expectations and values. But Diane, who was exposed to the range of feminine ideals then circulating in American culture, readily selected and appropriated from among them an image for herself. Diane's insistence on fulfilling her own ambitions and desires contributed, in turn, to transformations that her generation made in American expectations about the lives of women—including, of course, women with disabilities.

A rueful passage in Diane's autobiography laments her parents' failure to encourage their two eldest children, Diane and Debbie, in their abilities and to advise them about their future. Diane muses that this "could have been due to the fact that we were both of the female gender, and opportunities and expectations of females during the mid-'50s and '60s were isolated to the house and home." Yet Diane felt that in her case the omission was also due to her parents' incapacity to imagine a life for their disabled daughter.

> I never heard the words, "Wait till you become a mother," or "Someday when you are married, you will understand." Even though my toys represented the perfect socialization of a little girl into wife and mother, they were probably given to me with the belief that they would be the closest I would ever get to the real thing. Neither of my parents ever felt I would someday become a sexually active female, let alone marry. In that case, if they did not see a husband and children in my future, what did they envision for their eldest? A stylishly attired *cripple* sitting on the corner with her tin cup, or perhaps, an armless, legless version of Esther Williams?[5]

Diane wanted more than a tin cup. Born at midcentury, she was among the first generation to grow up with television, during one of the most socially conservative periods in the history of the United States. This was the era of *Father Knows Best, Ozzie and Harriet,* and *Leave it to Beaver*—situation comedies that promoted a dominant image of the American family as white, middle-class, nuclear, heterosexual, and suburban. Women in the sitcoms were supposed to experience complete fulfillment in the role of mother and housewife, an image that accorded with post–World War II domestic policies and ideologies.[6] But then there was also *I Love Lucy,* with its more complex representation of the tensions in this image. Comedian Lucille Ball played the zany television character

Lucy, an impulsive redhead always cooking up harebrained schemes. In every episode, Lucy tried to outwit her on-camera husband, Cuban-born band leader Ricky Ricardo, who was played by her real-life spouse, Desi Arnaz. Lucy's efforts often centered on subverting her husband's refusal to let her go out to work. Although she was always defeated, she never gave up.

In real life, however, Lucille Ball was the most independent and successful businesswoman in the entertainment industry of her time. She created *I Love Lucy* by proposing the television series to CBS, with which she and Desi Arnaz had separate radio contracts. Because Arnaz was frequently sent on tour with his band by CBS, Ball invented an entertainment vehicle that would allow them to perform together. Not only did she create the show's hilarious plots, but she produced them under the aegis of Desilu Studios, which she founded. When Ball became pregnant, she incorporated her real-life pregnancy into the show. In an episode broadcast to millions of viewers in 1955, the character Lucy gave birth to Little Ricky. At the time, television was not ready for a character who could combine a career with marriage and motherhood. But by continuing to perform, and allowing her pregnancy to be seen, Lucille Ball sent a subversive message that along with motherhood women could have an active and exciting life outside the home.[7]

Diane's mother's life story reveals the conflict during her era between the ideals of autonomy and domesticity for women.[8] In 1949, Irene Snow married Kenneth Fields, a handsome, easygoing enlisted man a year older than she. She had known Kenny since first grade, when his family came to live in her town in East Texas. Denison was a railroad town in an agricultural area with a few factories, near Paris Air Force base. There were the Levi Strauss clothing factory, the Kraft cheese factory, and a cotton mill. Denison also boasted three movie theaters.

Irene was a tomboy who spent hours in the smokehouse drawing and carving wood. She was reviled by her mother, a powerful woman born in Little Rock, Arkansas, who stood four feet nine inches tall. But she was indulged by her father, an affable, outdoorsy man born in Nashville, Tennessee, who stood six feet six. His position as a railroad agent on the Texas A&M line provided the family with solid middle-class amenities even during the Depression. They were among the first to own a radio, and her father had a beautiful Buick that he kept in fine condition. Although they did not see themselves as rich, the Snow family owned four acres that Irene's father had received in default for a bad loan. He built the house in which she was raised. They had a barn, the smokehouse, chickens and cows, and an apple orchard.

Irene was her father's favorite, and, as she recounts, he would sooner take her hunting or fishing than her brothers. She looked just like him, with brown hair and brown eyes, and also shared his relaxed temperament. He gave her a special knife to use only for carving wood, and he taught her how to carve. It was her father whom Irene cried out for during her frequent childhood illnesses. Irene recalled that when she returned home for a visit from California with Diane, then two years old, her father drove the ten miles into town just to bring Irene a pear, because she'd always liked them so much and wanted one. It made her mother angry.

"My father spoiled me," Irene summarized to me with a pleasant smile.

Before getting married, Irene worked for neighbors across the street, schoolteachers who also had a business selling canisters of oxygen and other pressurized gases. Her first paycheck was for twenty-four dollars. With it, she went right into town and paid nineteen dollars for an electric waffle iron with chrome finish for her mother. But her mother threw it out, saying, "What do I need that thing for?"

Kenneth Fields was the youngest of five children, son of a railroad man who had had to move his family out of their house and into a tent, and later into a boxcar, when he lost his job during the Depression. Kenny was a friend of Irene's brother, so the two knew one another as children, although, according to Irene, there was never a strong attraction between them. But one day after they had left high school and Kenny had enlisted in the Air Force, he turned up in town, looking handsome at a social event in his military uniform with his blond hair and blue eyes. Quite a few girls were impressed, but Irene didn't take particular notice until Kenny asked to walk her home. Irene and Kenny found that they liked one another and loved doing the same things—namely, going hunting and fishing.

One day, Kenny said to her, "Would you like to get married?"

Irene said, "I don't really know. Let me think about it."

She thought it over. One thing she considered very carefully was the fact that she could never get along with her mother and would like to leave home. She and Kenny were "very compatible," so she decided to accept his offer.

The three generations of women in Diane's family on her mother's side represent very well the changing patterns in American women's longevity, childbearing, and participation in the workforce.[9] Diane's maternal grandmother, Annie Beasley Snow, was born about 1890, had ten children, and did not work outside the home. She was about forty years old when she gave birth to Irene, her eighth child, in 1929. Women of Annie's generation had a life expectancy at birth of fifty years or less (Annie's own mother died giving birth to twins at age thirteen), and child-rearing took up most of their adult lives. But by 1950, when Diane was born, the average woman was getting married at twenty and bearing her last child at twenty-six. With a life expectancy of sixty-five years, she could expect to live for many years after her child-rearing responsibilities ended.

Irene Snow was right on target demographically: she was nineteen when she married Kenny Fields. Diane was born a year later, and Debbie two years after that. Irene had four children by the time she reached her mid-thirties. Her fertility was above the national average (three children per woman) for white women in her age group, but in line with the trend by which the number of large families with seven or more children, like the one in which she was raised, was declining. Irene worked before marriage, unlike her mother, but only because she wanted to. Like the vast majority of women in her age cohort, Irene did not have a paid job outside the home once she was married.

Diane Fields DeVries was several years older when she married than her mother had been. Diane deferred marriage until her late twenties while exploring life as a single woman and pursuing a higher education. Reaching puberty in the permissive era of the 1960s, when oral contraceptives were readily available, Diane freely engaged in sex with whom she pleased. When she and Jim DeVries were wed in 1977, it was after a long period of living together. Diane remains childless after having had two miscarriages and a hysterectomy. She spent many of her adult years as a university student preparing for a paid profession. These characteristics turn out to be common for women of her generation.

The self-image of a rebellious hoyden conveyed in the life story told to me by Diane's mother recalls the independent, slacks-wearing, wise-cracking female stars featured in films she must have seen as a girl.[10] Many female stars of the 1930s fit this mold, including Greta Garbo, Carole Lombard, Joan Crawford, Marlene Dietrich, Jean Harlow, Claudette Colbert, Myrna Loy, Bette Davis, Irene Dunne, and Katharine Hepburn. Irene Fields resembled them physically, with her trim, tailored look. These were self-reliant, assertive women who gave in and married the men who pursued them only at the end of their films. But, as feminist historian Lois Banner points out, "What would happen after Katharine Hepburn acceded to Cary Grant or Spencer Tracy was never made entirely clear: the vigorous independence of her character before marriage could lead her in a number of directions."[11] In Irene Fields's case, it led to divorce and a more autonomous lifestyle.

Changing standards of American femininity in Diane's childhood were embodied in "voluptuous, earthy" goddesses such as Ava Gardner, Jane Russell, Hedy Lamarr, and Dorothy Lamour. The prototypical earthy goddess was brunette, but blondes like Lana Turner and Kim Novak were soon added to the pantheon. This type was better matched to Diane's natural endowments than her mother's: "The 1950s sirens were bigger in build than those of the 1930s, and their breasts were heavier," writes Banner. "Women were to be homemakers, yet they were to be sirens to boyfriends and husbands, concerned with attracting men through sexual display."[12]

The personification of these ideals was Marilyn Monroe.[13] In a paean to Monroe written a decade after her death, Norman Mailer described the blond actress as "every man's love affair with America . . . the sweet angel of sex."[14] Diane was native to Southern California and the Hollywood look of the fifties: glowing, suntanned bodies in swimsuits and dark sunglasses. To my eyes, Diane, who has preserved her natural blond look with the help of Clairol, and who likes to dress in brief clothes that make the most of her ample breasts, embodies something of the 1950s feminine ideal.

That Diane to some degree internalized the desire for monogamy and fifties-style domesticity is apparent in a long, poignant letter that she wrote at age twenty-three about her foundering relationship with Jim DeVries. Diane and Jim had met five years earlier and fallen in love. Because she never felt truly loved by her mother, her pleasure in being cared for by Jim was profound. After they had lived together for some time, Diane became pregnant. She suffered an early miscarriage, but her pregnancy precipitated a serious discussion of marriage. Jim was a wanderer, but Diane felt she could keep him anchored close to her if she could fully enact the housewife role. In her letter to Cameron Hall, the much-loved orthopedic surgeon at the Child Amputee Prosthetics Project, Diane pleaded:

> I couldn't stand being Mrs. Jim DeVries and not being able to take care of him. You may think I'm being over romantic, but if you could only feel the pain I feel every time I see some other woman cook his meals, or just hand him a glass of water! . . . He has finally admitted our problem was my handicap. He said he lied about it because he didn't want me to think it made him love me less. He said we just can't go on this way because we are destroying ourselves as well as eachother . . .
>
> I have made up my mind this time that I have to *try* something for Jim and I. I have had many "boyfriends" but all of them, except for 2 just wanted to see what it was like to have sexual intercourse with a girl without arms and legs. God has been good to me. Not many people which are handicapped have such an exciting life as I do and not many are lucky enough to find a man to love me as much as Jim does. . . .
>
> I was brought from Texas when I was 3 years old to U.C.L.A. They trained me completely. They taught me everything I would need to know. They never thought of what I might do if I got married. I love U.C.L.A. and all the doctors, therapists, and surgeons connected with it. I know I was more or less their "guinea pig," but in order for me to survive I had to be. Now, I am asking for their help.
>
> They must have something which can help me *do* for my man. Even if they have to transplant arms and legs on me. No matter what they come up with, I'll try. I'll train for as long as I have to, but I guarantee I'll learn

sooner than they expect me to, just as I did when they were first training
me. . . .

Please help me. I can't lose the life Jim and I could have without trying.[15]

Diane did marry Jim just a few years later. But by 1973, when Diane sent
her plea to Dr. Cameron Hall, options for women besides cooking and
ironing were opening up rapidly. A decade had passed since Betty
Friedan's bestseller *The Feminine Mystique* had exploded the myth that
women were totally fulfilled by marriage, motherhood, and household
work. The National Organization for Women (NOW), founded in 1966,
was a major force on the political scene, raising women's consciousness
of their subordinate position and supporting demands for equal opportunities in education and employment. Battles over the proposed Equal
Rights Amendment to the U.S. Constitution often dominated news headlines. Moreover, in 1973, the U.S. Supreme Court handed down its landmark decision in *Roe v. Wade,* safeguarding a woman's right to choose an
abortion until the third trimester of pregnancy.

Diane's life certainly would be affected by the achievements of the feminist movement. Yet she was to benefit even more directly from a piece of
federal legislation that passed in September 1973, just one month before she
took her pen between arm and cheek to write to Dr. Hall. The Rehabilitation
Act of 1973 was the first major legislation to protect the rights of people
with disabilities, outlawing discrimination based on disability in the federal sector of the nation's economy.[16] The Rehabilitation Act called for affir-
mative action in hiring and advancement by the federal government, its
contractors, and institutions receiving federal funds. Section 504 of the act
broke new legislative ground by prohibiting discrimination against "otherwise qualified persons" with disabilities, and it required employers to provide "reasonable accommodations" to keep people with disabilities on the
job, except when doing so would cause an "undue burden."[17]

The concept of reasonable accommodation generated enormous con-
troversy in the next few years as it was applied and tested in the courts.
The appearance of curb cuts, ramps, reserved parking spaces for handicapped drivers, and wheelchair lifts on buses resulted in a huge shift in
popular awareness and perceptions of disability. The list of "firsts"

marking the inclusion of people with disabilities in the popular culture grew: *Coming Home,* a film released in 1978 in which the hero, a disabled Vietnam War veteran played by Jon Voight, uses a wheelchair and makes steamy love with Jane Fonda); television commercials for cars and fast food featuring customers in wheelchairs; and a Playboy centerfold featuring a model with a disability (a sexy blonde shown semi-naked in bedclothes and pearls, riding horses, and learning karate in her wheelchair).[18] People with disabilities—especially those with mobility impairments, like Diane DeVries—increasingly viewed themselves, and were increasingly recognized, not as objects of charity but as a political minority with rights to equal access and opportunities.[19]

The next legislative landmark for people with disabilities was the passage of the Americans with Disabilities Act of 1990. The ADA expanded the scope of the Rehabilitation Act beyond isolated pockets of federal authority to include public and private sectors fully. With respect to employment, it built on the earlier statute's Section 504 by including the mandate for private-sector employers to provide "reasonable accommodations" for workers with disabilities.[20]

Critics argue that the activists who founded the women's movement and the disability rights movement failed, in both cases, to achieve a truly inclusive vision and agenda. The leaders of feminist organizations, such as NOW, were primarily white and middle-class.[21] Similarly, the founders of the disability rights movement were white, middle-class, university-educated, younger men and women whose physical disabilities and experience as wheelchair users led them to pursue goals that enhanced the lives of people mainly like themselves.[22] But these were exactly the constituencies to which Diane DeVries belonged as a white woman, a wheelchair user, a university student, an aspiring professional, and an intended self-supporting member of the middle class.[23] She was positioned to derive full benefit from changes in the legal system brought about by the feminist and disability rights movements.

In order to track such changes, legal scholars David Engel and Frank Munger examined the life story of "Sara Lane," a newspaper editor and reporter who uses a wheelchair as a result of childhood polio, for evidence of the effect of the ADA.[24] Sara Lane's childhood was much like that of Diane DeVries; she claims to have participated in the full range of childhood activities, such as sleepovers at friends' houses, and she was educated in mainstream classrooms beginning in high school.[25] Sara Lane's first job application after college in 1973 was positively affected by her gender and disability: her employer thought hiring a woman with a disability was "cool." Her second employer, a few years later, responded similarly. As Engel and Munger point out, a cultural shift had occurred in which "civil rights became active in the employment decision, not because they compelled action, but because a growing disability rights movement succeeded in transforming the consciousness of some employers and employees."[26]

After being hired, however, Sara experienced typical forms of discrimination based on her gender and disability and had to struggle for more challenging opportunities than sitting at a copy desk writing headlines. Any breaks she received as a reporter came from other women who, despite having achieved the status of editor, were still fighting sexual discrimination. Although she hails the ADA as having "more teeth in it" than earlier legislation, Sara did not feel completely secure in exercising her civil rights to gain the reasonable accommodations she needed, such as an accessible bathroom and a protected parking space. She realized that initiating a court action might damage her relationship with an unsympathetic employer and therefore stymie her chances for success in the organization. She also wanted to avoid stirring up conflict that would make the climate less favorable for future job applicants with disabilities. But her grievances did matter, as Sara remarked:

> I did feel prejudice in the newsroom, and I did feel often to be an outsider, and I did feel that I had to work a lot harder to prove myself on a daily basis. . . . And you did get very, very, very tired of it after a while. When you're out in the real world and you take your kid to the mall and you find that everybody who walks past you stares at you, that really starts to get at you after a while. And there were times in the newsroom where that kind of staring was going on, that you just didn't feel they took you seriously or that they really wanted your opinion. And there were times when I would really lose my temper. . . . I said to the editors,

how long do I have to be here before we get beyond this point, before this is not an issue anymore? . . . Personally, it's been very degrading. . . . And the fact that they wouldn't give me a bathroom stall on my own floor for three or four years was just degrading beyond belief. It was infuriating; and you would just kind of go along for awhile and be a nice happy-go-lucky kid, but deep down it was really eating away at you. . . . I didn't feel that I could go to them one more time and say, I've got to have a bathroom stall on this floor, because you are perceived as a whiner. And you are perceived as someone, oh, well, we didn't realize you'd be so much trouble when we hired you. . . . We all have our little crosses to bear, but being a woman and being disabled and being a single mother with special needs has been very difficult.[27]

Reflecting on her life at age forty, Sara Lane was not ready to declare it a success story. Yet Engel and Munger point out that she has approached "the dilemma of rights and full participation in society" with "greater self-confidence and success than most."[28]

An overwhelming majority of Americans with disabilities surveyed nationwide in a 1985 Harris poll believed that life had improved for disabled persons in the previous decade.[29] But the playing field remains far from level, even for those like Sara Lane and Diane DeVries who have benefited the most and are part of an elite vanguard.[30] The report came to the stunning conclusion that: "Not working is perhaps the truest definition of what it means to be disabled." Sixty-six percent of all disabled people between the ages of sixteen and sixty-four were unemployed. No other demographic group in America had such a low employment rate, not even the group usually represented as at greatest risk for joblessness, young African Americans. The poll showed that the overwhelming majority of the unemployed with disabilities would like to work.[31] And there was a sharp contrast in the quality of life reported by those who were employed and those who were not.[32]

In the mid-1980s, when Diane returned to UCLA to finish her bachelor's degree in sociology, people with disabilities were on average very much poorer than non-disabled Americans.[33] They were less likely to get around and socialize with family and friends: the more severe their disability, the less often they left the house.[34] They were less likely to participate in the leisure occupations Americans typically enjoy, from watching movies, plays, and sports events to dining out.[35] They were less likely to do their own shopping for food.[36] Although a large majority of people with disabilities felt "reasonably satisfied" with their lives, they were less likely to feel this way than people without disabilities.[37] Most felt that their disability prevented them from reaching their full potential.[38]

The Harris poll did not report data by sex of respondent. Asch and Fine have shown that, as in the general population, women with disabilities are poorer than men with disabilities, less likely to be fully employed, and at greater risk of not living a satisfying life.[39] Disabled women are less likely to be awarded Social Security benefits than disabled men, even when they have similar individual characteristics and type of impairment.[40]

At age forty, in 1990, Diane entered the job market seeking full-time employment. After graduating from UCLA three years earlier, she had begun graduate studies in social work at the University of Southern California, but marital stress caused her to drop out for a while. Diane was separated from Jim and planning to divorce him. Living independently with the help of a personal assistant, she wanted to work in a field related to social work, such as discharge planning for hospital patients. With characteristic optimism, she went on interviews for two months. On July 4, Diane called to tell me the good news that she had found work as a discharge planner through a woman she knew who ran a placement service for social workers.

The director of personnel at Long Beach Doctors' Hospital had been impressed with Diane and hired her. But before her first week on the job was over, Diane was fired in a flagrantly discriminatory manner by the director of nursing, who had not met Diane until the day after she started on the floor.

When they did meet, the director of nursing said, *"You're the new social worker?"*

Diane said, "Yes, I am." And she thought to herself, "I'm going to have trouble with her."

The next day, at the nurses' station, the director of nursing noticed Diane turning a page in a chart with her lips. "Diane," she said. "Aren't you ever worried about infection—giving it or getting it? You ought to be careful!"

"My mouth is just touching *paper*," Diane answered back. "How many nurses sit there and lick their finger and turn the page? This isn't any different!"

The nurse said, "Can't you turn pages any other way?"

Diane explained, "I use my mouth like a right-handed person uses her left hand."

Diane had the phone on her left arm, the pen in her right arm, and was turning the page with her lips.

The nurse went to the hospital administrator, who called the registry that placed Diane, and fired her with the absurd-sounding complaint: "We're worried about infection control because she's turning pages with her lips."

Recounting these events to me, Diane was filled with anger and grief at her first experience of blatant discrimination.[41] She said:

> It all came from the Director of Nurses, who didn't like me. The charge nurses told me, "You did a fantastic job! You handled more work on your first day than your predecessor usually had in a week!" Nobody listened to that! Nobody saw what I did! They just listened to the Director of Nurses. They didn't even talk to me! They treated me like a non-person. They treated me like a dirty fuck.

At first Diane was wounded and panic-stricken. Not only was her self-confidence undermined, but she needed a job to help pay her rent. Her fear of ending up in a convalescent home made her physically sick. When she tried to eat she felt like throwing up. Her asthma became severe: "It was all balled up in me like a knot!" She couldn't sleep. A scalp condition, triggered by stress, appeared. But Diane's reaction soon changed from hurt to fury.

The idea of seeking legal remedies was not new to Diane. She had moved to Berkeley in 1978, when disability rights activism was in full swing. With the presence there of the highly activist Center for Independent Living (CIL), Diane found Berkeley to be more accessible than any other place she had lived. Ramps for wheelchairs were everywhere. She was impressed by a commercial she had seen there on TV that began: "Learn how to take care of the handicapped." Then there was a shot of a building with stairs; a judge slammed his gavel and pronounced: "Guilty!"

In 1986, as a student member of the California Association of the Physically Handicapped (CAPH), Diane helped to organize and placed herself on the front lines of a demonstration against discriminatory policies at UCLA—in particular, failure to comply with Section 504 of the Rehabilitation Act of 1973.

Diane now phoned the Western Law Center for the Physically Handicapped (since renamed the Western Law Center for Disability Rights). A lawyer told her that she had a remedy under the State of California's Unruh Act, which prohibits discrimination in all kinds of situations, including employment. (Although the ADA was signed by President Bush in 1990, before Diane's incident, the legislation did not take immediate effect.) As soon as she was able, Diane filed a claim of discrimination with California's Department of Fair Employment and Housing, while her lawyer wrote a letter to the hospital suggesting that they reach a settlement without litigation.[42] Diane also mustered newspaper publicity.[43]

Meanwhile, Diane called the woman who owned the placement service. By failing to back her as an employee under contract, she had violated Diane's rights. "Oh, Diane," the woman said, "I'm just as upset and livid as you."

"I doubt that," said Diane. "Why didn't you fight for me? The charge nurses and everyone said I'm fine."

"I didn't want to lose the hospital," the woman admitted.

"You've got ninety hospitals!" Diane shot back.

"I can't lose that contract."

"I'm going to do what I can," said Diane. "I'm not going to let it slide."

"I'll find you a job right away!" the woman countered.

Diane said, "It took you two months to find this one. . . . I just want to remind you, I have a deadline."

A month later, in August, Diane was still looking for work and feeling despondent. She told me:

> When I lost this job, it really did something to me. I don't feel as confident as I usually do. I'm self-conscious about the way I do things. I

know it's wrong, because I didn't do anything wrong to make me lose my job. I'm trying to deal with it intellectually, but it really has affected me. Everything I fought for all my life seems not to mean anything. I see myself now as a *handicapped* person. I've always known I was disabled, but now I feel handicapped. I notice people looking at me, I never bothered to notice before. I hear comments I never heard from people before. When I go for an interview, I think: There's 16 other people here trying for this job, why would they hire me? I'm just like a thousand other handicapped people.

Diane's loss of self-confidence was not helped by the fact that her younger brother Chris could not recognize the discrimination. Instead he questioned whether Diane might be at fault. He asked, "Wasn't there some other reason that you lost the job? Maybe you can't do the work." Sharing this with me, Diane commented: "He couldn't quite grasp the situation."

In October 1990, Diane's lawyer reached a settlement with the hospital for an amount that, as a condition of the agreement, may not be disclosed. After paying her lawyers, Diane calculated that with the settlement and her SSI income, she had enough to take care of her bills and live for a year. She did not go out and blow it, she said, except for treating herself to a beautiful leather jacket. She planned to start back at graduate school. Her last word on the settlement was this: "Hey, this many dollars for 4 days of work. . . . It's one way to look at it. I'm glad I got my bills paid. I feel good. I'm back to my normal self. I have enough strength to deal with whatever else comes."

I break off the narrative here to return to the question of how Diane's life should be viewed in the context of American life—in terms of deviance from the norm, as suggested by Erving Goffman, or as diversity within an overall pattern, as suggested by Margaret Mead. So far, I have followed Mead in treating Diane's life as perfectly representative of American culture, while carefully specifying her individual position and individual character as a woman with a disability. But the very terms *woman* and *disability* are problematic.

It is time to consider how Goffman's insights into American culture apply to Diane's life and to look more closely at how my methods of research might be implicated. Modern Western cultures have a history of confusing and merging images of people whose physical type varies from that of the European white male. The "Other" includes women, non-Europeans, and people with physical anomalies.[44] Consider, for example, the old epithet for someone with Down syndrome: "Mongoloid idiot."

Diane's bitter recognition that she was fired by the hospital because of her physical difference, rather than any deficit in her ability to do the job, was exactly like the experience of racism. But her experiences of discrimination also touched on the devaluation to which *women* may be subjected at any time: "They treated me like a dirty fuck." The hospital administration never spoke directly to Diane again; they didn't want to see her face, and they instructed her to return by mail the keys with which she had been entrusted. They acted like the respectable business-man on Main Street who pretends he doesn't know the prostitute whose sexual services he enjoyed only the night before—except that Diane wasn't a prostitute, she was a legitimate employee.

Presenting Diane's life in the context of changing American discourses and practices, as I have done in this and previous chapters, is an example of the method in the social sciences known as *Verstehen,* or historicism.[45] As proposed by the philosopher Wilhelm Dilthey, it is an effort to understand the meaning of events by reconstructing their historical context, including the subjective viewpoint of the individuals who took part. Dilthey argued that a true philosophy of life, and the human studies, should be based on the broadest possible knowledge, including psychology, history, economics, philology, literary criticism, comparative religion, and jurisprudence. Part of the *Verstehen* approach is to reflect on how the historian and her perspectives are bound by the horizons of her own age. My account of Diane's life is a historicist construction, based on selected facts and features of her life and times, guided by various movements and theories. Recognizing that my account is only one possible version of Diane's life makes it no less valid or valuable, but it does encourage new insights and questions. In particular, it may be asked: What discourses characteristic of my own historical period and Diane's frame my narrative?

This chapter has employed mainly the discourse of American liberalism, with its triumphal account of achievements toward equality for women and people with disabilities in all sectors of society under the law.[46] Liberalism is the source for the women's movement and disability rights movement as most Americans know them. Although liberal feminism has become synonymous with the women's movement in the United States, it is only one of several approaches to women's liberation to emerge during the late 1960s and 1970s. Others include cultural feminism, radical feminism, and Marxist or socialist feminism. Liberalism looks to the regulatory arm of the state to guarantee free and fair competition. Cracks in the liberal discourse begin to appear when other critical strategies for the liberation of women and people with disabilities are brought to bear.

To focus exclusively on eliminating sexist discrimination, for example, ignores class-based differences in women's resources that make it impossible for all women to compete equally.[47] In the United States during the 1990s, attempts by feminists working mainly within the Democratic Party to correct these basic structural inequalities have been soundly defeated. As one commentator put it, "The order of the day is welfare-state contraction, not expansion."[48] The trend is demonstrated by the defeat of President Clinton's proposal for universal health care during his first term and, during his second, the president's collaboration with the Republican-led Congress to dismantle supports for America's poorest citizens.

Marxist and socialist feminist analyses confront the effect of massive global economic restructuring on women and children, who disproportionately occupy the most impoverished sector of economies in the developing world and in advanced capitalist countries.[49] In the United States, for example, the percentage of jobs that pay decent wages and provide benefits such as health insurance is constantly shrinking.[50] The right to equal employment opportunities for women with disabilities in the United States is a meaningless victory unless more and better jobs are created. Clinical social work, the profession in which Diane was trained, is oversupplied as a result of the retrenchment of government welfare supports and the increasingly restrictive reimbursement policies of private health insurance corporations.

For Diane, this situation leads to a contradictory and confusing position. When unemployed, she is a client of the welfare state who survives on SSI, food stamps, and other entitlements. But when she is employed as a social worker, Diane becomes a member of the bureaucratic, mainly female cohort that administers and dispenses such services.[51]

In Diane's life, the achievements of liberalism—both feminism and the disability rights movement—must be weighed against the loss of entitlements and erosion of purchasing power for most Americans from the late 1970s through the mid-1980s. The effect of a global recession, the most severe since the 1930s, was jarring. Its impact was exacerbated by policies during the administrations of Republican presidents Reagan and Bush to withdraw the safety net that kept unemployed workers and members of the middle class from becoming part of a permanent underclass.

Fear of joblessness and homelessness lurks close behind the survival strategies of Diane DeVries, whose quest for appropriate employment in the mid-1990s amounted to brinkmanship. While attempting to maintain a middle-class lifestyle, she was constantly in danger of failing to pay the rent and lapsing into irremediable poverty. Her backup option, entering a nursing home, would drastically reduce her quality of life. Along with forfeiting her personal attendant and thereby losing control over her own schedule, Diane would also be obliged to give up her adapted van and relinquish control over her own finances, including the ability to save money to return to the world of independent living and paid work. It is her worst-case scenario.

It is liberal feminism that shapes my insistence on Diane's full status as an American woman (*woman* being the category that feminism has rehabilitated) rather than thinking of her first and foremost as belonging to the category *disabled*. I believe my view accords with how Diane sees herself.[52] But how effective is this liberal discursive strategy? Evidently it meant little to the director of nursing, who was also a woman but fired Diane. With one look at Diane she saw nothing but the potential for contamination.

When liberalism alone does not transform discriminatory social attitudes, discourses and practices that embrace difference come into play. Cultural feminism and radical feminism do not hold that women are essentially the same as men, or that equality means having the same opportunities without discrimination or special treatment. Cultural feminists believe women to be endowed with special gifts related to nurturing children and caring for others, such as intuition, emotional responsiveness, and empathy. They affirm these so-called feminine qualities as a source of personal strength and pride. And they have imagined alternatives to the institutions of society (such as religion, marriage, and the home) that the liberal theorists leave more or less intact.[53]

Radical feminism emerged in reaction to the contemptuous treatment women activists received from some of their male counterparts in the civil rights and peace movements during the late 1960s and early 1970s:

> In the civil rights movement, women rightly took offense when both black and white male liberationists aggressively refused to extend their ideals to the oppression of women. . . . Remarks like those of Stokely Carmichael: "The only position for women in the SNCC [Student Non-Violent Coordinating Committee] is prone" (1966), or Eldridge Cleaver: "Women? I guess they ought to exercise Pussy Power" (1968), contributed to the alienation of many women from the male-dominated civil rights movement.[54]

The same treatment was evident in the white-dominated peace movement. At the 1969 anti-inauguration demonstration in Washington, when feminists attempted to present their position at the rally, "men in the audience booed, laughed, catcalled and yelled enlightened remarks like *Take her off the stage and fuck her.*"[55]

Radical feminists argued that many supposedly private or "subjective" issues (such as rape and incest) resulted from the subordination of women within social institutions dominated by men, beginning with the family. They insisted on treating such issues as no less important than those of winning civil rights for all Americans or ending the Vietnam War. Radical feminism contributed the now commonplace, but still vital, wisdom that the personal is political.

Many disability rights activists have arrived at a similar radical stance. Psychologist Carol J. Gill, for example, depicts herself as an "ex-homogeneity-junkie" who formerly wanted to ignore or do away with uncomfortable differences:

But my black and gay and Jewish friends refused to go gently into that good blender. They insisted on being exactly what they were (and letting me know exactly what I was!). I got over the rejection and disillusionment to learn that it wouldn't kill me to be tense over differences. I even learned that I could be enriched by cultures I didn't understand, cultures that didn't exist for my enrichment. . . . If we've learned anything from other oppressed minorities it's that you gain nothing from efforts to assimilate into the culture that devalues you. We will never be equal if we accept token acceptance as slightly damaged AB's. Politically and psychologically our power will come from celebrating who we are as a distinct people.[56]

Any radical standpoint or identity politics based on opposing binary categories (such as *disabled* versus *able-bodied*) will ultimately raise practical difficulties about whom such terms *really* refer to.[57] The disability rights movement playfully subverts the boundary by referring to non-disabled young and middle-aged adults as "TABs": temporarily able-bodied.

Gill's message contains the important cultural insight that the category *disabled* exists only in relation to someone else's more powerful "AB" (able-bodied) position. It prompts us to ask: Can anything be done by people without disabilities who want to subvert their own AB position?

Gill's own experience suggests that it takes time and effort to change one's consciousness and accord respect to people with disabilities regarding their differences:

Respect is a key concept in accepting differentness. Many years ago, I was sitting on a stage with Judy Heumann and an interviewer asked us what we found most disturbing about others' attitudes toward us. Judy said she most resented their need for us to be nondisabled. I'm ashamed to say I didn't totally get it then, but I do now. There is a great lack of respect for who I am as a disabled person conveyed by people who either wish I could be normal or who need to see my disability as an unimportant part of me.[58]

Gill's testimony helps drive home my point that the usual ethnographic and historicist methods are not sufficient to understand the life of someone with a disability. Such methods do not necessarily free a researcher of unexamined assumptions and prejudices typical of the "AB" position. Most assumptions and prejudices originate in the common culture. Other assumptions and prejudices may have an additional, irreducibly personal layer of meaning rooted in one's own life history.

A radical practice of self-examination is needed by anyone—able-bodied or disabled—who hopes to transform the cultural legacy of disability oppression.[59] This reflective work cannot be purely rational; it must involve gaining access to feelings and unconscious predilections. One must become, in Ruth Behar's phrase, a "vulnerable observer."[60] My own practice while researching the life of Diane DeVries has included ongoing self-reflections (written and verbal, some with the help of a psychoanalyst) and dialogues with Diane to validate or invalidate my understandings through her comments and silences.[61] Such practices help to identify differences between Diane's consciousness and mine—and what differences they make.

6 "The Biography in the Shadow" Meets "Venus on Wheels"

FROM EMPATHY TO THE MIRROR PHENOMENON

When the eighteenth-century philosopher Jean-Jacques Rousseau wrote his famous *Confessions,* he boldly proclaimed that his self-portrait would be one of a kind. Laying bare his secret soul, he would display himself as "vile and despicable" when his behavior was such and as "good, generous, and noble" when it was so. Rousseau saw himself as unlike anyone he had ever met: "I will even venture to say that I am like no one in the whole world. I may be no better, but at least I am *different.*"[1]

Unlike the prototypical *Confessions* of Saint Augustine, almost a millennium and a half earlier, Rousseau's autobiography was not written to testify to his conversion to Christianity and to show the glory of God's grace.[2] Rousseau's motives were rather more secular and egotistical. "So let the numberless legion of my fellow men gather round me, and hear my confessions," he boasted to his God. "Let them groan at my depravities, and blush for my misdeeds. But let each one of them reveal his heart at the foot of Thy throne with equal sincerity, and may any man who dares, say 'I was a better man than he.'"[3] Rousseau went on to reveal his religious apostasy, adultery, and exhibitionism, and his refusal to support his five illegitimate children by a servant woman, Thérèse Levasseur. He assumed that those reading his life story would naturally reflect on their own. But to make sure, he challenged them to test their own sincerity by taking an unflinching look within.

Literary critics have already explored the interesting textual problem of how an autobiographer like Rousseau creates a coherent myth or "metaphor of self."[4] An equally important philosophical and anthropological question remains concerning the reader (or participant observer): How does the kind of self-comparison anticipated by Rousseau enter into understanding the Other? Personal introspection has expanded exponentially, so that James Joyce used as much space in *Ulysses* to describe the internal experience of half a day as Rousseau used to recount the story of half his life.[5] Rousseau would have been astonished by the flocks of writers who accepted his challenge to write their life stories. The writing, reading, and viewing of life stories are now a national pastime.

Following this wave of self-narration, scholars are turning in droves to autobiographies and life stories to understand the construction of lives and selves. In fact, numerous works by psychoanalysts and psychologists now suggest that there is no "self" apart from narration.[6] If so, narrative ethnographies produced from field notes over time have an edge over retrospective memoirs told only once.[7] Such narratives have greater potential to show the *biographer's* process of constructing and negotiating images of the Other. Successive field note entries and drafts become the evidence of the biographer's first impressions and of how these have been subsequently re-read and reinterpreted in light of greater familiarity with the subject's words and actions.[8]

Every life history contains a "biography in the shadow," as I realized early in my collaboration with Diane:

The life history may be thought of as a process that blends together the consciousness of the investigator and the subject, perhaps to the point

where it is not possible to disentangle them. . . . If the investigator relies
in a primary way on personal resources in understanding the subject of
the life history as another person, then in some sense the life history may
represent a personal portrait of the investigator as well. This portrait
would take the form of a shadow biography, a negative image, for which
the missing text could be found in the investigator's private thoughts,
interview questions, field notes, dreams, and letters home.[9]

Gaining insight into how I tended to construct images of Diane, based
on autobiographical self-reflection, was an important part of my study in
the late 1970s.[10] I was attempting not only to "locate myself" to readers
in the sense that feminist critics were beginning to do but also to clarify
my unconscious predilections and expectations.

Feminist literary critics in the 1970s had begun to study literature in a
sociological sense, focusing on images of women in fiction. Looking back
at those years, Toril Moi characterizes the critic studying "images of
women" as one who felt a duty "to present an account of her own life that
will enable *her* readers to become aware of the position from which she
speaks."[11] It remains a fundamental assumption of most feminist criticism that the reader has a right to learn about the writer's experience
because no criticism is value-free; it would be authoritarian and manipu-
lative to present anyone's limited perspective as "universal," and the only
democratic procedure is to provide the reader with all the necessary
information about the limitations of one's own perspective from the start.

The difficulty I found with the feminist practice of self-exposure was
its failure to go deeper, to explore the unconscious, and to offer methods
needed to do a more thorough job. The need for readers and critics of
women's lives to examine their own pre-understandings is one that Moi
grasps precisely:

Problems do however arise if we are too sanguine about the actual possibility of making one's own position clear. Hermeneutical theory, for
instance, has pointed out that we cannot fully grasp our own "horizon of
understanding": there will always be unstated blind spots, fundamental
presuppositions and "pre-understandings" of which we are unaware.
Psychoanalysis furthermore informs us that the most powerful motiva-
tions of our psyche often turn out to be those we have most deeply
repressed. It is therefore difficult to believe that we can ever fully be

aware of our own perspective. The prejudices one is *able* to formulate consciously are precisely for that reason likely to be the least important ones. These theoretical difficulties are not just abstract problems of the philosophers among us: They return to manifest themselves quite evidently in the texts of the feminist critic who tries to practice the autobiographical ideal in her work.[12]

The autobiographical work of feminist critics is often disparagingly labeled exhibitionist and narcissistic, contrary to its author's stated intention.[13] Even the most candid self-presentation can leave much out. My colleague Janet Hoskins comments: "Every 'confession' both reveals and conceals by focusing on one aspect at the expense of another. Every 'confessional moment' invokes vulnerability but is also a subtle defense and self-justification."[14]

In choosing to write about the life of Diane DeVries, I had to ask myself how it was that, as an anthropologist, I chose not to travel to some remote place, but to stay at home and study one individual, one with a congenital absence of limbs. Rehabilitation research after World War II demonstrated that exposure to persons with disabilities often stimulates feelings of distress in able-bodied subjects. These reactions tended to involve some identification, or disturbance of identification, with the disabled person. In one study undertaken with Navy personnel, perceptions of adult amputees and even of mutilated mannequins provoked anxiety and anger in able-bodied male subjects.[15] According to classic psychoanalytic theory, visible physical abnormalities threaten the body image of the able-bodied. A trainee in psychoanalysis, to whom I described my study, joked: "It gives me castration anxiety just to think about it!"

I knew that some people found it hard to encounter Diane face-to-face. For instance, Diane told me that she and a friend were once seated way in the back of a popular restaurant in Westwood, near UCLA. When they removed themselves to an empty table by the window, their waitress complained within earshot: "She'll make the people sick!"[16]

In a study by a Canadian sociologist, even mothers of children born with limb deficiencies due to thalidomide needed to learn to see their offspring in their own image: "The maternity of a thalidomide child was not simply a triumph of maternal feelings over abnormality; on the contrary, it was based on the mother's ability to find sufficient common ground between mother and child, in spite of the differences."[17]

In her study of parental responses to their children born with disabilities, Israeli anthropologist Meira Weiss notes that 68.4 percent of newborns with appearance impairments were abandoned by their parents, whereas 93 percent of the newborns suffering from internal defects were taken home.[18] Weiss concludes that the parents' body image must be the significant factor in determining whether parents initially bond with their appearance-impaired children, since no other information concerning the newborn really exists. This was exactly the situation of her parents that Diane imaginatively reconstructs in the dream she recounts, when her parents are about to hand over their disabled newborn to the nuns.[19]

Confronted by overwhelming evidence that contact with persons with severe physical disabilities evokes powerful emotional reactions for others, I set about uncovering my emotional responses to Diane, using methods derived from Edmund Husserl, founder of the phenomenological movement, for describing how perceptions of the world are constituted in consciousness.[20] Husserl's methods involve disciplined reflection, or introspection, on experience. In other words, phenomenology proceeds by means of intuition, rather than induction or deduction.

A study by Gaston Bachelard with an intriguing title, *The Psychoanalysis of Fire*, provided me with a particularly helpful methodological example.[21] Investigating the evolution of the metaphor of fire in Western culture, Bachelard began by free association of images that he later challenged, through further introspection. In such an inquiry, Bachelard found, his first impression was not likely to be a fundamental truth, but one that almost invariably was refuted. Therefore the investigator must decisively "bracket" or suspend first impressions. My first impressions of Diane DeVries were dominated by my reaction to her appearance as a disabled person. Following the example of Bachelard, I sought to bracket this impression and examine its contents, including its emotional content for me.

In autobiographical writings I began by exploring the earliest images I had formed of "crips."[22] Like Diane, I grew up during the 1950s and 1960s. My childhood took place in the Bronx, New York, where I was born in 1948. Many images came to mind, from passing close to a beautiful midget at the circus ("Ooo, Daddy! That little girl is wearing *rouge* and *lipstick!*") and being hushed, to looking up from the curb at anonymous veterans on crutches, with pinned-up uniforms, who marched down the flag-bedecked Grand Concourse on Memorial Day, to conversations with my much-loved junior high school English teacher, Edmund "Dante" Assante, with his tobacco-stained fingers, quick laugh, and forceful walk from years of dragging a brace. Dante was the first to take me (and my writing) seriously. As I dredged my memory, I knew when I hit the mark by the release of emotion: a burst of laughter, deep sobbing, dry retching.

Over the next several months, I examined, in turn, three broad domains of my experience. First, I tried to remember all the people I knew who were "crips" and my feelings about them: What was it about the veterans that interested or repelled me? What did Dante's disability mean to me? Next I examined the ways in which, on the basis of physical limitations, *I* could be considered a "crip": squinting and wearing glasses for myopia since I was a little girl, speech classes for my lisp, visits to Orthopedic Hospital for my pigeon-toed gait—and big, ugly, but very comfortable corrective shoes with a "cookie" inside and curved Thomas heels.

Finally, because I perceived Diane's body as *missing* something, I examined experiences of lack and loss in my life: unfulfilled desires, lack of power, lack of control, loss of innocence, loss of self-esteem (craving my mother's loving attention, being Jewish and learning about the Holocaust, allowing myself to be coerced around age five into a sexual act to please my brother, shame and distress about my homosexual longings). As my emotions were discharged, certain presuppositions became clear to me: I had expected to find a victim in Diane. Instead, as my psychologist pointed out to me, using a popular metaphor of the 1970s, I had found a survivor.

These strictly intuitive insights were among my pre-understandings, products of phenomenological reflection now available for further hermeneutic analysis. Traditionally, hermeneutic reasoning is described as a "circle" in which knowledge about the whole (text) is applied to understand a part (a word or phrase), which in turn is used to reinterpret the whole.[23] More recently, Hans-Georg Gadamer has argued that hermeneutics can never be a wholly rational process. Prejudices, or pre-understandings, are part of the interpreter's "horizon" of understanding—a horizon that is not fixed and rigid, but that advances and is transformed by new understandings.[24]

In psychoanalytic terms, it could be said quite properly that my image of Diane was affected by such processes as transference, countertransference, identification, projection, and splitting.[25] But I was interested in phenomenology, which emphasized neutrality and the suspension of judgments. I wanted little to do with the medicalized side of psychoanalysis that dealt with the correction of pathology. I called my project "psychoanalysis without a problem." This disclaimer hid the exact opposite truth, however, that I longed for a psychoanalysis because I felt that some things were indeed very wrong with me. The life history project allowed me to make myself visible to myself under the legitimating praxis of clarifying what was *not wrong* with Diane. It was a search for the self through the detour of the other. As for Diane, she had no interest, then or later, in being psychoanalyzed—at least not by me.

When we first worked together, Diane encouraged me to contact her former psychotherapist for information.[26] It was something I vaguely planned to do and never got around to. But about the same time I had begun seeing a humanistic psychologist; it was my second experience of being in treatment. My first experience with therapy was as an adolescent at a clinic in Manhattan, at a time when my older brother and I, who shared a room, were at each other's throats, everyone in the family was constantly yelling and fighting, and I began pressuring my parents to get a divorce. The only problem was that I couldn't decide which parent to choose. My mother was crazy, as far as I was concerned, but she had the more expansive approach to living. She was articulate and loved to talk. If only she had had the same gift of listening to me. She loved going to the theater and dining at elegant restaurants, bought beautiful clothes and expensive furniture, and argued with my father that I should be allowed to do the more adventurous things I wanted to try—things she had been prevented from doing.

My father, who left the house to open his garage business downtown every morning before six in every kind of weather, always made me feel loved, even though he was so uncommunicative as to be almost mute. I think I can remember every conversation I ever had with him because there were so few. A dreamer with artistic talent and an eighth-grade education, he was imaginative and playful in a childlike way, but as an adult extremely self-limiting. Never having gotten over the poverty of his early childhood on New York's Lower East Side, he lived simply and resignedly. One boyhood memory he shared was of standing in front of a bakery window, too poor to buy anything, but filling himself up by imagining eating the cake. We had often had a wordless alliance when my mother was making exhausting emotional demands. But his classic response to complaints from any quarter was: "I make the best of it."

I begged my parents to let me go somewhere else: to private school, to summer camp, to a therapist. My mother did a first-class job of researching the options, and I was accepted for treatment, on a sliding-scale fee basis, at the Alfred Adler Mental Hygiene Institute. At least one parent was expected to attend family therapy. My father, of course, refused. But my mother joined a daytime group led by one of Adler's disciples, Danica Deutsch. This was a new outlet for her tremendous verbal talents, and she shone with new ideas and new confidence. She felt that her marriage benefited enormously, and she also acquired new friends, well-to-do wives of professionals and successful businessmen—the class to which she aspired and should probably have belonged.

Thus my mother and I had a fascinating, oddly status-enhancing exposure to the mainly Jewish milieu of psychoanalysis, transplanted from Freud's Vienna to Central Park West. This exposure also unfortunately included for me a privileged insight into the absurd phallocentrism and self-deception possible among psychoanalysts. My mother was referred for a consultation with an eminent analyst whose last name was apparently "A-member-of-Freud's-circle." She thought I would be interested to meet him and left me to visit with him for a few minutes privately in his office. The kindly doctor in his eighties, with protruding blue-veined lips, whose name in German actually means "frog," in fact looked like one. I was disgusted when he gave me an erotic good-bye kiss and had the chutzpah to invite me back. I was angry with my mother for putting me in that situation and amazed at the frog's vanity.

In the mid-1970s I began therapy with the humanistic psychologist, who helped me explore difficulties I was experiencing with accepting my sexual orientation and establishing a compatible and well-functioning relationship. This reentry into therapy came as a result of an explosive event that occurred when I was visiting my brother's new in-laws, a former sheriff and his wife in an Alabama county light-years from the Bronx. The sheriff had a reputation for pawing his female kin, and on a little tour of the catfish pond he groped me.

"Give me some of that *good* sugar," he said. "I won't tell nobody if you don't."

I went back into the house and informed my father. He offered no help. "Forget about it. He's a sick man," he said.

"If it were *his* daughter," I said, "he'd get out a shotgun." I began to cry and gave myself over to the luxury of a hysterical outpouring that let up only when my mother returned from an outing with the sheriff's wife. When I told her what had happened, she consoled me and took the opportunity of this breakthrough to ask whether any improper relations had ever occurred between my brother and me. Then she confessed that when she was a girl, her brother had groped her in her sleep. At the time she pretended not to notice, but she resented him all her life and forgave him only on his deathbed—not that he ever asked for forgiveness. With my therapist I explored such experiences of powerlessness and how they might be related to the image of Diane as someone whose limbs suggested immobilization.

In the mid-1980s, with the breakup of a six-year relationship, I returned to therapy with a marriage, family, and child counselor who was recommended through the lesbian community. Later, on a field trip in Israel and the West Bank in 1986, I experienced a breakdown with symptoms of acute anxiety and depression and was encouraged by a psychiatrist there to return to therapy and begin "working with transference." Returning to the United States, I began an absorbing and productive analysis with a clinical social worker finishing her psychoanalytic training. It lasted seven years, with me on the couch for fifty minutes, five days a week. This treatment, which ended unsatisfactorily, was implicated in a paper I wrote about Diane, using a psychoanalytic approach to which she strongly objected. But that is to be discussed in the next chapter.

To take another's standpoint or perspective requires empathy, which makes a biography a highly demanding form of historicist research. It involves not just reconstructing a period or category of experience but also grasping the specific feelings and perspectives of an actual individual. In her study of empathy published in 1917, Edith Stein argued that empathy with another person's feelings is a direct intuition, an experience all its own, with no need for symbols.[27] In certain more complex states of empathy, however, Stein suggested that we assume the place of the other person as the "I" at the center of her world, orienting toward the same objects in the same way and using our imagination. Stein writes:

> As my own person is constituted in primordial mental acts, so the foreign person is constituted in empathically experienced acts. I experience his every action as proceeding from a will and this, in turn, from a feeling. Simultaneously with this, I am given a level of his person and a range of values in principle experienceable by him. This, in turn, meaningfully motivates the expectation of future possible volitions and actions. Accordingly, a single action and also a single bodily expression, such as a look or a laugh, can give me a glimpse into the kernel of the person.[28]

Stein's practice offered no guarantee that I would really have the same experiences as Diane DeVries. Deceptions of all kinds are possible, of course. But attempting to center myself in Diane's world did open up ranges of values that I might not have experienced otherwise, just by posing their possibility. This brought me closer not only to Diane's momentary states of feeling but also to understanding how she is constituted as a person, someone different from me.

In my practice of empathy, it has been as important to listen to Diane's silences as much as to her actual statements, as occurred when Diane commented on the first draft of my dissertation. Although Diane's comments on my work have never been effusive, she singled out one paragraph for praise: "Page 2, last ¶ was superb. I really liked that."

Turning to page 2, I found a description from my phenomenological investigations of what I imagined it would feel like to have a body like Diane's, not with arms but with stumps. The feelings I experienced were of physical ineffectuality and, if covertly, sexual inadequacy:

> It reminds me of the flippers on certain pinball machines which you jam with a button. These flippers are incredibly frustrating to use. You jam a button at the front of the machine which usually feels as though the spring behind it is broken—either because it was punched too often, or because it was designed not to work. The flippers are weak and the radius of their motion is somehow always too short. I get the same feeling when trying to roll film on a developing reel in a dark room, or worse, in a light-proof bag. If the film jams on the reel over and over again, I go berserk. My breathing gets fast and I start feeling trapped. I want to turn on the light, but that would spoil the film; so I am caught, angry and choking. That's how I feel playing pinball. That's what Diane's arms remind me of. A pair of ineffectual pinball flippers.

When I reread the paragraph I was amazed. This was probably the most narcissistic passage in my entire draft, in the sense that it was written with almost no regard for Diane's feelings. I had produced it very early in my acquaintance with Diane and wanted to suspend normal social restraint so that I could freely explore the distress that lacking arms and legs could cause me. I should have kept the results completely private, but I had allowed Diane to see it. Perhaps I wanted to see if she could take *my* standpoint and appreciate my efforts as an experimental ethnographer. I read the paragraph aloud to Diane when we next met.

"Was that it, the part you liked?" Diane hesitated and averted her eyes. There was not even a flicker of affirmation in her face.

Later, I found a different sheet, also marked "page 2," in the draft Diane had reviewed. The last paragraph on this page was undoubtedly the one she had praised:

> Diane Fields has managed to experience many if not most of the key life events that might be considered normal for a person of her age, gender, and social background. She has grown up at home with the rest of her family, gone to public schools, maintained a social life with her peers, lived in a variety of arrangements with friends, had relationships with lovers, attended a major university, lived independently in her own

apartment, has been pregnant, and has been married. Diane has lived in institutions for the disabled, attended special schools and clinics, struggled with prostheses and abandoned them, undergone frequent and painful surgeries, confronted the progressive debilitation of her body, depended on the assistance of others for her most basic subsistence needs, and more than once has attempted suicide. To me, the life history of Diane Fields underscores, among other things, the power of norms to order a person's life even against the strongest pressures to adopt other standards. I would say that a feature of Diane Field's success in living has been her ability to innovate so freely in meeting these standards.

The shift in my perceptions, as I clarified my empathic projections on Diane, was encapsulated in my choice of a title for the life history. I first proposed calling the study *Devil's Daughter*, referring to the exorcism held by Diane's grandmother at her birth. Diane immediately objected to this title, despite my intention to show how misguided the expression was. As my research progressed, it had become evident that Diane's self-image was very positive. But it was only through a leap of imagination, and a shared metaphor, that I was able to grasp the essential fact that Diane conceived of herself as lovely.

It came as a surprise to me, even though I had initiated the conversation with a visionary perception. Sitting with Diane, talking in the half-light of her apartment, I relaxed my gaze and let my eyes fill with light. This dissolved the image of Diane before me into a pale, pretty haze. In that moment I perceived her resemblance to the famous statue of the Venus de Milo. I told her what I saw, and her response came back with the force of an epiphany.

G: I got a weird image, letting my eyes flood with light. You got pale and looked like the Venus de Milo.

D: My mother's friend one time gave her a candle of the Venus de Milo. And I came home and they lit it. I thought there was something symbolic there. That was terrible.

G: Did you identify with it?

D: Oh yeah! I was going with a black guy named Rico and I gave him a big statue of the Venus de Milo for his birthday. He loved it. His wife got mad and broke it over his head. He re-glued it. It was pretty, too.

G: She's an image of you, really. She doesn't have legs.

D: And also the one arm is shorter than the other. That's what's so weird,
      too. Also Diane is Greek. Or Roman. Diane is the other name for
      Venus.[29]

As we talked, Diane and I discovered that we shared the feeling that
the Venus de Milo did not seem to be missing limbs but was intended
that way—and that she was beautiful in her own right. This experience
permanently altered my perception of Diane as disabled. Her body need
not be seen from the point of view of its deficits but as integrated and
complete. That is how Diane herself seems to experience her body.[30] In
this way, by clarifying my empathic constructions, I came to rename my
study of Diane's life *Venus on Wheels.*

In Western psychology, and in popular culture, empathy has been
associated with so-called feminine qualities such as love, nurturance,
and intuition.[31] Consequently, its application in philosophy and the
social sciences has been treated with suspicion not only by masculinist
thinkers of both sexes but also by some contemporary feminists who
want to break down gender stereotypes.[32] Empathy needs to be rede-
ployed against entrenched ways of knowing.[33] Taking the other's perspective is a necessary step in constructive social change. This has been
argued in regard to the unconscious racism of white Europeans, but it
applies also to ablism:

> What we are asking for is that the hegemonic discourses, the holders of
> hegemonic discourses should de-hegemonize their position and them-
> selves learn how to occupy the subject position of the other . . . rather
> than simply say, "O.K., sorry, we are just very good white people, there-
> fore we do not speak for the blacks." That's the kind of breast-beating
> that is left behind at the threshold and then business goes on as usual.[34]

Perspective-taking of this kind has been recommended by scholars in
law and medicine to deal with the "dilemma of difference" in their fields.
Arthur Kleinman, a psychiatrist and cultural anthropologist at Harvard
School of Medicine, proposes that an attitude of "empathic witnessing"
by physicians should be at the very core of patient care.[35] Effective treatment, especially of the chronic conditions that predominate in developed
countries like the United States, requires that physicians learn to listen to

patients' and their families' stories about the meaning of their illness to them. They must treat the person in the story, not just the biomedically defined disease.

Harvard law professor Martha Minow argues that the justice system must strive to reconstitute the excluded perspectives of people who are "different," including women, children, nonwhites, and the disabled.[36] Such perspective-taking is needed to correct the standard liberal assumption that everyone is the same and equal before the law. Minow is aware that when judges use empathic imagination, it may lead inadvertently to stereotyping and to obscuring the range of differences in a group, but she argues that "the very effort to imagine another perspective could sensitize the court to the possibility of a variety of perspectives. Once judges recognize that they do not possess the only truth, they may be more ready to acknowledge that there are even more than two truths, more than two points of view."[37]

As a practice, empathy must be tried and tried again to comprehend differences through a hermeneutic circle of experience, introspection, and clarification. Cultural biographers, ethnographers, and life historians working face-to-face with people whose experiences of discrimination they are trying to understand—such as people with disabilities like Diane—are often able to clarify their empathic feelings and imaginative constructions through dialogue. This ability carries the responsibility, however, to listen well and respond meaningfully.

The role of empathy in understanding others is particularly important for anthropologists trained in the United States, but is rarely examined in such terms. Self-reflection in fieldwork is part of the American anthropological tradition shaped by Franz Boas and his many students, including Ruth Benedict and Margaret Mead.[38] In 1896 Boas established the nation's first department of anthropology at Columbia University. A Jewish-German immigrant fleeing a reactionary political regime and growing anti-Semitism, Boas stamped the discipline with an empathic approach to people perceived as racially and ethnically different.[39] Having studied cultural geography and physics in German universities, Boas brought to American anthropology a legacy of methods from both the social sciences (*Geisteswissenschaften*) and the natural sciences (*Naturwis-*

senschaften).[40] One of his intellectual biographers points out that Boas was clearly influenced from his youth by "the historicist spirit of romantic idealism."[41] Another points out that Boas was directly influenced by the leading exponent of historicism, Wilhelm Dilthey.[42]

In a tribute to Boas, Robert Lowie, one of Boas's early students, identified empathy, or "seeing from within," as a core operation in ethnology.[43] Describing how Boas learned to interpret native life "from within," Lowie stresses Boas's reliance on natives and locals to provide data and validation for his basically historicist reconstructions.[44] Boas gathered information from Europeans who had become long-term members of native communities (such as the "squaw man," James Teit, who lived among the Salish of British Columbia), and he trained indigenous ethnographers (such as the "half-blood" Kwakiutl informant George Hunt and the Sioux anthropologist Ella Deloria).[45] Lowie writes: "Material of this sort has the immeasurable advantage of trustworthiness, authentically revealing precisely the elusive intimate thoughts and sentiments of the native, who spontaneously reveals himself in these outpourings. Boas aims at ascertaining the true inwardness of aboriginal life, not by the uncontrollable intuitions of romantic outsiders but by objective documentation."[46]

Ruth Benedict, author of the best-selling books *Patterns of Culture* and *The Chrysanthemum and the Sword*, was similarly interested in understanding the world of others as experienced from within.[47] In an address as president of the American Anthropological Association, in 1947, she recommended the use of biographical methods to see how other cultures were actually experienced by individuals. There are more direct and efficient approaches than the life history for collecting general cultural information, she pointed out. What a life history uniquely conveys, Benedict argued, is the self-understanding gained by a person over a lifetime: "The unique value of life histories lies in the fraction of the material which shows the repercussions the experiences of a man's life—either shared or idiosyncratic—have upon him as a human being molded in that environment."[48]

The best-known of American anthropologists, Margaret Mead—who was Benedict's student as well as Boas's—extended further the use of the method of "seeing from within" in the profession. It was necessary, she argued, that participant observers gain self-understanding:

> Advances in the application of scientific knowledge to our understanding of man have been dependent on two developments, methods of observing other human beings and methods of observing ourselves, as observers. Articulateness about the observed, unrelieved by articulateness about the biases and blindnesses of the observer, gives us arid material. . . . either devoid of all meaning or so heavily weighted with unacknowledged emotions that they are meaningful only to those who share the same biases.[49]

Many contemporary ethnographers—Barbara Myerhoff, Vincent Crapanzano, and others—have continued the tradition, arguing for the need to go more deeply into the self in order to understand others.[50]

It is only within this well-elaborated tradition of empathy in American anthropology that the 1976 polemic by Clifford Geertz, "From the Native's Point of View," can be fully appreciated.[51] Geertz argued persuasively in favor of basing the discipline in an interpretive approach. In doing so, however, he made the explicit claim that understanding (*Verstehen*) is wholly distinct from empathy (*Einfühlung*). This was a mistake based on too limited a concept of empathy as simply an intuition or feeling, and not as part of the hermeneutic circle.[52]

The starting point for Geertz's argument was the public's shocked reaction to the posthumously published field diaries of Bronislaw Malinowski, the founder of the modern school of British social anthropology.[53] Malinowski's diaries from his stay in the Trobriand Islands showed that he felt distant and often contemptuous of the natives he studied. Malinowski was not "an unmitigated nice guy," writes Geertz: he had "rude things to say about the natives he was living with and rude words to say it in," and he often wished he were elsewhere. Geertz argued that the diaries prove that *Verstehen* has nothing to do with empathy:

> The discussion eventually came down to Malinowski's moral character or lack of it; ignored was the genuinely profound question his book raised, namely, if anthropological understanding does not stem, as we have been taught to believe, from some sort of extraordinary sensibility, an almost

preternatural capacity to think, feel, and perceive like a native (a word, I should hurry to say, I use here "in the strict sense of the term"), then how is anthropological knowledge of the way natives think, feel, and perceive possible? . . . If we are going to cling—as in my opinion, we must—to the injunction to see things from the native's point of view, what is our position when we can no longer claim some unique form of psychological closeness, a sort of transcultural identification, with our subjects? What happens to *Verstehen* when *Einfülen* disappears?[54]

Taking understanding to be positive and rational, Geertz fails to appreciate how attitudes and feelings, even negative ones, might be implicated in *Verstehen*. But feelings are involved in cognition as unclarified "pre-understandings." Wouldn't Malinowski's diaries, which obviously served to help him discharge his uncomfortable feelings, also have helped to separate his pre-understandings from his professional writings? The diaries may be seen in another light, in terms of Malinowski's "magnificent courage to face himself with enough awareness to write it all down."[55]

Some of Geertz's own possible pre-understandings in relation to the four key figures he discusses in his book *Works and Lives: The Anthropologist as Author* have been suggested by feminist sociologist Susan Krieger. Focusing on the writings of Claude Lévi-Strauss, E. E. Evans-Pritchard, Bronislaw Malinowski, and Ruth Benedict, Geertz continues his exploration of the contributions and limits of first-person experience in shaping anthropological understanding. Geertz writes:

Anthropologists are possessed of the idea that the central methodological issues involved in ethnographic description have to do with the mechanics of knowledge—the legitimacy of "empathy," "insight," and the like as forms of cognition; the verifiability of internalist accounts of other people's thoughts and feelings; the ontological status of culture. . . . It is not merely that this is untrue, that no matter how delicate a matter facing the other might be it is not the same sort of thing as facing the page. The difficulty is that the oddity of constructing texts ostensibly scientific out of experiences broadly biographical, which is after all what ethnographers do, is thoroughly obscured.[56]

Krieger observes that Geertz begins by putting aside anthropologists and authors as "real persons" (the quotation marks are his) in order to focus exclusively on how they function inside their texts.[57] Geertz views

Benedict as most interesting when seen as an atypical woman writer with manly qualities: the "vein of iron in Benedict's work," the "determined candor of her style," "the mordant." Less favorably viewed by Geertz are Benedict's "soft-focus lyric poetry" and the "onward and upward sermons" with which she began and ended her books. It is the iron satire, the "incised lines, bitten with finality," which Geertz admires and compares favorably—if with fainter praise—to the work of men like Jonathan Swift. Geertz writes, "She did not have Swift's wit, not the furor of his hatred, and, her cases before her, she did not need his inventiveness. But she had his fixity of purpose and its severity as well."

Krieger questions: "Why did he [Geertz] use the generic "he" throughout his volume, written, as it was, in the 1980s? Why did he interpret his one central woman as a man?"[58]

Anthropology's reconsideration of empathy must move beyond a narrow technical definition of the immediate intuition of a shared feeling (although it is sometimes only that) to a wider appreciation of the *mirror phenomenon* in human understanding. Following the direction in which Edith Stein led, we need to clarify how we construct others through imagination, as well as through immediate flashes of intuition. Empathy takes many forms. It is not always a feeling of oneness but often a pure projection of the self onto the other. Its affective content includes not only nice warm feelings but all sorts of unclarified affinities and repulsions that come with face-to-face encounters. It is necessary to use hermeneutic methods to validate or revise our first impressions and pre-understandings.

For about a hundred years psychoanalysis has been giving us information about the mirroring that occurs precisely when concrete individuals are engaged with one another face-to-face: transference, countertransference, projection, love and hate.[59] Because of the analytical bias of our scientific worldview, and a corresponding passion for technological control, we insist on breaking down these "processes" into finer and finer distinctions without returning to a more synthetic appreciation of the overarching phenomenon.

We need a term—*mirroring*—to grasp what happens when concrete individuals confront and experience others as like or unlike themselves. When the objects of study are other persons, an empathic element may be irreducibly present, conditioning the tone and attitude with which one confronts and engages with an alternative reality. The very inability to think, feel, and perceive like a native can be a source of insight. It is often the failure of conventional empathy that forces an anthropologist's effort to understand things "from within."

Several years ago, I went to the Sisterhood Bookstore in Westwood to buy copies of *With Wings* and *With the Power of Each Breath*, books of first-person narratives by women with disabilities. I put my keys down on the counter to write a check, and when I picked them up, a woman standing next to me quickly challenged me for picking up her keys instead. "This could be fun," I said. "I'll just step into your life, and you can step into mine."

"I don't think I'd like that," she said sharply. "You're straight."

"Well," I said, looking at her notebook. "What's your book about?"

"I'm not writing a book. I'm compiling a bibliography for a professor at UCLA. He's writing the book."

"Working for the enemy!" I needled.

"I'm adding sources on women of color. Otherwise, they wouldn't get included. What's your book about?"

"I'm writing about a woman with a disability."

"I hope it's a woman of color," she said righteously.

"No," I sniped back. "She's white, like you."

As I left the store, what fascinated and disturbed me about our encounter was how many hostile assumptions this woman had made about me. She didn't know that much of my life has been spent as an "out" lesbian; but I also have had meaningful relationships with men. She had no idea that I have a daughter whose father is African or that, although I am white, most people regard my daughter as black.

It seemed a shame that two women should have had so harsh, so needlessly ugly an encounter. I reflected on the inadequacy of our concepts of identity. The interests that this woman presumed I ignore have actually been central to me. Even more astounding, as disability scholar Harlan Hahn noted when I told him the story, was that so many assumptions about our identity had been made in a matter of seconds, based only on appearance.

7 I-Witnessing Diane's "I"

TIME, ETHICS, AND EPISTEMOLOGY

In the 1920s and 1930s anthropology was reinvented by Boas and Malinowski as a discipline characterized by prolonged periods of living in the field with the natives. Ever since, ethnography has been a confessional genre founded on the claim, "I was there."[1] Clifford Geertz, who in *Works and Lives* calls this style of ethnography "I-witnessing," points out as its hallmark the requirement that the ethnographer establish himself (or herself, I wearily add) as an "I."

Geertz addresses this as a specifically literary problem: how to construct a text that successfully negotiates what one has been through in the field and what one may say credibly to an academic audience.

> The problem, to rephrase it in as prosaic terms as I can manage, is to represent the research process in the research product; to write ethnography

in such a way as to bring one's interpretations of some society, culture, way of life, or whatever and one's encounters with some of its members, carriers, representatives, or whomever into an intelligible relationship. Or, quickly to refigure it again, before psychologism can set it, it is how to get an I-witnessing author into a they-picturing story. To commit oneself to an essentially biographical concept of Being There . . . is to commit oneself to a confessional approach to text-building.[2]

I base this cultural biography of Diane DeVries largely on the experience of "Being There." But I have chosen not to cut the connection between "Being There" and "Being Here."[3] That cut, which characterizes a literary approach, equates "text" quite literally with the written product. The text I want to keep in frame is the still unfinished, quite irreversible co-construction of lives that the ethnographic relationship has set in motion between Diane and me.[4]

In this work, I am trying to resist a literary model that makes the ethnographic text a trophy, something I place on the mantel as proof to my friends back home of a struggle from life in the field. Consequently I frame the problem of text-building somewhat differently from Geertz.[5] Some of his own informants have read Geertz's books, which are now all translated into Indonesian, but I contend that a description of a culture is more removed and has other implications for the author's responsibility than a biography of a living individual. Diane remains always in my frame, with her own experiences inside and outside the bound covers of this book, face-to-face in a double mirror, "I" to "I."

The issues of representation for my project are not only epistemological and literary but also part of an ethical situation that Diane and I share. Vincent Crapanzano put it this way: "As anthropologists, we have a responsibility to the people we study, if not to our readers, to recognize the ethical and political implications of our discipline. Every interpretive strategy, including those implicit within description itself, involves choices and falls, thereby, into the domain of ethics and politics."[6]

The finite temporal structure of our human situation has conditioned my project with Diane.[7] Together we have moved forward through time. Our association over twenty years has helped to shape our realizations of who we are and can be—and to rule out who and what we are not. Of course, the intentions and outcomes of this process have been different for each of us. The completion of my Ph.D. dissertation in 1981 was followed by several published articles and book chapters specifically about Diane. Each of these celebrated the importance of Diane's life, affirmed the value of her struggles, and supported her feelings and aspirations.

I documented Diane's life in all seasons. She wanted me to bear witness to her triumphs, especially her graduations in 1987 and 1993. In June 1987, I braved the early morning traffic flooding the parking structures at UCLA as crowds assembled for the ceremony in the massive outdoor stadium. Arriving in time for the pregraduation ceremony of the Department of Sociology, I watched as Diane was honored with a bouquet of roses and a speech testifying to her remarkable achievement. A CNN television crew was on the spot to capture Diane's proud moment. But as I stood beside her husband, Jim, I realized that none of Diane's immediate family—mother, sisters, or brother—was there to celebrate with us and that she needed me.

When she received her master's degree in clinical social work from USC in May 1993, I roved about Bovard Auditorium, from the grand balcony down to the flower-bedecked dais, to assemble an album of photographs from every angle—a token of my solidarity with Diane's accomplishment. Afterward I was at the dockside restaurant in Long Beach's Shoreline Village to help celebrate with family and friends. Jim was no longer on the scene, and Diane's current boyfriend was absent. But Diane's former film documentarian, Michael, now a businessman, had flown in from Arizona for the occasion with his beautiful wife and handsome young son. Diane's lawyer and friend from the Western Law Center for Disability Rights was there with his wife, as was Diane's longtime friend Alice and her daughter. Diane's personal assistant, who had become like a family member, was present to celebrate with her daughter. Diane's own family was represented by only one member to celebrate her achievement, a grown niece.

Diane wanted me to be there when the breakup of a relationship or chronic health problems made her feel so beaten and low that she was almost ready to give up living. Through my commitment to Diane and our project, I expressed my belief in the fundamental value of her exis-

tence and in her ability to move through difficulties, no matter how challenging. I joked that Diane needed to give the book a happy ending or it
wouldn't sell.

One of the worst times was in spring 1989, when Jim went on a long
and nasty drinking binge, stole Diane's van, and left her in the apartment
with no attendant. I talked often on the phone with Diane and visited her
in the outlying community of Covina, where she was hospitalized for
weeks for severe depression.

I remember Diane's sadness when it appeared that she would be discharged earlier than anticipated, on Easter Sunday—less than a week
after her thirty-ninth birthday—and nobody in her usually impressive
network of supporters was available with a vehicle big enough to accommodate her wheelchair so that she could go home. That day I had
planned to take my daughter, Rebecca, then only one and a half years
old, to a Purim party before going to visit one of my friends. I canceled
my plans, put on a silky dress and pearls, dressed Rebecca in a pink
party frock with white anklets and Mary Janes, grabbed her diaper bag
and toys, and went. We were the perfect incarnation of Easter celebrants,
a particularly good stunt for our little Jewish family.

As I was filling Rebecca's bottle with juice, it occurred to me to take
some wine to bless the coming occasion of Diane's return to the community. I took a half-empty bottle of Manischewitz kosher blackberry wine
from the kitchen cabinet, along with a couple of slices of fresh rye bread,
and stuffed a few candy bunnies for Rebecca into a Ziploc bag. Rebecca
drank her bottle in the car and then cried the rest of the way, so I stopped
at a Lucky's market near the hospital. Entering the deli section, I passed
the barbecued chickens and thought about bringing some real food to
Diane, then decided against it; Diane had probably already eaten, and,
besides, I could just imagine what would happen with Rebecca, the juicy
chicken, and my expensive new clothes.

As I cruised past the counter I saw some of the marinated mushrooms
that I know Diane likes, and I couldn't resist having a quarter-pound
packed up for her. By the time I was finished, I had also picked up some
crab salad, something else I knew Diane fancied, coleslaw, potato salad,
plates and spoons, soft drinks and, of course, the chicken. I packed these

strictly contraband items into Rebecca's toy bag, hoping that the strong and alluring aromas wouldn't result in their immediate confiscation by the hospital authorities.

I arrived at Parkside West and was beeped in, met by a nurse who summoned Diane, and shown into the social worker's office. The other rooms were full with other families and visitors, as was the hallway just outside the unit.

Diane commented with delight on Rebecca's dress, a Christian Dior hand-me-down in pristine condition. "How cute she looks!"

But there was a harsh, distracted quality to Diane's presence. She launched into an account of how things at dinner earlier had been just horrible. Some of her table partners had used profanity. Diane recounted her angry response, to groan and demand that someone "pass the *fucking* sherbet."

As self-appointed master of ceremonies I wanted to move us from these recollections of unpleasantness into a shared experience of surprise, pleasure, and release. "Was dinner good? Are you full?" I asked. "Because I brought us an Easter dinner."

Diane's look confirmed that a smuggled meal is one of the few possible highlights of being on a locked ward. I walked to the door, flamboyantly locked it, and began unpacking the food from Rebecca's bag onto the social worker's desk.

"What did you bring?" Diane asked.

"Barbecued chicken," I answered, stripping back the wrappings from the steamy, fragrant meat.

Then came the side dishes. "What's that?" asked Diane.

"Oh, marinated mushrooms," I said casually. With some help from my spoon, they came tumbling onto Diane's plate.

"I love marinated mushrooms," Diane said.

"I know. Remember when you ordered them at the Black Angus?"

"I love that place," Diane said. "What's that?"

"Crab salad."

"I love crab salad," Diane said.

I reminded her of the time she insisted that I try the crab salad at the Sizzler.

I placed a bib around Rebecca's neck and gave her a marinated mushroom to distract her from grabbing our plates. From the backpack hanging behind Diane's chair, I removed her adapted fork and placed it on her lap board.

"This is a feast!" Diane said.

"I brought some wine for a blessing. Would you mind?" I asked.

"Not at all," said Diane.

"And here's some good Jewish rye," I said reverently. "I don't mean Mrs. Levy's packaged bread."

Diane laughed.

I poured a cup of wine and I held it in one hand. Diane bowed her head, put her arms on the table, and leaned toward me. I put my other hand on her arm, exactly as we had held hands many times during grace before dinner by ourselves or with Jim. "Baruch atah Adonai," I began, pronouncing the Hebrew blessing over the wine. Then I blessed the bread.

I asked Diane if she would like to make a blessing. She looked at me quizzically. "In Jesus' name," I explained.

"Yes," she said.

Diane thanked Jesus for the food and asked Him to bless the hands that had made it and the hands that had brought it. "Bless my friend, Gelya," she added, "whose friendship has been a blessing to me. And help our friendship to continue to grow."

"That was nice," I said happily. "Thank you."

By now, Rebecca had caught the spirit of the meal and was sitting nicely in a chair at the desk between Diane and me as she ate.

"I feel we've become much closer through this," Diane said.

"I do too!" I said.[8]

Although conducting research in any formal sense was the furthest goal from my mind that Easter Sunday, such experiences provided access to information about who Diane and I were. This information was not based on identifying traits that supposedly already existed in us, but through the joint creation of a relationship. I welcomed closeness and felt committed to Diane as a friend.[9] And, as a friend, Diane has much to offer. She is intelligent, sympathetic, insightful, a good listener, and immensely fun-loving, with a twisted sense of humor. Diane is conscientious about remembering birthdays, and, when she has the money, exercises her distinctive taste by selecting thoughtful gifts. Diane was given a huge challenge in life, yet she has the guts to live her life to the fullest. She wants to try everything, won't let anyone hold her back, and has a gift for telling interesting stories. Diane is just plain interesting to know. Yet, along with our friendship, and often as an area of tension within it, I have striven to keep my self-definition as a researcher.

My researcher role involved, for example, clarifying my empathic projections or mirroring of Diane, a practice that helped to make my personal suffering in life less inchoate. It launched me on a self-integrating project through which I could understand and ameliorate my own sense of being disabled. Learning and writing about Diane helped me to construct my professional identity and career. It was inevitable, of course, that I should commit myself as an anthropologist to some topic of library research, some group of "natives," or some field site. But for two decades, my primary research commitment centered on one person, Diane, and the related area of disability studies.

My focus on Diane's life created a situation of enormous dependence: my dependence on Diane. My plan to write a book about her was delayed until long after articles had been published from the initial study. This was a career decision because tenure in my department required the publication of peer-reviewed articles rather than a monograph. The longer my association with Diane continued, the greater the incentive to maintain it on good terms. Because of the efforts we had already invested, the project became more and more valuable as time passed, taking on the dimension of a longitudinal study. It also required a commitment of time and resources that I no longer had the chance to devote to another topic.

Because of my dependence on Diane, my field situation was utterly dissimilar to what I had experienced as an ethnohistorian for the Tule River Indian Tribe. I had worked on the reservation in the foothills of the Sierras near Porterville, California, between 1972 and 1974, at the invitation of the Tule River Tribal Council.[10] And if one family on the reservation might view me with suspicion because they didn't trust whites or disliked my friendliness toward someone from a rival faction, another family would welcome me and support my efforts.

It was also different from my ethnographic work in Israel and the occupied West Bank in 1986.[11] Excellent personal references and a reputation for trustworthiness were needed with Israelis and Palestinians on both sides of the "Green Line," but if relations proved unproductive in one place, there were other possible field sites.

But while I was studying Diane's life, once I met my own standards, it was she whom I had to please with how I conducted myself and what I wrote. I had promised from the start to show Diane any manuscripts I planned to publish and to validate them with her. These ethics of research meant placing myself in an asymmetrical relationship that compelled me to put Diane's interests first. She could reject my work at any time.[12] Contrary to most of what has been written about the power dynamics between ethnographer and "native," these ethics have made me subject to Diane—giving her the ultimate power, appropriately, over me.

I found a resonance with my stance in the writings of philosopher Emmanuel Levinas. While a doctoral student at Strasbourg, in 1928 to 1929, Levinas attended a series of lectures given in Freiburg by Husserl on phenomenological psychology. He wrote his dissertation on Husserl's theory of intuition and was taken with the problem of intersubjectivity: how individuals understand and share an experience of the world.[13] Later, building on Martin Heidegger's theory of temporality, Levinas devoted himself to challenging its central tenet, the preoccupation with being that has characterized philosophy since the classical Greeks. Western philosophy's preoccupation with being sets up categories based on the uniformity or identity of things, and tends therefore to enforce sameness and eradicate differences.

Writing in the shadow of World War II and the Holocaust, Levinas placed ethics first, prior to an ontology and epistemology of being.[14] Levinas's ethics supposes an asymmetrical relationship in which each individual has an unlimited obligation face-to-face with every Other. This relationship relies on a mirroring practice or, in his terms, a "substitution." One must be ready to see oneself as having already been substituted in the Other's place and to question one's enjoyment of privileges that might just as rightfully belong to the Other.[15]

I don't know whether—or how many times—Diane may have considered firing me as her biographer. Only Diane can speak definitively about what she may have thought and felt, or discussed with other friends but didn't state directly to me. I *can* comment with gratitude and respect on Diane's generous attitude. Her enthusiasm for life and its possibilities is contagious. She allowed me the broad latitude I needed for my study, in which her portrayal is frequently thrown off center by theoretical concerns and my own self-presentation. She never squelched me when I approached her with a new idea but has been enthusiastic and open to possibilities. Yet my wide-ranging interests and idiosyncratic style have made my treatment of her life unpredictable, the antithesis of an "as told to" story; I never promised to act simply as Diane's scribe.

Writing a life history involves objectification and appropriation. For the life history subject, seeing oneself as perceived by another usually results in some degree of shock and alienation.[16] It must have been nerve-racking for Diane to wait and see what I would come up with next. Although Diane had the power to withdraw from our association at any time, she did so only twice in twenty years—and then neither formally nor permanently. Her willingness to continue showed tremendous courage and persistence. These qualities were most clearly evident in May 1992, when I presented a long paper using psychoanalytic concepts to discuss Diane's autobiography at a Norwegian conference on "Constructions of Childhood."

Diane read the paper only after I had left, and she was furious. Her first reaction was: "Since when did Gelya become an expert in psychoanalysis?"

Diane felt that, true to classic psychoanalytic theory, which she had studied in school, my paper was "very subject-blaming." She also found some of my views condescending. She disagreed strongly with my interpretations about how she represented her mother and father. But mainly she felt that such interpretations were hers to make, not mine. One-on-one therapy sessions would be the proper place for them. A paper was not the place to start, even if my interpretations had been valid. She also objected strongly to my basing the paper on a manuscript that she had written some years ago, without stipulating how she has changed since then.

Diane voiced these concerns to me in an angry phone call when I returned from the conference in Norway. I had sent Diane a typical Norwegian tourist souvenir, a tiny pair of Lapp reindeer boots, symbolic of the journey on which I had taken her story. Dripping with sarcasm, Diane told me she had indeed received the gift: "Little boots. How cute."

She expressed dismay that the audience at the conference would tend to accept my interpretations over hers. She complained that she did not feel "present" in my text. I pointed out that the presentation I had made was to a very small group, perhaps twenty people. Every one of them had the opportunity independently to read Diane's autobiography, which I had circulated with my paper in advance, along with earlier published articles. I was ready to make any and all necessary revisions. In fact, I informed Diane, there were numerous concerns and criticisms of my paper from among the other scholars. James Olney, the dean of autobiographical studies, shared a story in which irreconcilable differences of interpretation with a subject kept an oral historian's work from being published. The feminist literary and film critic Birgitta Holm, from Sweden, while not at all unkind to me, asked why I would want to write an "ordinary psychoanalysis" of Diane.

The paper focused on Diane's self-construction in terms of gender, tracing her transition from girlhood into womanhood. In a strictly academic sense, I had intended my psychoanalytic reading of Diane to respond to the chapter by Adrienne Harris and Dana Wideman, "The Construction of Gender and Disability in Early Attachment," in *Women with Disabilities*, the book by Fine and Asch.[17] Looking back, however, I think it is significant that these events, in which I used psychoanalysis to do violence to Diane's self-interpretation, occurred while fatal disturbances were brewing in the transference relationship with my psychoanalyst at home.

Toward the end of my ten-day stay in Norway, I suffered a severe attack of anxiety and depression. It was worse than a similar breakdown near the end of my research in Israel and the West Bank in 1986, because this time I was so desperate that I felt I wanted to jump from my hotel window. My focus on jumping from a window was overdetermined by the fact that this was how my maternal grandmother Gussie Gordon (born Gelya Boxer), ended her life.

When I returned to the United States from Norway, I felt sure that I required additional treatment that my lay analyst could not provide. This claim exacerbated existing tensions in our relationship and eroded my trust in her. I insisted that I needed medication because my symptoms were at least in part a physical syndrome, not merely a mental state that I could analyze and control. Irreconcilable differences led us to end the analysis on an uneasy truce in 1994. My analyst wanted to be rid of me.

A few months later, I sought treatment with a psychiatrist for renewed symptoms of depression. An important part of this treatment was his suggestion that there was likely a genetic component to the history of social dysfunction and psychiatric instability that was prominent in my mother's family, stemming from her mother's side. This insight allowed me to experience some closure in the search for a label for my disability. Weekly therapy sessions, along with the stabilizing use of antidepressants, allowed me to reach a more satisfying conclusion than in my earlier analysis.

Returning from Norway in May 1992, despite the anxiety and depression, I had been eager to tell Diane about Birgitta Holm's extremely enthusiastic reading of her autobiography. She felt that Diane had a distinctive voice, should be encouraged to write more, and must publish her completed autobiography. But this message was swamped by Diane's fury.

Although Diane and I agreed to talk again soon to continue working out our extremely uncomfortable situation, a month passed before she responded. I felt punished by her silence and also enraged.[18]

"I'm a scholar, not your press agent," I rehearsed telling her.

It was not that I really expected to utter those words.

Still, I insisted to myself, "I have a right to my independent point of view!"

In reading an essay about the writing of biographies, I underscored the following lines:

To identify too closely with a life, to collapse into adulation, is to give up the distance that allows the writer to become something more than the agent for a reputation. One can fall into the role willingly, as in the authorized biography where objectivity may be qualified for the sake of the cooperation of family and friends and of access to restricted materials. But more often it is the force of the subject's personality, its power to fascinate or to dominate, which binds the biographer. The threat is all the greater when biographer and subject know each other. . . . The major struggle between writer and subject is fought here, in the arena of reputation. A modern biographer may or may not choose to reveal the intimate, the amorous details of a life, but he must, if he is good at what he does, probe beneath its public, polished self.[19]

I phoned my office regularly from home during the summer break to check whether I had received any mail. I feared that Diane would send a letter revoking her consent to the publication of her life history. But when Diane finally called, it was to give me some upbeat news. She had a new boyfriend, Dave, who had moved in with her. As far as I was concerned, the air between us hadn't been cleared; I couldn't share her excitement. I asked bluntly why she thought a man would move in so readily with a woman lacking arms and legs.

I promptly wrote a letter of apology. Diane wrote to me, in turn, about her "disillusionment and shock" concerning me and my comments of late. I owned that I was acting on feelings and reactions that ideally did not belong in any relationship, certainly not a professional relationship. In anthropology, as in medicine, the first rule must be: Do no harm.[20]

Diane's letter was tough and articulate:

What made your comment so painful was that it came from my biographer—someone who is highly intelligent, educated, and supposedly sensitive to individuals with differences. My initial reaction was, "How can I permit someone who sees me as 'someone without arms and legs' present me to the academic world?" This thought was perhaps strengthened by your "psychoanalysis" of my autobiography. There seems to be something lacking in our work together, because it seems you truly do not accept or see me as one who is confident in myself, or if it's there, it is fantasy. Friends, who have not delved into my life history as you have, know me as self-confident, weak and strong, open-minded, and living it all with positive body-image. I've never needed—nor do I now—need

undivided approval of my behavior, politics, or belief system from anyone; just acceptance of my right to be. It was neither here nor there that
you approved or disapproved of Dave and I. It's only been just recent
that you and I have developed our relationship into a friendship, so I
shared this with you as I did with my other friends. Unfortunately,
Gelya the biographer/intellect took it and scrutinized, analyzed,
degraded it, instead of allowing Gelya the friend to hear it, offer friendly,
optimistic comments, and let it go. I read a lot of projection in your letter.
I don't need your mirrored approval but I do know how important my
approval is to you, but if you notice, I never offer approval or disap-
proval regarding your personal life. Why should I, unless asked? It hurt,
Gelya, but I do understand how people can say things they don't really
mean. I'm not a supporter in Freudian psychoanalysis, but you appear
to be so, and if that's the case, somewhere in your conscious or unconscious, you did mean it. It is something we are going to have to work
through before further progress can be made.[21]

By Thanksgiving, six months later, we were still cautiously circling
around the issues that the Norway paper had raised. We exchanged letters, had conversations, and met for a talk with the tape recorder on. By
this time, the acrimony was gone, although the sore feelings and mistrust
were still palpable. Our relationship was salvageable, but the paper I had
written definitely was not. I withdrew the manuscript from the volume
in which it was to be included and wrote a new paper from scratch, using
an entirely different type of narrative analysis, hermeneutic case reconstruction.[22]

Diane's reaction to the manuscript that I finished one year later was
more positive, I felt, than to anything I had written previously. Not only
did she like the paper, but she offered the ultimate validation: affirmation that I had really understood her. "I liked it because that's kind of
how I wrote it," she said, "to have it be interpreted that way."[23]

The Norway incident remained important to Diane and to me for
many reasons; not least, it had raised the opportunity to examine the
dynamics of power in our relationship and the question of what kind of
relationship we were having anyway—stranger, friend, or what?[24]

At our face-to-face meeting, which I tape-recorded, Diane expressed
very clearly her experience of the asymmetrical power embedded in our
positions. She also confirmed her commitment to the project:

D: First of all, you probably don't even feel you have power over me. But
    in a sense I feel you do a lot of times. Number One, intellectually and
    educationally and academically, you are way up there, and I respect
    that and I always have. So sometimes that can be very intimidating. So
    maybe because of that, maybe I might tend to relinquish more power
    than I think I should. . . . And then when something like this happens,
    it just all mushrooms into this one thing because I feel like sometimes I
    have given up too much, or given over too much because of who you
    are and what you represent. . . .

G: As an author, I couldn't really go forward with the writing of the
    book without some sense that I would have some control over the
    product. . . . But what if I give it to you and you say, "Well, you know,
    I don't really like that at all." . . . I mean, would you do that to me?

D: No, and the reason I don't think I would do that to you is because I
    want to see this come out just as badly as you do, this book. I want to
    see it completed. I want to see that all these years were worth some-
    thing and are going to come to some kind of fruition. And I am not
    real sure, I mean I have asked myself, too, why I do this. I mean it just
    seemed right. I think it is a valuable project because I think people
    need to know about things like this. Different ways of life and differ-
    ent ways of handling and coping. I really believe that that is truly
    important. I believe you can handle it well . . . but . . . I would like to
    see it over. I feel like it has been too long now. But it will be nice when
    it is done—I'll be glad. But I don't regret doing it. And I would never
    stop now.[25]

Turning Diane's life into a life history raises an issue of appropriation,
although somewhat different from that word's common meanings of
political co-optation or economic exploitation, which imply the crass
misuse of others' property for selfish gain.[26] Appropriation also refers to
a process inherent in the structure of life itself, involving the differentiation of self-consciousness through encounters with that which is not-self.
Gadamer writes:

> Life is determined by the fact that what is alive differentiates itself from
> the world in which it lives and with which it remains connected, and
> preserves itself in this differentiation. The self-preservation of what is
> alive takes place through its drawing into itself everything that is out-
> side it. Everything that is alive nourishes itself on what is alien to it. The

fundamental fact of being alive is assimilation. Differentiation, then, is at the same time non-differentiation. The alien is appropriated.[27]

A focus on self-differentiation as the condition for knowing things is a peculiarity of the Western tradition. In Western philosophy the transcendental "I" (the *cogito*), or consciousness, depends on the idea of a self that is discrete and bounded. The importance of this concept originates with René Descartes's *Discourse on Method,* which includes rules by which the truth of propositions can be ascertained by adopting an attitude of radical doubt. The only thing clearly beyond doubt to Descartes was the fact of his own existence, because to have doubt means that he is thinking, hence his dictum *cogito ergo sum* (I am thinking, therefore I exist).[28]

The importance of the transcendental "I" continues through the philosophy of Kant, Hegel, and Husserl. Although there are many sources of the attack on the transcendental "I," the modern existentialist philosopher Jean-Paul Sartre continued to posit subjects whose difference from one another occurs precisely because they experience their consciousness as separate, bounded, and whole. In *Saint Genet,* a biographical study of the playwright Jean Genet, Sartre wrote: "Man, says Marx, is an object to man. That is true. But it is also true that I am a subject to myself exactly insofar as my fellow man is an object to me. And that is what separates us. He and I are not *homogeneous:* we cannot be part of the same whole except in the eyes of a third person who perceives us both as a single object."[29]

An ontology or theory of reality based on a unitary (male) subject is at the core of Western autobiography. James Olney has noted that the common task of Western autobiographers as diverse as Michel de Montaigne, Carl Jung, Charles Darwin, John Stuart Mill, and T. S. Eliot has been to create "an order and meaning that is not always to be found in experience itself"—that is, to construct coherence around some metaphor to make a complete whole.[30] A new generation of scholars with a feminist viewpoint has argued that this ontology and its related theory of knowledge reflect the bias of elite white men who have been the self-appointed guardians of the philosophy club.[31] These feminist scholars question whether autobiography must depend on methodological individualism, a sense of one's own isolated being and a belief in the self as a discrete, finite unit.

Yet such individualistic practices of the self are ingrained in American culture, for women as well as men. Women whose consciousness has been "raised" are probably more likely than other women to be sensitive to appropriation in daily life and to resist it. Yet in my relationship with Diane, each of us found elements from our lives and writings being appropriated and redefined by the other.

Diane's use of the expression "my biographer, Gelya Frank" sounded different to me from my self-description as her life historian. Diane has since repeated the phrase lightheartedly many times. But the first time I heard her use it, at her camp reunion, I felt momentarily humbled, a Boswell scrambling with my notebook after the exalted Samuel Johnson. Yet why should that image bother me, when it is a very fair description of what I do as a life historian? At other times, I found myself insisting I was "really" a researcher, most often when Diane seemed to suggest that I was "really" her friend. I don't know how Diane might describe me when she deals with these years in her autobiography, which I hope she will continue to write and publish one day soon.

Diane has struggled to keep her life story distinct from my life history of her. Tensions over the appropriation of Diane's life may actually have helped fuel her efforts to write her own autobiography. The more energy I have put into describing and defining Diane's life, the more Diane may have needed to resist my narrative authority and maintain control over her own life story. When Diane was writing her autobiography most actively, through the 1980s, she would point out how different her book was going to be from mine. Hers was not going to be a scholarly book, but an off-the-wall black comedy like Carrie Fisher's *Postcards from the Edge*, something you would want to read while lounging around the swimming pool. Her book would be popular, funny, and entertaining. The oppositional character of Diane's assertions left the possibility of writing something unpopular, unfunny, and a yawner entirely to me. My book would be something you would read because your professor assigned it—perhaps in a mausoleum.

These undertones of competition make perfect sense, however, as a stance Diane may have felt forced to take in order to protect or defend her position as the originator of personal meaning in her life. No matter how well I might write about Diane's lived experiences, my voice could only be an after-trace: illuminating but not generative, necessarily limited and a little hollow. It is Diane alone who has the authority, like any autobiographical subject, to inflect endless meanings by what she decides to include and exclude from her story, and how she chooses to say those things.

8 The Women in Diane's Body

NARRATIVE AMBIGUITY IN A MATERIAL WORLD

Two stories I tell late in this chapter might be seen as bookends to the relationship between Diane and me. They help me to reflect critically on my efforts to get a clear understanding of Diane's experiences over time. How can I seek clarity when there are obvious limits to my ability to know myself, let alone another person? Was the Diane whom I observed in a university lecture hall in spring 1976 the same woman with whom I shared a date in Hollywood almost two decades later? If I had only a snapshot of the Diane I first noticed, and no record of our encounter on that later occasion, what would I really understand about the woman in her body?[1] I find myself wondering what are the possibilities and limits of narrative itself for my understanding of Diane. I turn to philosophy to help me explore whether words can capture the richness of embodied life.

The rich narratives possible when loose ends and multiple versions of a life are allowed to proliferate were recognized by the novelist Virginia Woolf, who kept putting off her plans to write a conventional memoir. Instead, as critic Shari Benstock observes, Woolf favored keeping a diary like "some deep old desk, or capacious hold-all." She did so to keep her internal censor at bay and permit the possibility of later finding significance "where I never saw it at the time."[2] Woolf valued play—the play of her unconscious and the play of time—as sources from which new meanings could, indeed must, emerge.[3] She was willing to sacrifice the illusion of clarity for another kind of truth.

In describing Diane DeVries and the cultural implications of her various images, I have especially wanted to clarify the mirroring process that takes place in biographical descriptions.[4] My images of mirroring—and of the biography in the shadow—are metaphors of cast light and visual sensation.[5] My taste for establishing clarity reveals the metaphorical preoccupations of Western philosophy speaking through me. The inherited language of the academy tends to emphasize the presence of things. Sifting through the manifestations of things, which it leaves behind as chaff for historians and anthropologists, philosophy has aimed to describe only the essential kernel of being.

It has been argued, however, that a metaphysics of presence and being does violence to actual beings who exist yet often are different from what the language of being would suppose them to be.[6] Take, for instance, the case of a woman born with a visual impairment. For her, a mirror can be tactile or abstract but not visually reflective. A philosophy of being, expressed in ordinary language, usually puts in question her full inclusion in the category of "a person" by adding a qualifier: "a blind person." It also distorts whatever experience she actually has of mirroring, which the sighted presume must be essentially visual. Fortunately, as the deconstructionists of language have argued, language contains the tools for subverting its own tendency to posit essences.[7] All we need to begin is to listen to the silences.

I want to point my way to the very margins of language. I will not summarize who or what Diane DeVries is. Neither will I try to list her "differences." Both strategies play into the trap of being. Instead, I refer the reader backward and forward in time—back to the biographical situations described so far, and forward into the future that is yet to be known. The historical manifestations interest me as much as the essences. Even the term *manifestation* corrupts my intended meaning, because I do not see Diane's lived experiences as fundamentally a "reflection" or "representation" of anything.

Nor do I see Diane's life as merely a narration. Her life is neither an ethnographer's thick description nor the thin fiction suggested by postmodern theories of the self.[8] Derrida's deconstruction of the protean possibilities of language has been taken to imply that the "self" is infinitely changeable, fragmentary, self-contradictory, and open. But, as feminist philosopher and critic Elizabeth Grosz points out, Derrida's logocentric approach, which invites us to see the self as a text, does not do away with the self or "subject." In Derrida's own words:

> I have never said that the subject should be dispensed with. Only that it should be deconstructed. To deconstruct the subject does not mean to deny its existence. There are subjects, operations, or effects of subjectivity. That is an incontrovertible fact. To acknowledge this does not mean, however, that the subject is what it says it is. The subject is not some meta-linguistic presence; it is always inscribed in language. My work does not, therefore, destroy the subject; it simply tries to resituate it.[9]

An amazingly flexible and fragmentary "postmodern self" has been claimed to arise in relation to the uprooting and dislocation of populations resulting from wars and the migration of wage laborers in the late stages of global capitalism.[10] The late twentieth century is a period characterized by drastic alterations in the experience of time and space associated particularly with instantaneous electronic information systems. The advanced capitalist economies require constantly expanding markets for goods and services. Rapidly changing patterns of production and consumption make styles, habits, behaviors, and even "the self" highly mutable. Some of these theories about the postmodern self strangely recall the "rational man" of liberal economics, appearing to put the "self" within the realm of an individual's conscious choice.[11]

There is reason to doubt sweeping claims about the demise of the unitary "I." People do stabilize their existence within areas of relative coherence. Here is where philosophy needs not only introspection but the kind of work done by ethnographers over time, in local contexts, as observing participants. For example, Diane's "I" has been firmly anchored to the conditions of living as a woman with a disability. Mine has been anchored at least in part to the project of writing about Diane's life. Certain key projects and occupations do define us to a great extent. It is also not easy to change one's individual consciousness—as almost anyone will attest who has been seriously engaged in psychotherapy or some other transformational practice.

It might be worthwhile to think for a moment about the implications for biographical understanding of Lyotard's often-cited manifesto *The Postmodern Condition.*[12] Lyotard's argument was a challenge to fellow philosopher Jürgen Habermas and his theory of a "legitimation crisis" in late modernity. According to Habermas, the Western democracies have failed to engage the allegiance of their various constituencies because of public alienation from elites and experts. The willingness of citizens to believe and participate in common goals has been destroyed by the failure of experts to communicate effectively, giving way to the incoherence and apathy that now characterize civil society in Europe and North America.

In *The Postmodern Condition,* Lyotard shifts the grounds for the debate away from Habermas's concern with authority, consensus, and the ability of scientists to communicate clearly. The ability to mirror the truth is no longer the key question. As Fredric Jameson explains in a commentary on Lyotard: "I am referring to the so-called crisis of representation, in which an essentially realistic epistemology, which conceives of representation as the reproduction, for subjectivity, of an object that lies outside of it—projects a mirror theory of knowledge and art, whose fundamental evaluative categories are those of adequacy, accuracy, and Truth itself." Making a radical break with realism, Lyotard substitutes a theory of knowledge that is nonrepresentational. The goals of science should be, in Jameson's commentary, "not to produce an adequate model or replication of an outside reality, but rather simply to produce *more* work, to generate new and fresh scientific *énoncés* or statements."[13]

For anthropology, and in my project about Diane DeVries, the crisis of representation raises important problems. A critic who begins with the modernist view of Habermas would ask whether my reconstructions of

Diane's life are accurate and well founded.[14] There is the question of her truthfulness as an informant: What if Diane's memory is faulty, or if she lied to me? And there is the problem of my diligence and skill as a reporter: Did I get enough information? Was it the right kind? There is also the matter of my credibility: Did I understand the experiences of another, someone who is necessarily "different"? Finally, there is the democratic questioning of expert authority: When and how should I be allowed to speak about Diane? Does my expertise involve appropriation and suppression of her autonomous voice and self-determination?

But in Lyotard's postmodernist view, these would no longer be the most important questions. Critics would concern themselves less with the problem of accurate representation of the subject's life and more with evaluating what is accomplished by the narrative itself. They would ask: What kind of life story did Diane DeVries tell about herself? What kind of narrative did Gelya Frank write about Diane? Did it offer new perspectives leading to the production of more narratives—new discourses—about disability, about Diane, about biographical understanding? How has Diane's story about herself been shaped and changed in the course of her relationship with Gelya, a relationship based on the production of texts? How has Diane's story affected the cultures of which it is a part?

Since the mid-1980s, narrative experimentation and cultural criticism have increasingly been used to justify anthropology as a liberatory or progressive discipline seeking to distance itself from the colonial past.[15] This trend has led to ideas of "writing against culture" and "writing against the grain"—a practice that has come to challenge even the male, presumably able-bodied Western theorists who first announced the "experimental moment" in ethnographic description.[16] It seems to me that the old problems of representation also remain, however, as in my conflict with Diane over the paper I presented in Norway. My data were credible and my interpretations were reasonably valid within standards of conventional scholarship, but Diane would not authorize them for the purpose of representing her. The Norway incident suggests that postmodern epistemologies have different ethical and political implications for actual human beings than they do for "texts" and even "cultures."

The "legitimation crisis" has not ended because of the shift in perspectives from modernism to postmodernism. One way to think about this situation was anticipated by Thomas Kuhn in his history of science, *The Structure of Scientific Revolutions,* one of Lyotard's sources. Kuhn argued that science does not proceed in a strictly cumulative manner but undergoes periods of crisis in which problems arise that can no longer be solved using existing theories and methods. A radical shift to a new set of perspectives and practices—a *paradigm shift*—occurs only when a framework for further scientific activity is introduced that can explain phenomena under the old paradigm as well as solve the anomalies that provoked the search for a new paradigm. A paradigm shift may occur in which it is suddenly understood that air is composed not of one element but many, or that the earth travels around the sun rather than the reverse. These perspectival shifts have had tremendous technological consequences. But people continue to need air to breathe, and the sun still comes up at dawn.

Such material conditions of life—and the physical embodiment of actual individuals—provide inexhaustible sources for the meanings embedded in narratives.[17] They also ground the possibilities for deconstructing meanings. Embodied life is the source of countless ambiguities that spill over or resist filling the outlines of narrative strategies.[18]

The term *ambiguity* has had an admittedly pejorative meaning in English, implying equivocation. But Maurice Merleau-Ponty, in his inaugural lecture at the Collège de France, characterized the true philosopher by an equal taste for clarity (*évidence*) and ambiguity, which he distinguished in a positive sense as the repudiation of absolute knowledge.[19] The body as a source of ambiguity in that positive sense is what I now want to address, affirming the ethical primacy of Diane's ultimately unnamable, lived experience as the definitive source for my narration about her.

To do so, I need to return to the beginning of our story. But which beginning? Diane and I have different memories of our first encounter; not different versions of the same event, but memories of different events entirely: my story begins in the lecture hall, while Diane's begins with her visit to my office and challenge to study the disabled woman and the disabled culture.

The first life history interview that I tried to conduct formally with Diane was itself characterized by ambiguity.

I asked Diane, "What do you want to talk about?"

"You start," Diane replied. "I work better when you ask me what you want to know."

My attempt to gain access to a pure phenomenology of Diane's consciousness—her "I"—was immediately foiled.

Diane suggested that perhaps I should just talk and she could break in.

"Then begin at the beginning," I prompted.

"Like when I was born and things like that?" Diane asked.

"Fine," I said.[20]

And that was how our interviews began, an entanglement of intentions resolved by the most conventional narrative device of Western autobiography: "I was born . . ."

Many of the experiences Diane eventually described did not fit neatly within the conventional concept of the "body." For example, Diane's interdependence with others—particularly her younger sister Debbie, who was expected to help her with daily tasks of dressing and toileting—engendered an intimacy and identification that defied normal definitions of the bounded body. Consider Diane's participation in Debbie's learning to dance: "It's true that there is a Diane within this Diane who can dance which enabled me to teach my younger sister Debbie. But there's another reason I could coach her so well. I saw her body move from childhood's awkwardness to adult gracefulness and strength. But not only did I *see* this. I felt her movements in a sense, part of her body (the part I lacked on the exterior) was mine too. So, since I *knew* how her body moved, I could coach her in dancing."[21]

Such instances of ambiguity have arisen through the very configuration of Diane's physical body. The clinical term *congenital amputee* has been applied to Diane. But to call up an image of Diane in the company of people who have had an arm or leg cut off leaves something to be desired. Her arms and legs can only be postulated. They exist in a state of potential as much as in a state of loss. This is clearest with respect to Diane's arms. She does in fact have arms, in the form of two upper stumps of about equal length.

Diane's legs are both present and absent. For all practical purposes, she was considered to be lacking legs. At the Child Amputee Prosthetics Project, Diane was first diagnosed as having "congenital absence of both legs at the hips." In an early clinical description, however, she was reported to "ambulate" or walk by alternately swinging the left and right sides of her pelvis forward.[22] As a little child, Diane was given a platform with short legs that she used to walk by using this method of pelvic rotation.

The language used to describe Diane's lower limb deficiencies evokes the presence of limbs. A note at Diane's admitting examination at CAPP in 1955 states: "There appears clinically and by x-ray to be a femoral head only on the right, and no bony components on the left lower extremity." Thus there is the suggestion that Diane has at least a rudimentary right lower extremity. Some years later, however, a physician noted: "The legs are represented only by soft tender nodules in the anterio-inferior aspect of the groin-buttocks area. There's good anterior and posterior flexion of this tissue mass."[23] What happened to the rudimentary right leg? Diane's ambiguous body structure didn't change, but the description did.

In summer 1998, Diane underwent two surgeries to clean out a supposed infection in the area of her left hip that had been tender for over a year and had begun oozing a black secretion. The first surgery did not correct the problem. A month later, a second surgeon reopened the area and found no evidence of an infection. He did, however, discover an embryonic foot about two inches long. He removed the foot, which was perfectly formed except for the toenails. Diane's hips have been scrutinized by x-ray and CAT scan more intensively than most people will ever have a photograph of their face examined. A competent surgeon had opened Diane's hip area just one month earlier. How is it that her embryonic foot was never noticed before? Having "decided" Diane had no legs, the surgeons simply were not looking for, and therefore did not see, new evidence that she might have them. And the ambiguity of what she did have made recognition difficult.

Medical anthropologist Cheryl Mattingly, in her remarkable study of occupational therapists in practice, observed how experienced practitioners co-construct with their patients an implicit narrative about the patient's future that they enact together.[24] Mattingly calls this phenomenon "therapeutic emplotment." As Diane grappled with the implications of her clinical description as both having legs and not having legs, difficulties arose over the emplotment of her rehabilitation goals, particularly concerning her ability to walk. Over the objections of her clinical team, Diane continued to believe through adolescence and early adulthood that she could walk with lower extremity prostheses—if only her team would fabricate an appropriate pair and teach her to use them.

When I interviewed her in the 1970s, Diane described herself as having the ability to walk and in some sense as having legs. She reported: "They discovered I had hip bones when the doctors were standing around in preparation for my first surgery. I was walking already."

G: Walking?

D: Walking. On the floor. Scooting around.

G: How?

D: I just moved my hips back and forth. I still do it when I have to.

G: Give it to me in more detail.

D: I sit on the floor on my butt, and I move each. . . . Well, these, I call them legs, 'cause they *are* in a way. Just move each one with your hip. Just like anyone else would. Just move the top of their leg. And I got around like that. You know, around the house, not outside.

G: Walking on the front part? What would be your thigh? Or on the point of it?

D: Just like I'm sitting now. Except walking.

G: It's hard for me to visualize exactly what you have there.

D: When I was younger, it was just my butt. But then I realized I could move each and they were separate. So they were legs, you know. I walked on them. When I was younger and thinner it was easier. I could bounce around. I used to be able to stand on my head! That amazes me when I think about it. I was really *light* then. They discovered I had hips and that surprised me, because I figured that if I'm walking, of course I had them.[25]

The ambiguous presence/absence of Diane's legs is even more dramatic in what might be considered the more symbolic and *dis*-embodied modes of being. In 1981, for example, Diane described to me a vision in which she was "restored" arms and legs.

"There's a woman minister in the church. She's highly anointed and has the gift of healing, and she's been promised a miracle," Diane told me. "I had a vision that God promised to restore my arms and legs. That minister was standing at the foot of my bed."

"That's great!" I said.

Perhaps wickedly, I added, "Did you ask Him when?"

Diane laughed and replied, most reasonably: "In His own eternal time."[26]

Attempts to describe Diane's legs heightened my awareness that narratives involve a surplus or deficit of meaning relative to embodied reality. Other events also showed that the physical body—disabled or not—is a source of narrative ambiguity.[27]

In spring 1987, I spent a week visiting with Diane and Jim, spreading my sleeping bag on the floor of the living room in their one-bedroom apartment in Long Beach, with the goal of observing how they handled their daily routines. Their marriage was still in pretty good shape, and their lifestyle was stable. Diane was enrolled at UCLA and just about to finish her bachelor's degree in sociology. Jim drove her the fifteen or twenty miles to campus in the morning and picked her up after classes, sometimes spending the afternoon with his sketch pad at the beach to avoid dealing twice in one day with the bumper-to-bumper traffic on the 405 freeway. Then he went to work at night driving a cab.

As on many other occasions, Diane asked me one afternoon to help by wiping her after defecating in the toilet. Bending over her in the bathroom, I felt suddenly nauseated and gagged involuntarily. I was surprised at myself. Feeling bad about the episode, I wrote about it in my field notes, which I am afraid Diane may have viewed on my laptop computer screen. Diane became emotionally distant and cold. She wouldn't let me help her again during my visit. She later made a deprecating comment that I was always running to the bathroom to urinate, whereas she has trained herself to control her bladder for long hours. Two days later, Diane completely blew up at me when I responded to Jim's complaint of sore muscles in his neck and back by giving him a massage. She revved up her wheelchair and stormed out of the house. I packed my things. Diane's body language told me clearly that it was time to go. Only months later did it occur to me why I had gagged in the bathroom. It wasn't a comment on helping Diane, although that is how we both saw it: I was pregnant but didn't know it yet.

Ambiguities are also embodied in material conditions beyond those of the physical body—within an economic or class structure. The contingencies of our class positions were not simple matters of fact to be put into field notes. Rather, they fundamentally constituted our experiences of each other, shaping the ways Diane perceived me and I described her. Diane has lived true to the philosophy of the independent living movement, which includes the right to take risks, and that philosophy has at times led her into financial difficulties. On occasions when she has phoned me to say that she needs hundreds of dollars in a hurry to pay her rent, or asked me to cosign on a bank loan when it seemed unlikely that she could make the payments, my relationship with Diane has been uncomfortable. How much easier and more pleasant everything might have been if her financial situation had been consistently closer to my own.

I have had to struggle intensely with my sense of responsibility for Diane's well-being during her crises. I have wondered whether I would feel less responsible for Diane, and less guilty about sometimes turning down her requests for money, if she were not disabled. Yet there seems to be no clear answer about the part her disability "should" play in my ethical obligation to her, an ethical obligation that I feel would be mine regardless of whether or not we had a research relationship, simply by virtue of the fact that she is someone in my life whom I care about. But I have needed to resist trying to fulfill all of Diane's manifest needs. Naturally, this has created strains in our relationship, especially at times when she has suggested that a nursing home or suicide might be her best or only option. Although I have helped Diane financially, I try mainly to use my skills and academic position, including my contacts with occupational therapists and other colleagues, to be of unique assistance. Over the years, I have tried to give only what I would not resent. I would guess that Diane has tried not to resent my limits in responding to needs that were imperative for her. So it is important to consider the material conditions of our lives, and how shifts in our class position may have affected our experience of one another.

Although I had met Diane in spring 1976, I visited her home for the first time in the fall, just before taking my doctoral qualifying exams. This encounter forced me to revisit, in almost textbook fashion, the question of how natives survive in harsh environments. It was "Anthropology 101: Introduction to Material Culture" with an emphasis on food, shelter, and transportation. Since I didn't own a car at the time, I arrived at Diane's apartment by bus. I found her in the midst of difficulties and feeling depressed. Not knowing her well, I could not assess whether her current problems were usual. Diane told me that Jim had been unemployed for some time and was getting drunk frequently. His sister and her two children had moved temporarily into their ground-floor apartment, which Diane and Jim had been able to rent at a reduced rate because they were the building managers. Jim and Diane possessed an old van provided by the Department of Vocational Rehabilitation for her transportation to and from school. Diane told me Jim would drive me home after my visit. All I had to do was call him at a certain neighborhood bar.

Diane agreed to hire Jim's sister, who had just left her husband, to work as her personal care assistant. Diane bought the groceries and paid for rent and utilities, while Jim's sister, she complained, ran up steep bills for long distance phone calls and demanded cash to pay baby sitters. Diane often went without breakfast, or with only a glass of instant breakfast, because Jim's sister was late to her other job at a department store. If she cooked, Jim's sister prepared frozen TV dinners, pot pies, and "shit from a can" like ravioli. When I opened Diane's refrigerator it was empty except for a leftover cheesecake. Jim's sister restricted her attendant care services to dressing Diane in the morning and giving her a bath two or three times a week.

"I know you don't like to be told things, but this place is a mess," Diane had complained to Jim's sister. "This floor has got to be scrubbed."

Jim's sister swept it and was resentful all day. Diane was concerned because an excess of dust aggravates her asthma. She asked Jim's sister to strap on her artificial arms so Diane could try to clean things up herself.

Meanwhile, Jim had been coming home drunk, acting disgusted with life. Diane accused him of giving up while she kept striving.

"You've got it made," he told her at one point, when her monthly SSI check arrived.

When Jim announced that he planned to leave, Diane asked her former roommate, Alice, to move in.

"Is she a student, too?" I asked Diane.

But I meant, "What's wrong with *her?*"

Diane fully intuited my question.

"No," she replied. "She has a bad leg."

Over the next month, whenever I spoke on the phone with Diane, I kept expecting that Jim would be out, Alice in. But Jim was still there. Meanwhile, Diane had a full academic schedule.

"Is there something I could do to help?" I asked.

Without hesitation, Diane replied, "I need a place to live free for a month."

Diane's directness put me in shock. I was living in a one-bedroom walk-up apartment.

"Can you go up stairs?" I ventured. I was too embarrassed to express the image that suggested itself to me: Diane hoisting herself up the steps, one by one, using her arms.

"If you carry me," she said.

I pointed out another stumbling block, that I lived quite a distance from campus, in the Pico-Robertson area, and lacked a car. "The van is mine," she reminded me. "It goes where I do."

The thought of caring for Diane struck me heavily. I didn't want the responsibility. Perhaps I could handle it for a day or two. But to drive Diane to school five days a week, care for her, and live my own life—no way.

As for Jim, I hadn't even met him yet.

"If I knew Jim," I said, "I'd talk to him and you about how you're getting along. That's what I'm good at."

I asked Diane to call me when she wanted to talk. I felt bad about having made an open-ended offer and then refusing to help.

At the end of October, Diane invited me to a birthday party for Alice in East Los Angeles. Diane needed cash to put gas in the van and wanted to buy Alice a present—a bottle of booze. She said she planned to write a rubber check. That, she said, was what she and Jim had been doing right along.

"You sound like you're in a bad way," I remarked.

Diane replied that she hadn't slept that night. Jim had come home drunk and punched her up, and her face was swollen.

In November, Jim entirely gave up taking care of Diane, leaving the job of personal assistant to his sister. Diane began to press Jim to leave but he wouldn't budge. Diane decided that the situation was critical and that she had to get out of the house immediately.

She invited me to lunch at a bistro on the Venice boardwalk to discuss her options. It was a cloudy weekday. Dogs sniffed around our table and tanned regulars breezed past on Rollerblades. Diane said she could stay with Michael, the filmmaker who was making a docudrama about her life, and his girlfriend. Or she could ask her mother to let her live with her in Long Beach.

Staying with Michael was not a real possibility, Diane had decided. Not only was Michael's apartment located inconveniently upstairs, but Michael and his girlfriend were not getting along well. Michael's girlfriend would not take care of Diane, and Diane didn't want Michael to act as her attendant. I surmised that this was because of Diane's attraction to Michael. Undoubtedly she did not want him to see her in the unromantic light of toileting and other self-care activities. Moreover, Diane and Michael had not been getting along well lately concerning his film.[28] Yet Diane did not want to turn to her mother, Irene, for shelter.

I simply did not know what to do. I asked for more information, deliberating from moment to moment about what action I should take. At the same time, I was learning more about Diane's life—in fact, gathering data. Without actually inviting Diane to live with me, I reminded her that, like Michael, I lived upstairs. I said I couldn't conceive of taking Diane, her electric wheelchair, and its battery up and down the stairs . . . more than once a day. Diane would have to spend longer days at school from drop-off to pick-up time. Also, she'd have to spend a lot of time at home alone. If Diane wanted to come over . . . look at the place . . . try the stairs . . . I was willing.

Diane sounded eager to try, but she reminded me of my difficulty when she taught me how to carry her one day. I had to pick up Diane by holding her against my body, both of us facing forward, with my arms wrapped tightly around her waist. She weighed eighty-three pounds. Although I was tall and strong, and weighed more than the one hundred fifty pounds on my driver's license, there was reason for both of us to fear that I might drop her on the stairs. Her cautious response to my half-hearted offer left me a respectable out.

Still, I tried mentally redesigning my apartment to meet Diane's special needs. I lowered shelves to floor level, removed the legs from the couch to make a bed that Diane could climb on and off independently. Regrettably, I would have to give Diane my place at the kitchen table, with its full view of the treetops, since it was the only space accessible to her electric wheelchair. I considered turning the tiny utility room into a study for Diane and pictured myself giving her a bath and cooking her a delightful, nourishing meal.

These thoughts of turning the calm, peaceful atmosphere of my apartment into a humming household were pleasant—until it occurred to me that Diane might have other habits, plans, and needs. She might want to bring her own furniture. Probably she would want to have her coffee table that she used as a desk placed in the sitting room by her bed. Her bed would no longer serve as my couch, and her linens would make the entry messy. As my bed was in the living room, partitioned by a half-wall, I would lose my privacy. And, of course, Diane would bring her TV into the sanctity of my peaceful surroundings. How would I handle my resentment at these everyday disruptions and intrusions, not to mention the inevitable visits from Diane's many friends? What, I contemplated further, if Diane were to act seductively toward me? Somehow I pictured myself passive, unable to resist.

I brought up the situation in my Tuesday night group therapy session. My therapist bluntly asserted, "You don't have the time."

She reminded me that I was writing a dissertation, working as a research assistant, and living my own life. She wanted to know what I was going to get from having Diane move in.

"Why doesn't Diane get a paid attendant?" she asked.

As I tried to explain, I realized how complicated things had become. I planned to let Diane be my guest for two months, paying only for groceries, phone calls, and gas for her van. She could then save up to get her own place.

If Diane were a roommate paying half the expenses, my therapist argued, the arrangement might be taken more seriously.

But if I took money from Diane, I countered, she would need more time before getting out on her own.

My therapist suggested that I might take such good care of Diane that she'd never want to go. Letting Diane move in, she argued, would be the same as giving her money. That was the problem I should address if I wanted to help her.

I phoned Diane as soon as I got home. I didn't say that I would or wouldn't take her in, although I felt that I had already made an offer. Instead, I echoed my therapist's phrases.

"We have to work on getting you in control of your situation," I said. "With your own apartment and attendant."

I was surprised that Diane did not challenge this view.

"Yes, well," she said, "that's always been my problem."

Her response seemed to confirm my therapist's view—that I had been overly involved with my own emotions rather than thinking clearly about Diane's problem. I told Diane I would help her work on getting money. Of course, as a struggling graduate student I had no better idea how to do this for Diane than for myself. I offered to pay an outstanding bill of eighteen dollars to the Santa Monica *Evening Outlook* so that Diane could advertise there again for a driver or attendant.

Meanwhile, Diane's problems mounted. She used the deposit on her apartment to pay November's rent. December's rent would be four hundred dollars, plus a new deposit. Diane considered getting rid of Jim, who was abusing her, by calling the sheriff or getting an injunction against him. But she realized she could not stay in the place anyhow. Jim was supposed to be the building manager, overseeing the trash collection, painting, and doing repairs. So Diane gave notice to her landlord.

Then there was the phone, which was registered in Jim's name. The bill, now overdue, was one hundred dollars. If the service were disconnected, Diane would not be able to answer calls for a driver or attendant. She could not get a phone registered in her own name because of a prior unpaid bill.

On top of this, Diane's electric wheelchair broke down, causing her to miss classes for several days. She also complained of asthma and a pain in her arm, which she attributed to the growth of a bone spur.

Finally, I had an accident while driving Diane's van, causing damage to another vehicle while parking at UCLA. Diane was intensely anxious that her worker at the Department of Vocational Rehabilitation might take the van away.

After the Thanksgiving weekend, I phoned Diane from my office at UCLA's Neuropsychiatric Institute. A meeting had just occurred at the Socio-Behavioral Group, where I worked for Lew Langness as a research assistant. Some graduate students hired on a grant to conduct ethnographic research about women with mental retardation living independently in the community had become so deeply involved in their informants' lives that the principal investigators now questioned the validity of the data: Were they recording the actual behavior of the women or only how they acted in situations that the researchers set up? The graduate students themselves were in a quandary about what to do with the information they had collected.

To anyone outside the ivy-covered walls of the academy the situation might seem obscure and trivial. But the story, as Lew recounted it to me, contained a powerful caution to an initiate about transgressing sacred taboos of the anthropological profession. I told the story to Diane in turn, emphasizing how the researchers had gotten "too involved."

I was confused and scared. I wanted Diane to pick up my allusion to our project. But I didn't want her to feel bad.

So I equivocated: "We know what to do with *our* data."

Diane was silent.

"Are you mad at me?" I asked.

"No," she said. "If I'm thinking a lot, I might seem unfriendly—but it doesn't mean I feel that way."

"If you really are my friend," I said, "I should do anything necessary to help you."

Diane listened.

"I talked to my shrink and to Lew, my dissertation advisor," I continued. "I wish I could have you come and live with me. But I had to agree with them—I couldn't handle it."

"Don't feel bad," Diane said sympathetically. "So many people have been giving me advice—Michael, other friends, you—that I know I'll do what I want, anyway."

Her response gracefully shifted the conversation away from confrontation and blame. It affirmed Diane's responsibility for her own course of action.

"How was your Thanksgiving? How are you feeling?" I asked.

"My asthma is acting up. I had it bad last night," Diane said. "I think the money problems are making it worse."

"I'll advance the eighteen dollars for the *Evening Outlook*," I reminded her.

"Are you planning for us to work tomorrow?" Diane asked. Tuesday was our regularly scheduled research day.

"You want to?" I asked.

Diane affirmed her willingness, once she took care of an appointment at the Student Health Service for the bone spur. It was causing tenderness in her arm and interfered with her functioning.

I offered to take Diane to campus and help her.

The next morning, I took the bus to her house at 8 A.M., then drove her to campus in her van. We planned to swing by the *Evening Outlook* offices, keep an appointment at the Placement Center with a special vocational counselor, get an extension on the deadline for her incomplete grade at the registrar's office, and show up for her appointment with the orthopedic surgeon at the Student Health Service at noon. I did not have a chance to leave Diane's side because her electric wheelchair was still in the shop for repairs and I was needed any time she had to move in her manual wheelchair. Afterward, I drove Diane home and took the bus from Westwood to the mid-Wilshire district for my group therapy session at 5:30 P.M. We never found the time for our scheduled interview. Audiotaped interviews were the "real" work of my research at this stage, because from audiotapes come transcripts, the most authoritative kind of text known to life historians, ethnographers' gold. But I reckoned I owed Diane something because I had retracted my earlier offer of help.

Diane resolved her immediate crisis by moving to her mother's house in Long Beach for several months. While living there she reconciled with Jim and soon married him; they moved to the Bay Area. Through these events I developed a knowledge of Diane as forceful, creative, and a skilled organizer of resources. I was amazed at how quickly she had cast me as a key player in the drama of her life. But I also discovered my fear of being overpowered by Diane and her assertion of her needs. It was stunning how Diane's housing crisis had both mobilized and immobilized me. Yet perhaps I had exaggerated her needs and amplified her distress. Diane had never asked directly to move in with me. I jumped into her dilemma on a hint and almost got stuck in the awesome possibilities.

Many years later, in April 1994, a very different situation existed. By now, Diane had established herself as a professional social worker and was living in Hollywood. The shift in her circumstances opened up possibilities for interaction, and for knowing one another, that were more equal than ever before. Diane was a single woman, having finally broken off her relationship with the account executive and musician she had met just after I returned from Norway. Diane had fallen in love with Dave because he was not only a good lover, she said, but also a good communicator. I remember Diane expressing her appreciation that Dave "did everything for me." I guessed she meant all the things that she cannot do alone involving her mobility, lifting and carrying, cooking, serving food, and her personal care.

Jim was long out of the picture. Diane had initiated the divorce because finally alcohol had gotten the best of him. After leaving Diane, Jim became a street person, a wino drifting through the skid rows of various western cities, on his gradual way back east. He called sometimes, on Diane's birthday and other occasions, to say he still loved her. His attentions were not greatly welcomed by Diane. Her feelings for him were gone and she was not sentimental. If Jim wasn't a man who communicated his feelings well, part of Dave's appeal was that he did. But Dave, Diane learned, had other problems. He was addicted to an expensive street drug. He had moved into Diane's place, used her credit cards, moved out, and left her in debt for the back rent.

Once Diane tried crack, Dave's drug of choice, with him. It was orgasmic, she said. The feeling lasted for hours even though they did not have sex. In fact, they had no sex drive while on the drug. Instead, they felt an incredible pleasure in just talking.

Dave was conflicted about his relationship with Diane. He left her several times but kept coming back: a yo-yo.

Diane told him, "You just can't handle the fact that you fell in love with someone with a disability."

He agreed.

Then, in a bizarre twist of fate, Dave had an accident on his motorcycle that led to the surgical amputation of one of his legs below the knee. This was a scenario worthy of the most maudlin daytime soap opera, except that it was real. After his accident, Dave drew closer to Diane, although he still used drugs and was as unreliable as ever.

Although we were in touch by phone, Diane and I had not seen one another since her commencement nearly a year earlier. Finally one Saturday we arranged to go to a movie. We were just two old friends getting together. I no longer had any particular research interest in the details of Diane's life, although I continued occasionally to jot down notes out of habit. I knew Diane very much wanted me to see her new place on Franklin Avenue, the street just north of Sunset Boulevard that snakes along the foot of the swank Hollywood Hills. She had moved there with her attendant, Lupe, after getting a job as a social worker at Partners, a West Hollywood agency that provided services to elderly people who were homebound and to gay men with AIDS. I know she was eager for me to see her in her new life as a full-time paid professional.

Diane suggested we could walk from her place to a nearby theater on Hollywood Boulevard or, if I parked my car at her place, we could go elsewhere in her new van. The van was another part of Diane's exciting "new me." She received it from the Department of Vocational Rehabilitation when she graduated from USC, and it was precision-designed like a space capsule for her eventually to drive independently. I wanted nothing to do with driving it myself because of my accident in her van so many years ago. I would wait to go for a spin when Diane learned to drive.

I arranged for a baby-sitter for my daughter Rebecca. But before leaving, when I phoned Diane, she informed me that there were no movies worth seeing in walking distance, only a couple of violent macho flicks and an insipid romance. All had gotten bad reviews. Also, she was feeling down.

"Would you mind just coming over to visit and talk?" she asked.

Now I wanted to see Diane, but I also wanted to see a movie. As the single parent of a six-year-old child, I wasn't getting out on weekend nights very often. I had recently ended my relationship with a man I had been seeing and considered marrying. Although glad to be rid of him, I was feeling down, too.

"Isn't there anything else playing?"

"There's *Schindler's List*," said Diane. "I saw it already, but I wouldn't mind seeing it again with you."

I hesitated. *Schindler's List*, Steven Spielberg's attempt to make the definitive Hollywood film about the Holocaust, had just been released. I wanted to see it, but I was also reluctant. Because I knew the movie would tear me apart emotionally, I had already made a mental list of the people with whom I might bear to see the film, whose hand I would clutch while sobbing. Diane wasn't on it. I realized I would have to give up the idea of physically holding someone's hand but decided that seeing *Schindler's List* with Diane would be all right anyway.

I got a little lost when driving to Diane's place, since I had not been there before. I realized my mistake only when my route took me to an odd side street where my friends Carol Lynn and Marcy, musicians, had lived for years before they broke up. That was in the 1970s, I had just started graduate school and was living only a few blocks away with my artist girlfriend. Had Marcy and Carol Lynn's house seemed so tiny then, the street so shabby? There had always been plenty of laughing there, fantastic duets on the violin, health food, kisses, and Marcy's outrageous toy frog collection.

This was my nostalgic Hollywood reverie when I pulled up to Diane's actual address on Franklin Avenue, a luxury apartment house with a doorman in uniform under a canopy. The day had been quite hot but the street was shady and cool, protected from the glaring daylight by tall leafy trees, the densely wooded grounds of a mansion in the foothills across the street. The grounds must have been just watered. I parked and got out of my car, felt the refreshing coolness, and breathed in the moist smell of land and leaves against the concrete street. It reminded me of Central Park West in deep summer. I felt as though the moment I stepped inside Diane's apartment, someone would hand me a Schweppes with lime or a martini.

Diane must have averaged at least one change of address for every year that I have known her. I have seen a lot of her apartments, but this was by far the nicest, a one-bedroom with a balcony overlooking a bricked indoor courtyard with trees in leaf and a sparkling blue pool. While Diane's attendant helped her with the finishing touches to her makeup and accessories, I looked around the compact living room. Everything was immaculate and strictly in order. The thick rust-colored rug gave the room a rich, warm feel. A beautiful fireplace in ceramic tiles was built at an attractive angle in one corner of the room. Above it hung a black-and-white portrait of Barbra Streisand, one I had first seen in Diane's room at a convalescent home around 1980; it had been a reconciliation gift from Jim. The poster looked right: a touch of Hollywood, but restrained and tasteful.

When Diane appeared in her motorized wheelchair from the other room, she did not look depressed at all. Her blond hair was freshly brushed, her brown leather jacket was draped casually over her shoulders, black mascara brought attention to her blue eyes, and she was enveloped by a mist of wonderful perfume. We left feeling happy and joking loudly as we turned corners along the corridors. Waiting for the elevator to arrive, we turned to discover that a beautiful young woman in tight black pants was observing us with the most delightful smile. The three of us got into the elevator together.

Diane and I emerged into the strong shadows of late afternoon on Franklin Avenue and headed toward the unimpeded brilliance of the sun reflecting upon stucco buildings and cement sidewalks. Diane commented on how much she missed living near the beach. Heading to get a bite at the Hamburger Hamlet, we arrived at the entrance to the Hollywood Roosevelt Hotel. Why not go inside, I suggested, and check out the piano bar?

The Hollywood Roosevelt is remembered by members of the first television generation as the place from which *Queen for a Day* was broadcast live. Diane, like me, is old enough to recall the tragic stories housewives told, pitting their suffering against one another to win a Norge washing machine or leg braces for Billy. Each time the audience clapped to rate a contestant's merits, the needle of the Applause-o-Meter jumped across the screen. Tears streamed down the face of the lucky winner while a gorgeous model put a wobbly crown on her head and draped her in ermine, and mustached host Jack Bailey thrust a dozen long-stemmed red roses into her arms.

The Hollywood Roosevelt had been renovated. Its piano bar now had a reputation as the place to go for smart renditions of classic Gershwin numbers. A feeling of freedom and adventure came over me, prompted by a sense that Diane was ready for anything.

"Maybe we should ditch the movie," I proposed, "if there's a good set."

Diane agreed. But an ordinary band was playing the smoky room, and the idea lost its appeal.

There was sparkle in the air between Diane and me as we surveyed the lobby with its columns, polished wood appointments, and soaring ceiling. The dining room was empty but ready for service with sprays of flowers, white tablecloths, stemware, and elaborately folded napkins. We browsed the menu outside with the satisfied air of people who have money and choices.

"I love room service," Diane commented.

"Me, too!" I said. "Have you ever heard of the writer Anaïs Nin?"

"I'm reading a book about her right now," Diane reported.

"Really? Her father used to say that people should live their life every day as if they were on vacation."

"That's good," Diane said approvingly. "I like that."

The Hamburger Hamlet on Hollywood Boulevard is a middle-priced hangout where Diane knows the food is good. She likes the Caesar salad with grilled chicken and the butter-drenched artichokes. Getting settled was a variation on a familiar routine. I went up half a flight of stairs to get the manager to turn on the electric wheelchair lift that makes the Hamlet accessible from the street. We selected a booth by the huge window across from Grauman's Chinese Theater, where throngs of tourists and street people walked by. Diane drove her chair up to the booth, wiggled around, and slipped onto the upholstered seat. The handsome gay waiter was aloof to me but warm to Diane, and he willingly found her a couple of fat telephone books, which is her standard request so that her plate can be propped up to a height that she can reach with her special fork. Outside, a black guy passed, stopped cold, and passed by again, breaking into an approving grin at the sight of Diane. Sitting with Diane behind the plate glass window was more instructive than an entire course on the sociology of disability—and definitely more entertaining.

"Have you seen *Boxing Helena?*" Diane asked. "I heard it was pretty bad, but I kind of want to see it." I hadn't heard of the movie, so Diane gave me a synopsis. It was by a woman director. A man traps his lover in a box and removes her extremities one by one. Controversial.

"Speaking of movies," I said, "you remember my cousin Amy? I was talking to her the other day about including photos in the book. She's working as a gaffer and offered to do makeup and lighting for glamour shots of you . . . and me."

"That's great!" said Diane. "But you know what?"

"What?" I said.

"Ever hear of the photographer Joel Peter Witkin?"

"The guy who photographs hermaphrodites?" I said.

"And amputees," Diane added.

"You know, I happened to see his one-man show at the San Francisco Museum of Art."

Witkin poses hermaphrodites and amputees like Greek gods surrounded by broken statuary draped with snakes, cloying vegetation, and severed body parts. An air of Saint Sebastian's martyrdom pervades everything he does, tortured head thrown back, blood dripping from the arrow wound in his side.

"Well, I've been dating someone. He owns a gallery. He likes amputees," Diane said. "Anyway, he knows Joel Peter Witkin."

"Yeah?"

"He told me Witkin is looking for a woman just like me."

"To photograph?" I said.

"Right."

"Unh. Would you do it?" I asked.

"I don't know," Diane said with a smile. "What do *you* think?"

"I think he's a little weird. Would you feel comfortable about, you know, the way he would handle your disability?"

"I think so," Diane asserted.

"Then do it," I said. "But tell him you have to have your biographer with you. Just think, a Joel Peter Witkin photograph on the book jacket! Do it!"

"Do you think I could still ask him?" Diane mused. "This man I was dating, he's married. I told him I didn't want to go out anymore."

"It's business, Diane," I said knowingly. "Of course he'll want to help you out."

Getting out of the Hamlet was not as easy as getting in. The wheelchair lift jammed before reaching street level with Diane in it. Busboys speaking various languages tried to get the switch working. Finally a manager found a way to trip the mechanism. I felt appreciative for the assistance but could see that Diane was angry. She's come to a point, I realized, where she has a right to expect these things to work.

I paid for dinner to belatedly celebrate Diane's birthday, and Diane insisted on buying the tickets for *Schindler's List* to belatedly celebrate mine. We left the electric wheelchair at the back of the theater after Diane transferred into an aisle seat beside me. When the Nazis rounded up the Jews in the Warsaw ghetto, I began to cry. I watched the rest of the movie with my knuckle in my mouth, sobbing. Mingled with my intense feelings was an awareness that among the victims of the Holocaust must have been family members I had never known. Had I been there, one of the victims could have been me.

In 1976 I made a reflexive investigation of the meanings I attached to Diane's disability to understand the issues that first attracted me to work with her. I discovered feelings of victimization, vulnerability, and marginality that I had projected upon Diane's disability, as if on a screen. Some of my feelings were related to being born a Jew in the period immediately following the Holocaust. For many years in my nightmares Nazis pursued me over rooftops and down blind alleys. Sitting with Diane in *Schindler's List*, I noted that a full circle had come around from the time when I first met Diane and began my study of her life.

Hearing me sob, Diane turned and asked whether I wanted to stay through the film. I nodded and thought, Diane has never seen me so vulnerable. It felt good to be with her in that unguarded state. But it was almost impossible for me to shift gears to casual conversation once the movie was over.

"It affected me, before," Diane commented. "But I knew it would be harder seeing it with a friend who is Jewish—you or Michael."

I had the curious feeling, for the first time, of what it would be like to have Diane study *me*—as a Jew, for example.

When we reached Diane's apartment, she invited me to visit before helping her to get ready for bed. I had earlier agreed to do this so that her attendant could go home. Diane turned on the TV, but I asked her to turn it off. I wasn't ready yet for mundane sounds and images to obliterate the film experience. I sat down on the couch while Diane sat in her wheelchair across from me.

She began telling me about Christopher, one of her clients with AIDS. He was dying in the hospital, and this was partly why she was feeling so depressed. Christopher had been chary of Diane when she joined the agency as its social worker, she told me. Finally, one day, she challenged him.

"You're not comfortable with me, are you?" she said bluntly.

"No, I like you," he said.

"But you won't look at me. It's because of the way I look, isn't it?"

Christopher admitted that it was. After that, he became very close to Diane and phoned her every day. Through Christopher, Diane became personally acquainted with a dwindling cohort of gay men ravaged by AIDS. She was hoping that Christopher would last the night so that she could visit him in the morning and say good-bye.

"Anyway, look at this," Diane said, indicating a book on an end table. It was an album of photographs by Joel Peter Witkin.

She drove her chair up to the table and looked over my shoulder. I turned page after page of black-and-white images celebrating the mysteries of the odd and freakish: hermaphrodites, the grossly obese, a mummified, dismembered male organ on a pedestal.

I must have stopped when I came to a photograph of three young women, nude, with long dark hair and beautiful breasts. Between their legs short fat penises sprouted from dark patches of pubic hair.

"Doesn't that satisfy all your bisexual fantasies?" Diane interjected.

Mine or yours? I thought defensively.

Maybe I wasn't so vulnerable after all.

To help Diane get ready for bed, we went into her room. I was aware, as I know she was, of the possibilities for mutual seduction.

First, at Diane's direction, I leaned over and gently removed her dangling gold earrings. One by one, I placed them on the special rack where Diane's glittering collection hung neatly in pairs. My breasts had nearly brushed Diane's cheek and I inhaled her perfume.

"That's the book I was telling you about," Diane said, indicating a hardbound volume on her desk.

I picked it up: *The Erotic Writing of Anaïs Nin.*

"Now I want to read all her work," Diane said. "Especially *The House of Incest.*"

"I have it at home," I said. "I'll lend it to you."

"Now my nightgown," Diane said. "It's on the bed."

Diane slipped one shoulder out of her leather jacket, then the other. She was wearing a low-cut lacy stretch blouse, very pretty. She raised her arms for me to pull it off, revealing her full breasts in a lacy black bra.

"Diane," I said, bemused. "This is very sexy!"

Diane smiled and said, "Of course!"

Before leaving, I asked Diane if she needed help in the bathroom. But she asked me only to set out her toothbrush and a cup of water on the marble counter where her perfume bottles were arranged. I would have been happy to help her use the toilet, but I sensed Diane's wish to let things end here, preserving the glamour of our evening.

I suppose either of us could have suggested making love in those last exciting moments of our date.

(In my first draft I mistyped: "In those last exciting moments of our *data!*")

We had come a long way, I thought. We were friends, more equal than ever before. Was this simply a result of our long relationship, particularly as I looked forward to resigning from the researcher role? Was it the gender-bending ambiance of Hollywood that sultry evening in April? Or was it the embodiment, I wondered, of a more equal distribution of resources and status now that Diane was a professional and employed?

9 Conclusion

Twenty years ago, as a graduate student in anthropology, I began a journey with a question: What is involved in understanding another person? I met Diane DeVries, who had the imagination to see herself as far more complete a woman than others might expect of someone born without arms and legs. She had the courage to live out her ambitions and desires and the strength to invite people to examine her life and, through it, themselves. I have learned much from knowing her since we met in 1976. What I have learned is embraced by the approach I call cultural biography. Now it is the reader's turn to reflect.

My first impression of Diane, before we had been introduced, was the point where my journey of understanding began. A number of my assumptions were soon proved wrong. I had imagined, for example, that Diane was dependent on her parents, lived at home, and would never marry. But it soon became obvious that I was not capable of imagining the life Diane actually led without getting to know her. It was necessary to be there, as on the day in July 1978 when Diane called from Berkeley to tell me that she was getting married.

"Need I ask to whom?" I joked.

"No," she confirmed. "Jim."

Actually, I was surprised, because Diane and Jim had been having problems. Now they were going to be married the next afternoon in the judge's chambers. For their honeymoon, they planned a two-week train trip across the country, with stops to visit family along the way.

Jim wanted to talk to me. He got on the phone.

"Congratulations!" I said. "You decided to tie the knot!"

"It's something Diane wants," Jim said shyly.

"Are you planning to have kids?"

"We would have had one by now," said Jim. "If we wanted one." He added his doubt that Diane would have an abortion if she were to get pregnant. "Guess who would wind up taking care of it," he continued. "I hate changing shitty diapers."

"No kids," I summarized.

"If I got a really good job, then we could afford someone to take care of all of us."

"Are you working again?" I asked.

"I'm going to look for a job when we get back," Jim said. "How are you?"

Diane picked up the phone again.

"Jim says you're the one who wants to get married," I said.

"He asked *me*," Diane asserted. "I asked whether he wants it, too. He said Yes."

Diane said that her mother, Irene, was surprised when they called to tell her the news. Diane recounted their conversation. "Why do you want to get married, when you've already been living with Jim for nine years?" Irene asked.

Diane told her mother: "Just because we want to."

"What do you want for your wedding?"

"A house."

"No, seriously," Irene responded. "What do you want?"

I arranged to join Diane's family at Union Station at dinnertime one day in early August to meet Diane and Jim on the first segment of their train trip from Oakland to Los Angeles. From there, the couple was going on to Texas to see Diane's grandmother and aunt. Then they planned to stop in New Orleans, in Philadelphia to see Jim's sister, in New York, and Chicago. They would return west along the Canadian border, then down the west coast to Oakland.

A couple of weeks afterward, Diane and Jim had a small party at her mother's place in Long Beach, to which they invited Michael and me. We got together in the den, a comfortably furnished, converted garage with wood-grain paneling.

Jim was usually a quiet, even silent, man. But this night he told captivating stories about the trip on the train. He and Diane had spent a lot of time between the cars, smoking tobacco and weed, listening to the rhythm of the track, catching the passing scenery. These were timeless images evoked in the country twang of Jim's soft raspy voice, as he sat on the blue couch in his chambray work shirt and jeans. Sitting beside him in a demure white piqué camisole top over her cut-off jeans, shoulders and arms attractively flushed and exposed, Diane glowed with happiness.

Diane mentioned how the seats on the train had been amazingly comfortable, more comfortable than any in which she had ever sat. She had suffered no back pain the entire time they were away.

"The train crew adopted us," Jim said.

A conductor gave them a sleeping berth even though they hadn't paid for one. Diane spent a whole day just lying around.

When Jim had to take Diane to the ladies' room, the conductor led them to a car in which the restrooms had been closed off. He opened one just for them.

One evening, Jim went back to the dining car and asked if he could bring a plate out to his wife. Otherwise he would have to carry her into the dining car. The maître d' didn't believe Jim. He said he couldn't make an exception to the rules.

Pretty soon Jim carried Diane into the dining car and set her in a seat. They ordered and ate.

When the bill arrived, the maître d' came over.

"This one," he said, "is on me."

As Diane and Jim recreated their ride through an endless field of sunflowers, I felt a mythic aura enveloping them that boded well for their future. In the morning the sunflowers were facing one direction, toward the sun. In the evening, they were facing the other way. Jim slowly turned the flat of his hand one way and then the other to show the sunflowers' devotion to the sun. When I first saw Diane in a lecture hall at UCLA, I could not have imagined this scene with Diane and Jim, their stories, our conversations. Without being there, I could not have understood that someone might love Diane as much as Jim did.

Biographers should strive to reconstruct the contexts in which individuals have lived, including the particular family milieu in which their subject developed. People who hear about Diane often assume that she must have had a wonderful family. This is a part of Diane's life that could use more elaboration before this book ends. Diane's successes in life might be viewed by a psychologist in terms of her "resilience"—the result of having had at least one consistently nurturing figure in early childhood who helped her acquire self-esteem and self-efficacy.[1] That figure in Diane's life story is her father, Kenneth Fields.

The family scrapbook kept by Diane's mother contains a page on which Kenny wrote his life story as an engaging spoof. Kenny's resilience in response to rural poverty during the Depression helps fill in a meaningful background to Diane's ability to take hard knocks.

"MY STORY"

by Kenneth Fields

My story "The life and loves of K. L. Fields," begins back in the year 1927. That's when I was a kid, a very young kid. I was born (some people find that hard to believe) in or around the vicinity of Kingsville, Texas, the town that was built for the King's Ranch, the largest Ranch in the Country.

But getting back to that unfortunate Date, Jan 14, 1927 as I said that was when I was born. It was pretty cold that day. how do I know?! Well its usually pretty cold about January. We moved from there to someplace else, I don't know, I was to young. I started knowing things when I moved to Ambrose. (I took my family too!). That was that sad day when I had to start to school my Ma & Pa made us kids go get something for supper. Of course you'd think we would get a kick out of going to the store and looking at all the goodies. But No! We had to hunt for our food. If it had been left up to me we would have probably starved to death. I was a little feller then (6 years old) and it was kinda hard for me to ketch them rabbits, so I just poked along waiting, and watching the race, between my older Brothers and the rabbits, it was kinda hard for them to catch jack rabbits so they kinda kept to chasing cotton-tails, We usually wound up getting a couple of rabbits and three or four chickens (neighbors!) So I didn't go entirely hungery, but I never did get used to eating rabbit skin.

So we finally moved from Ambrose, Date Unknown, which left the population one family less but I don't think they knew what census was in them there days. But a pretty close guess would be about 50 head, the population up to date is,—about 50!!! As I was saying, from Ambrose to a place very seldom heard of "Carpenters Bluff" and I believe that name fits the place and vice-verse, from the looks of the houses there, it did have all the carpenters bluffed off. If you don't believe me go see, Just drive about 5 or 6 miles east of Denison and look around. I went to school there too about the 4th or 5th grade, played basketball too. The rabbits around there got so used to us chasing them, we finally got us a system a ketching them. We'd go out into the woods, (Didn't have dogs then, they were to slow) and when we'd see a rabbit, we'd start walking the other way, they'd follow to see what was wrong, then we'd suddenly turn and they'd break their necks turning to run, got lots, didn't have to eat skin. We moved from there to Denison Texas, then I had to put on shoes Concrete was hard & hot & cold. I went to school at Lamar & Peabody & finally High School, If I was still going I'd probably still be there, teaching the teachers of course. That was where I started going with gals. I didn't care so much about them before I went to the Army in 1945 then came out I started giving them all a buzz. I got in pretty bad with one but it finally came to a halt when she married a soldier for his money, she thought. But I kept messing around until I met Irene Snow, She's Mrs. K. L. Fields now and we're happy about the whole thing. She's happy about the thing I'm happy about the *whole*.

Well Dear readers I could go on & on but as you see this here page ain't much longer. So I'll just stop.

Of Course this is a very brief story of my life.

K. L. Fields

Description
Height—6' 2"
Weight—170 lbs
Hair—yes
Eyes—two
Age—year older than last.

Diane's most enjoyable experiences during childhood were facilitated by her father. In her unpublished autobiography, Diane suggests that she never conceptualized herself as being handicapped before the age of five, when she became a patient at the Child Amputee Prosthetics Project. Before then she saw herself merely as "someone who had to do things differently" from others. "Participation was not denied me," she wrote. "It was simply approached very creatively, while at the same time highlighting my 'uniqueness.'" Her examples of participation usually include her father or his influence:

> Every summer our family used to have "bike-riding" nights. Instead of me trying to keep up in my tri-wheeled scooter, I rode on the basket attached to the handlebars of my dad's bicycle. One of my dad's favorite activities to do when camping was to go hiking. In order to share this with me he took his skin-diving bag which was made of rubber, and then attached shoulder straps to it to use as a papoose-carrier. Sitting safely atop his 6'2" back provided a perfect view.

Kenneth also facilitated Diane's independence in other ways. Diane discovered how to take her first independent mouthful while still in a highchair by balancing a spoonful of food on the rim of her bowl and depressing the handle. As she grew up, she eventually needed to develop more sophisticated ways of eating, which she found difficult with artificial arms and hooks.

> Fortunately, my dad's creativity came to my rescue again. Always aware of the aversion I held towards doing anything with my prostheses he designed a very effective fork and spoon, which could be used without the usual array of bowls, or my hooks. By taking an ordinary fork and spoon and welding an extension of metal onto each of them, he could then bend it so that it fit over my arm like a cuff. It was ingenious. When I received my first electric wheelchair in 1966, he designed a raised lap-

board which I could place and remove independently. This became my dinner table, as well as my desk. To this day, both his fork and spoon, and lap-board—though modified to accommodate my growth—is what I use.

When she was twenty-four years old, her father, who was then terminally ill with cancer, said, "You do know, Diane, that I've always liked you? Don't you?" And Diane did.

She felt much less secure in her mother's love and support. Although Diane shared some wonderful times with her mother, designing and shopping for fabric for the fanciful outfits that Irene sewed, these experiences were not sufficient to Diane's emotional needs. All their fun in creating new fashions for Diane—"strapless and backless blouses," "hot pink two-piece bathing suits," "pink and black lace blouse-top bathing suits"—did not make up for something that was missing in their relationship.

Irene was the parent who dutifully stayed at Diane's bedside during her numerous surgeries and did the drudge work of driving her to therapy appointments and carrying out the home program. But Diane resented and felt it was unfair that much of her caretaking—including dressing, grooming, and toileting—was delegated to her younger sister. And it was her mother, Diane tells us in her life story, who sent her away.

After dinner one evening in 1964, when Diane was almost fourteen, her father asked her to join him on the couch to have a little talk. Diane knew it was a matter of importance because of his formal demeanor and serious expression. She wondered what she had done.

"Honey, you know your mother has a hard time taking care of you." Kenneth told her. "She says that her back just can't take much more."

"She has a hard time taking care of me?! Yeah, I guess driving me to UCLA for therapy and sitting through the sessions, and driving me to the prosthesis man is a lot of work. The only time she lifts me is in and out of the car. She lifts her bowling ball more than she lifts me! Is she gonna quit bowling? What does she think it is for Debbie, a picnic?! She doesn't take care of me—her eleven year old daughter takes care of me!"

"I know, I know. It's just *that*, Diane. You and your mother just have a hard time with each other. I don't know what it is. It's always been there though. She thinks, uh well, we think, it would be better for everyone if it could stop."

"Stop? What's she gonna do, get rid of me?" Diane taunted.

"Uh, well, we heard of a place in Downey that might be the answer. It's a hospital—but not like most hospitals—called Rancho Los Amigos."

"What am I supposed to say? It sounds as if it's all set."[2]

Family dynamics such as these are as important as individual psychology for understanding Diane. But a cultural biographer will look beyond individual psychology and family dynamics to focus even more on the cultural milieu as the source of discourses and practices in the subject's life. Diane's life precisely maps major cultural transformations in American society concerning people with disabilities. Her exposure to the "crip" subculture at Rancho Los Amigos Hospital, where she lived almost continuously from 1964 through 1968, also set the stage in important if unanticipated ways for her future independence. A rehabilitation hospital was not a place where Diane wanted to live, but to her family it seemed the most likely place of refuge. She was not put in a convent, locked in an attic, or boarded on a farm—nor did she become a circus performer or a prostitute. Like the Child Amputee Prosthetics Project, the "Ranch of Friends" provided Diane with the possibility of trying out (and exhausting) the best remedies that people then believed possible.

When I met Milo Brooks, the founding medical director of the Child Amputee Prosthetics Project, I asked him whether he thought CAPP's work with Diane had been successful. Although Diane had rejected most of what the rehabilitation paradigm had offered her in the way of artificial limbs, Dr. Brooks responded: "I think we've been successful in that we've kept the lines of communication open and never rejected Diane."[3] Despite the imperfect fit between Diane's needs and the early goals of pediatric amputee rehabilitation, CAPP remained her supporter, bending the rules because of her family situation to continue providing services to her even as an adult.

When Diane applied for admission as a student to UCLA, for example, the new medical director, Yoshio Setoguchi, successfully petitioned on her behalf for funds to buy a second powered wheelchair, costing $1,350, that could fold to fit in a car. Diane was eligible for MediCal and

Medicare at that time, but neither insurance program would pay for a second wheelchair. The folding wheelchair would allow Diane to live outside Westwood, where rents would be more affordable on the ATD (Aid to the Totally Disabled) stipend she then received from the State of California. Dr. Setoguchi described CAPP's commitment to Diane and the importance of the facility as a place for her to turn to:

> Diane has been a patient at the UCLA Child Amputee Center for the past twenty years. Normally we only treat patients until they are twenty-one, however the hardship that Diane has had to endure due to a poor family situation has caused CAPP to bend the rules and continue to provide services although she is nearly 25. Diane was born with both legs and most of both arms missing. She has attempted to use artificial legs, but they are too cumbersome and require too much energy to make them practical. Since the age of ten she has used a powered wheelchair as she cannot push a standard one with her upper extremity prostheses. Diane lived at home until the age of twelve at which time she was placed in Rancho Los Amigos Rehabilitation Center for extensive training and because it was the only living situation suitable for her age. She returned home and attended Jordan High School in Long Beach and received excellent grades. During this time her parents separated. The home situation worsened following high school and Diane had to move to a nursing home where she still lives. Last year it was found that her father whom she was close to had cancer. Diane wanted to show her dad that she had not given up and would make something of herself before he died. It was at this time that she initiated her application to UCLA. Her father has since died, however Diane still feels she must make the effort to gain an education so she can help others and become a teacher or counselor.[4]

Although independent living activists have criticized its paternalism, the rehabilitation paradigm did put Diane in contact with professionals who let her know that her life mattered.

Diane commented as a UCLA student in the mid-seventies, "There's nothing about the disabled woman and the disabled culture." This insight registered the emergence not only of the "second wave" of feminism but also of the disability rights movement created by people with needs that were not met or were sometimes even exacerbated by medical rehabilitation. Whether disabled in the Vietnam War, born with cerebral palsy, or injured in a car accident, they recognized that society was sidelining them because of architectural barriers, lack of simple accommodations, stigmatization because of their appearance, and segregation based on the idea that they were sick and incapable. The disability rights movement called attention to the inequality in power between people with and without disabilities, and between physicians and their patients.

Through media, legislation, and cultural products like Diane's life story that "pass the word," the movement continues to empower people with disabilities to perform the range of occupations that are needed for survival and make life worth living in ways that work best for them. Challenging and transforming what is required to be fully included in society may mean different things to different people. Diane's goals are ones that other Americans of her era will find familiar: the right to fulfill her sexuality, to have meaningful relationships and marry if she pleases, and to have a remunerative career. Through her well-publicized actions to fulfill such goals, Diane has resisted people's expectations of American women with disabilities and contributed to changes in the culture. A cultural biography is not complete, then, until it examines how a subject's actions and image affect her culture and transform it, if only locally.

Diane's life has always been public—the subject of news reports, articles in academic journals, and this book. She was a poster child: the earliest of these appearances, preserved by her mother in the family scrapbook, shows three-year-old Diane with a frilly dress, three-wheeled scooter, crutches, and a Padres baseball cap, posed with members of the San Diego team to announce a benefit game for crippled children.[5] Diane was featured the following year, in 1954, as guest of honor at a Kiwanis Club benefit dance at the Mission Beach Ballroom with orchestra leader Lawrence Welk. The event was promoted in a cloying San Diego *Evening Tribune* news feature headed "Pair of Red Shoes Tiny Girl's Dream":

> This is the story of a brave little girl and her dream of a pair of red shoes.
> She's a pretty little girl with golden blonde hair and her name is Diane.
> You might even call her Cinderella.
> For some day, she's sure, her fairy godmother will come along with a magic wand and brush all the tears away.

It's a story, too, of heartache, of love, and of the courage and devotion of a mother and father, Mr. and Mrs. Kenneth Fields.

You see, Diane was born without arms and legs.[6]

Diane *was* blond and cute. Her appearance even with her disability could be made to fit a cultural formula of attractiveness by normative standards. Freddie Thomason, a boy two years older than Diane, born with quadrilateral limb deficiencies, was similarly described in newspaper articles at age two as "blue-eyed, tow-headed" and a "shy, blond youngster" and, at four, as a "sun-loving, unspoiled child." Children like Diane and Freddie, who lacked facial disfigurement, speech impairments, mental handicaps, neuromuscular incoordination, terminal illnesses, excessive body weight, or noticeable scars from surgery or traumatic injury, were prime candidates for celebrity. Simply being blond was an advantage.[7]

By imperceptible degrees Diane acquired a persona based on the meaning of her disability in popular culture, the stardom reserved for certain handicapped persons. In 1954 she appeared twice with her mother on Harold Keen's local San Diego television program, which showed her using artificial limbs and a scooter with crutches donated by the Kiwanis Club.[8] At age eleven, Diane was a poster girl for the March of Dimes fund-raising campaign in the city of Lakewood.[9] A publicity photo shows her posed uncharacteristically in a long fancy dress, with her three-wheeled cart and crutch and a sour expression on her face. Diane continued to participate in March of Dimes events and two years later was one of four "charming handicapped youngsters" who were "honored guests" at a fund-raising campaign luncheon.[10] Yet another news photo in Irene Fields's scrapbook shows Diane in shorts and a sleeveless top, with artificial arms and legs, being lifted onto a bus among 134 handicapped children headed for a two-week trip to Camp Paivika.[11]

For several years, Diane was the star of swim shows sponsored by the Shrine Club and other organizations to benefit an aquatic program started by Evelyn DuPont.[12] Three-time winner of the Mississippi River National Swim, DuPont contracted polio in the 1950s and rehabilitated herself by swimming. DuPont made the small orthopedic pool in her backyard available to handicapped children and donated her instruction, but had the larger ambition to build a well-equipped and properly staffed thirty-thousand-dollar facility to meet the needs of thousands of persons with handicaps in the Long Beach–Lakewood area. The beauty of swimming as an occupation for Diane was that she could move through the water like a dolphin without the need of artificial limbs or flotation devices. DuPont coached Diane in diving and swimming routines. Her confident performance at age twelve, the last year she participated in the program, was rendered in effusive terms by a reporter:

> A pretty blue-eyed blond with a happy smile, in a deep blue bathing suit, pauses at the end of the diving board. . . . She catapults into the water, a beautiful dive, either front or back. She swims the length of the pool. She swims on her face, and flips over on her back to get her breath. . . . She is Diane Fields, 12, born without arms or legs, and she will be the star of the Handicapped Children's Water Show, next Tuesday before the Shrine Club at the Lafayette hotel pool.[13]

But even if Diane's life had not been mediated in this way, she remains visible, rarely blending into the crowd, always exposed. The crisis of representation is never far from her, as she points out in her autobiography: "Before I enter a room, or am introduced to someone, I know my presence is merely a formality—they have already heard of or about me. I consider this a phenomenon because I am not a celebrity, nor one who has somehow improved society; or an inventor of a technological wonder. What I am, is a wonderfully unique conversation piece, which, if need be, can be converted into an attractive centerpiece."

Any work of historiography is culturally bound by the horizons of its own age. The idea that ethnographers trade in partial truths relates to such perspectival shifts.[14] Popular discourses and elite theories may last decades and sometimes centuries, but they do change. The nature of narratives is to impose order and coherence on a prolific and narratively unstable embodied reality. This is true even of the subject's life story, as a narrative that constructs an "I." The material that is included will always mask or exclude something else that could have been said. And it is true of my understanding of Diane's life, which is necessarily contingent on what I bring to it.

Sidney Mintz has written a bemused commentary, "The Sensation of Moving, While Standing Still," about changes in critics' perceptions of his classic life history of a Puerto Rican sugarcane laborer.[15] In 1948 Mintz began a field project that eventually resulted in a book about his friend and informant, Don "Taso" Zayas, called *Worker in the Cane*. The book was reviewed in *American Anthropologist* by Joseph Casagrande, who criticized the work for its lack of objectivity because Mintz and Don Taso were friends. Holding to a representational theory of science, Casagrande believed that Don Taso could be described objectively, but only if Mintz's biases as an observer were kept in check. Because Mintz was aware that Don Taso "must always have been on his guard to try to protect the image he would have me retain of him," Casagrande argued that the study had been compromised by Mintz's obligation to honor his friend's image.[16]

Two decades later anthropologist Kevin Dwyer also criticized the methods used in *Worker in the Cane*, but seemingly for the opposite reason.[17] One of the first to view the problem of representation as a matter of politics, not just science, Dwyer was concerned that Mintz had edited Don Taso's interviews into an artificially coherent autobiographical narrative. Dwyer argued that only a faithful reporting of dialogues could begin to even out structural inequalities between anthropologists like Mintz and their often much poorer and less powerful informants like Don Taso. The text of *Worker in the Cane* remained the same as in 1960, when it was published. But, as Mintz summarized, the book was now criticized "not because the anthropologist was too friendly, but not friendly enough." Mintz's portrayal of Don Taso was twice put into question as contingent and incomplete because of readers' shifting theoretical commitments.

It is important for a biographer to reflect critically on the dynamics of power when rendering an account of another's life. Including the subjects' own words through dialogue is important. But as anthropologist Parin Dossa suggests, despite claims to have accommodated the voices of the Other through dialogue and new genres, such textual devices may still constitute "a mask for the perpetuation of asymmetrical power relations between those who do the studying and those who are studied."[18]

Contemporary ethnographers and life historians face this challenge: to be faithful in dialogue and committed to ethical action within the contentious arena of the liberation of oppressed peoples. Because liberation and self-determination imply struggle, it seems unrealistic to me that ethnographic texts should be devoid of such tensions. As I have implied by including a description of the Norway incident, after which it took about a year for Diane and me to work through our conflict of interpretations, texts should retain evidence of conflicts and negotiations. It is necessary to add the dimension of power, which was overlooked by Dilthey in developing *Verstehen,* to the cultural biography approach.

Although psychoanalysis offers useful practices of self-reflection to identify the dynamics of power, the conventional psychoanalytic case history is a model to avoid. Inequality of power between the biographer (clinician) and subject (patient) remains the most stubborn problem embedded in psychoanalytic-style narratives. In regard to clinicians getting consent from patients to publish descriptions and interpretations of case material, psychiatrist Robert Stoller cautions:

> When someone says "yes" to a powerful figure, what parts of the "yes" come from love, fear, insight, possession of the facts, the state of one's digestive tract, the season of the year, the phase of the moon? Exhibitionism, vindication, revenge, desire to help humanity, desire to help me, fear of reprisal from me, to solidify things learned in treatment? All could play a part. Is informed consent possible? . . . I end with one strongly held opinion. We should not write about our patients without their permission to do so and without their view of the matters about which we write.[19]

Reclaiming the term *native,* rather than *subject,* is sometimes a useful strategy when thinking about who should have the last word in a biographical account. Diane is native to her body and the conditions I have studied in her life—that is, growing up and living as an American woman in the second half of the twentieth century with a particular disability. The right to narrative self-determination has become an axiom of our times, and only Diane can define the meaning of her experience to her. Diane alone determines the metaphor of self—the myth or myths— by which she lives as a woman who happens to have been born without arms and legs. She is the sole legitimate author of her life story. Yet it has been clear over time that a great deal of sharing, borrowing, and cross-fertilization has taken place between her version and mine. It is only when the power relationship becomes unbalanced that such sharing has been experienced negatively as objectification and appropriation.

A cultural biography would elaborate on Dollard's recommendations in *Criteria for the Life History*. A psychologist by training, Dollard was an important contributor to the culture-and-personality movement in anthropology who acknowledged his intellectual debt to Edward Sapir and his friendship with Margaret Mead. After reviewing and comparing a number of biographical works in psychoanalysis, sociology, literature, and anthropology, Dollard recommended seven criteria as indispensable for the life history. His approach, which is basically historiographic in the *Verstehen* tradition, calls for reconstruction and analysis of the subject's life and experience in terms of culture, biology, and psychology:

1. The subject must be viewed as a specimen in a cultural series.
2. The organic motors of action ascribed must be socially relevant.
3. The peculiar role of the family group in transmitting the culture must be recognized.
4. The specific elaboration of organic materials into social behavior must be shown.
5. The continuous related character of experience from childhood through adulthood must be stressed.
6. The "social situation" must be carefully and continuously specified as a factor.
7. The life-history material itself must be organized and conceptualized.[20]

Dollard's criteria provide a strong foundation for a cultural biography, which is a blend of life history and ethnographic methods resulting in descriptions that are both retrospective and contemporaneous. However, I suggest that the following criteria must be added, to the extent that they are relevant and feasible for a given project:

8. The subject's life story should be explicitly presented and analyzed.

9. The biographer's ethnographic observations and life history interpretations over time should be reviewed by the subject, whose
responses must be presented.

10. The historical context of the project must be analyzed reflexively
and critically regarding: (a) the biographer's interpretive horizons;
(b) changes in the ongoing relationship between biographer and
subject, including the dynamics of power; (c) clarification of the mirror phenomenon; and (d) the effect of the subject, including the subject's image, on the culture.

These new criteria should be used not simply to add and stir in new
facts, but to allow for a fuller analysis of the cultural processes by which
biographical images are created and propagated. Reflectiveness in
anthropology, a social science, is consistent with the relativity of the
post-Einstein observer's role as a participant in different frames or
contexts in the physical world. Contemporary anthropologists must
focus not only on images of the other but also on the cultural processes
by which such images arise. Yet the mirror phenomenon is the least recognized source of contingency in most biographical descriptions. It
operates in several ways. A biographer brings predilections and pre-
understandings to the research situation that are not only cultural but
also rooted in her own life history and life story and in the relationship
developed over time with her informant. Gilbert Herdt, an expert on
gender and sexuality among the Sambia in Papua New Guinea, models
the introspective work required to examine these dimensions of understanding:

Talking: who talks to me: Why are my friends the most verbal Sambia?
Interviewing: who talks? How much, when, where, how loud or soft,
about what? What topics (e.g., parents) are avoided? Does someone
make eye contact? If a woman or a boy looks away or is bashful, how is
this done: matter-of-factly, nervously, quietly, coquettishly? Why is
someone quiet? What kind of silence is it—cold, warm, angry, or inviting? Why does someone only get quiet when angry? Why do I feel
someone is talking too much or too little? What is the overlying mood of
the interview: contentment, passivity, aggressiveness, brooding, fearful-
ness, or combinations of these? Joking: who makes jokes—men, boys,
women? With me, too? When alone? Who laughs? With what kinds of

laughter (amused, hysterical)? What do I joke about? How do I make light of events, of myself, of my anxiety? What amuses me? Appalls me? I sense someone is hiding something from me but have only empathy to go by: what are my associations (fantasies)? Do I forget names? Why don't I trust someone's dream reports? Resistance: why am I reluctant to ask something? Why do I consistently avoid some topics? What fascinates me? Bores me? Why am I afraid to ask someone about a particular experience?[21]

I was attracted to study Diane's life because of her appearance. My first impressions were of a person with enormous limitations, a victim. With clarification of my mirroring, I found a survivor. Writing about her life while reflecting on my assumptions helped me to understand my hidden disabilities, come to terms with my own limitations, and grasp how they affected the images I was constructing of Diane. It was my job in life to untangle the elements of my suffering that were related to a history of family dysfunction (grandmother's suicide, parenting styles, sibling incest), intergenerational effects of migration and other cultural patterning (the Jewish diaspora, class background and aspirations, the Holocaust), and biological components (mood disorder and, perhaps, sexual preference). In turn, my study of Diane's life was enriched and informed by this self-reflective and clarifying work, using the same techniques of cultural biography in her case and in mine. For example, my sudden identification of Diane with the Venus de Milo was, I learned, one that Diane herself had made long ago. This discovery led me to a new appreciation of how Diane viewed herself: "a modern-day Venus," not on a pedestal but in a wheelchair: Venus on wheels.

The mirroring a *reader* brings to an ethnography or life history has hardly been examined at all. A cultural biography should provoke readers to clarify their empathy, projections, and transference related to the images in the text. If it does not, it has probably failed. So now, it is the reader's turn. Why not step up to the mirror of this text and tell yourself what you see? Biographical images proliferate in these pages. It is important to ask: With whose images and stories did *I* identify? What did I find when I dwelt inside Diane's body, if briefly? What resonance did I bring to each narrator's voice? What repulsed, confused, or frightened me?

Reader, this may be your last chance to catch yourself in the act! The Diane portrayed in this cultural biography depends on what you take away. She is very truly *your* Diane.

Diane and I once spoke at a seminar taught by my mentor and colleague Barbara Myerhoff at the University of Southern California in 1979. I picked up Diane at the convalescent hospital where she was then living. We had to take Diane's manual wheelchair because her power wheelchair would not fit in the trunk of the white 1967 Chevy Impala that my uncle had recently bestowed on me.

We soon discovered that the classroom was located upstairs in the Physical Education Building. One of the oldest buildings on campus, facing the track, it had a tall flight of grey stone steps leading to its front entrance. Diane and I wheeled around the brick building in the glaring sun, looking in vain for a side entrance with a ramp or even a service elevator. I was afraid we would be late for class.

"This is outrageous!" I vented. "It's against federal law for a campus to be inaccessible." Diane calmly listened to me rave. She sized up some athletes running up and down the stairs. "That's okay," she said. "We'll just get us some jocks to carry me up."

Diane entered the classroom in her wheelchair, as if on a palanquin, borne by four handsome, proud, and sweaty young men.

I spoke about my research approach and Diane talked to the students about her life experiences, particularly about her ambitions and her struggles to achieve her goals. She described how demoralizing and boring it was to live in a convalescent hospital. Before her father died from cancer in 1975, she told the students, she had made a promise to herself that she would do something with her life. She did not want to spend it sitting around in a nursing home.

At the end of the class, Barbara invited the students to reflect on their reactions to Diane and write them down. Reflexivity of this sort was central to Barbara Myerhoff's approach as an ethnographer and teacher. Several weeks later, Diane and I both received thank-you notes from Barbara, along with the papers by the students. There was a range of reactions, as might be expected, all thoughtful and honest. Almost every student who wrote confessed having had difficulty at first with seeing

Diane, and most reported evidence of the mirroring phenomenon. The students generally found Diane to be "powerful," "confident," and "courageous." One wrote directly to Diane:

> I admired your acceptance of your body and your realization that you have a good one because those of us with arms and legs often can't seem to get this together no matter how good our bodies are. Overall, the experience was very poignant for me not only because I saw that you are in so many ways a normal individual (foolish of me to think you wouldn't be), but because you show an acceptance of and a determination with life that I wish I could always possess.

Another student's response also showed evidence of mirroring. But it objectified Diane's existence in terms of theological problems. Diane became only a symbol, an image distanced from her engaging personal presence:

> What is it in the unusual, the deformed that we may find fearful? Why is it that some sights seem to be manifestations of God—and others manifestations of evil. The sight is what it is—our own mind, informed by our culture and experience, tells us what is evil and what is holy. . . . I could not look at Diane when I first noticed her; of course my emotions were torn between staring and blinding—what was so threatening and appealing at the same time? . . . She is one of us, yet not one of us; is she above, below us, inside us—she has no place, she must be hidden for we cannot place her and categorize her. . . . It is I who am crippled not she— she can tolerate me but I can't tolerate her. . . . Why is she evil then— because she points to my inadequacy.

A third student saw Diane in terms of suffering and dignity, drawing on a personal background as the child of a Holocaust survivor:

> Some of us are subject to more of the pain that the "human" condition can inflict. In light of this I was not shocked or repelled . . . but rather sympathetic to the unique problems a multiple amputee experiences. I have always been attracted to beggars, especially those that are physically disabled. . . . I think a lot of my attitude has to do with all the stories I have grown up hearing from my mother about Nazi concentration camps. I realize from this that under certain conditions human beings can suffer a total loss of respect and dignity. I firmly believe in light of

this that each person's soul is sacred and deserves to be valued. . . . [The presentation] was a rare insight into the world of a very different yet very similar human being.

Perhaps most interesting, because it offers such a striking contrast, is the response of the sole student who reported having friends with physical disabilities. This student's comments appear to have the least unclarified projection and greatest grasp of Diane's self-presentation. In addition to a friend called Jayne who uses a wheelchair, the writer also mentioned having another good friend "who broke his neck and is in a wheelchair." This student and her sister took care of Jayne and visited her in the convalescent home where she stayed. The student reported that "knowing Jayne first as an individual and then as someone in a wheelchair has greatly broadened my perspective of people who do not have the mobility of their arms and legs." She envisioned having begun a relationship with Diane that might well continue after the buzzer signaled the end of class:

> When Diane talked about the bizarreness of such [convalescent] homes I was reminded of the fascinating mixture of human experiences in such places. I think Diane has it together in many many ways. She has separated herself from those who have said she is marvelous all of her life, crazy nurses who do exercises in front of immobile patients and those who have hurt her—and by doing so has developed an individuality and thoughtful objectivity. She's very down to earth and doesn't seem to harbor a lot of bitterness. These are tremendous qualities. . . . I hope our paths will cross again.

Someone born with Diane's disability only a few decades earlier might have made her livelihood by exhibiting herself as a freak.[22] The shift in American culture is marked by the story of Otis Jordan, born in Georgia in 1926 with "poorly functioning and underformed limbs" and better known in the carnival world as "Otis the Frog Man."[23] Jordan, who performed feats such as rolling his own cigarettes, was banned in 1984 from appearing in the Sutton Sideshow at the New York State Fair when a high-minded citizen challenged the anachronistic exploitation of people with deformities. In a newspaper interview, Jordan defended his right as a showman to make a living rather than live on welfare. Life in the United States for Diane's generation appears to be very different from that in which pioneer disability performers like Otis Jordan were raised. Diane is the most highly educated of her family. But what about the following unsolicited letter from a well-wisher that Diane's mother saved and pasted in the family scrapbook?

The writer of the letter saw Diane's appearance on television in the summer of 1954 and wrote suggesting that Irene Fields try to arrange for Diane to meet a certain circus performer who was, she said, "the same as Diane."

> I thought I maybe could help you a little with my added information, perhaps you already know of this other girl who is the same as Diane, we saw her last year at the Barnum and Bailey Circus side show, she was so accomplished in being able to do things for herself and her autograph was done right before our eyes by holding the pen in her teeth, beautiful writing and much better than many who use the hands, of course that girl is 31 years old now and didn't have the advantage of the new equipment that your girl will have. If Frieda is still with the circus this year when it comes to San Diego, I think it would be a wonderful morale builder for Diane to see and meet her.[24]

When I discovered this letter in the scrapbook Irene entrusted to me, Diane was repelled by its patronizing tone and implicit suggestion that she belongs in a circus. She was shocked and outraged that her mother would have kept the letter rather than destroy it. Reflecting further on the letter's contents, however, Diane later wrote:

> I have read this letter numerous times and each time it has exorcised different thoughts and feelings. My very first reaction was that of indignant outrage! How dare this woman compare me to someone in a "freak side-show!" Next, I was amused by the woman's audacity at referring to herself as one offering "knowledge" when all she was doing was what she did at the circus: Gawk at the "freak." However, once my sensitivity and self-righteousness vented itself, I saw this woman as not unlike many people confronting something alien to themselves who are overtaken with contradictory feelings of remorse, fear, admiration, and guilt.[25]

It may be unnerving to realize that people with disabilities like Diane are acute observers of the often unflattering behavior others exhibit in response to them. As a child performer in swim shows, she eventually noticed that "it was my physical disability and deformity, rather than my aquatic talents" that the director of the program used to draw the interest of the public and the media. At the annual gala Golden Crutch Ball, supporters of the program donned formal attire to dine and dance, paying fifty and one hundred dollars per ticket to raise money for an Olympic-sized pool. The ceremony included calling the children by name to the podium to receive a congratulatory hug or kiss from Mrs. DuPont and a trophy of a diver.

> Each and every year, I was the "dessert." Not because of anything I personally did, but because of duPont's extensive words of introduction, my appearance at front and center evoked a more emotionally charged response from the spectators. Not only did the applause seem louder and to last longer, but a mist began to form over their eyes, as well. After they had all taken their seats, the flashbulbs had stopped flashing, and the trophy and "special award" had been placed in the seat of my wheelchair, I was then placed in front of a microphone and a hushed audience. I was the only child actually expected to speak. . . . There was no shame or regret upon receiving my swimming trophies. I worked and prepared very hard to be at my best for each show. I deserved the trophy. However, internally, I knew it was because I was the most obviously "physically deformed" child present that constituted the "extra-special" awards, the extended publicity, and the emotional audiences. Not my aquatic talents or acrobatics. Those children with multiple sclerosis or severe cerebral palsy were truly the deserving performers. It was much more physically demanding for them, than it was for me.[26]

The crisis of representation is a dominant issue in the social sciences, related to the rise of liberation movements all over the world, including feminism and disability culture. Postcolonialism has brought questions of power into the academy, privileging voices previously silenced or suppressed. The postmodernist response has been to recognize diversity and claim difference. But the same postmodernist movement also has generated a climate of epistemological instability by challenging all authorities, while uncovering hidden possible meanings in the textual practices common to Western cultures. When applied to liberation movements such as feminism and disability culture, postmodernism can be either empowering or disempowering.

Disability is arbitrarily constructed and imposed on people, relegating them to a lower status and sometimes to an inescapable caste. Civil rights laws and other liberal policies of inclusion are bringing about positive transformations in American culture for people with disabilities. Yet it would be a mistake to assert that Diane and others with disabilities are just like everyone else, or that "all they need are the same opportunities." Such a homogenizing approach threatens individuals who do need accommodations, which often are simple, cost-effective solutions.[27] In view of that dilemma, it is important to consider one last time: What differences do Diane's differences make?

According to a Harris poll in the mid-1980s, half the people in the United States who are disabled, according to the definition of having a limitation in one or more major life activities (such as work or keeping house), do not consider themselves disabled.[28] Cross-national studies among the Western liberal economies show that the category of the disabled is elastic, expanding when the job market declines and shrinking when it rebounds.[29] Such data indicate that most people would rather work competitively than rely on government support for "disabled" people. Joan Ablon reports in *Little People in America* that most people with profound short stature did not consider themselves "disabled" despite the many challenges of functioning in average-sized environments.[30] But some were willing to accept the label of disability to be eligible for reduced rates on public transportation. These statistics and observations underscore the fact that disability is an artifact of culture and an identity responsive to material conditions.

Since the 1980s and 1990s, the field of disability studies has been radicalized by the influx of scholars and critics who are themselves disabled. As "natives" have become the experts, they have pushed disability studies far beyond questions of managing stigma and psychological adjustment, producing an identity politics based on images of the everyday lives of people with disabilities, as individuals and a distinct cultural group. Never entirely abandoning concerns with personal coping and public attitudes, they have added a new thrust toward civil rights and social policy. New images of people with disabilities in popular culture have followed.

Diane offers her life and experience as a mirror for all people, how-ever, not just those with disabilities. As she stated in an interview with the *Los Angeles Times* in 1987, when she received her bachelor's degree from UCLA, "I really believe I have a purpose in life—to use my disabil-ity to encourage people to live their lives out as best as they can."[31]

Crossing over, back and forth, between a common humanity and the distinctiveness of cultural difference is the only sane path that I have been able to find. It is what Diane does in her life story. It is what I have done by reflecting on the feelings and presuppositions I bring to writing about her life. And it is what I invite readers to do with their own mir-roring phenomena. Lila Abu-Lughod calls efforts to respect sameness and difference "tactical humanism."[32] Tactical humanism is not a replacement for political action but a way to place empowerment in a broader human context, keeping in mind that cultural constructions of difference—and theories about them—are useful for a limited time, an imperfect overlay upon a fundamentally mysterious and prolific embod-ied reality.

In rummaging through my files about Diane's life, I found some field notes recounting a conversation about justice and disability with my daughter Rebecca, who was then about age five. Rebecca proposed a delightfully paradoxical image of disability, a vision of culture toward which the disability rights movement and its critique of ablism are lead-ing us. In her vision, in Diane's, and in mine, disability is more a matter of diversity than deviance, and life for people with disabilities can be fair.

The children in Rebecca's preschool had picked up the expression, "Life is not fair."

Rebecca said to me: "Some people say life is not fair, but life *is* fair."

"I'm glad you feel that way," I said. "What does that mean, Life is fair? Can you think of another word?"

Rebecca thought a long time: "Life is peaceful."

So we began a game. "Life is a smile," I said.

"Life is a tree," Rebecca said.

"Life is a tree with fruit on it," I said.

Rebecca laughed.

"Life is a person with no arms and legs," she said.

Notes

CHAPTER 1. MY INTRODUCTION TO DIANE

1. Key discussions of ethnography as a method and genre include Geertz, "Thick Description," 1973, and *Works and Lives*, 1988; Marcus and Fischer, *Anthropology as Cultural Critique*, 1986; Clifford and Marcus, eds. *Writing Culture*, 1986; Clifford, *The Predicament of Culture*, 1988; Stocking, "The Ethnographer's Magic," 1992; Behar and Gordon, *Women Writing Culture*, 1995; and Van Maanen, *Tales of the Field*, 1988.

2. Barbara Tedlock (in *The Beautiful and the Dangerous*, 1992) defines "narrative ethnography" thus:

> During participant observation, ethnographers move back and forth between being emotionally engaged participants and coolly dispassionate observers of the lives of others. . . . In the observation of participation, on the other hand, ethnographers use their everyday social skills in simultaneously experiencing and observing their own and others' interactions within various settings. This important change in procedure has resulted in a representational transformation where, instead of a choice between writing a personal memoir portraying the Self (or else producing a standard ethnographic monograph portraying the Other), both Self and Other are presented together

within a single multivocal text focused on the character and process of the human encounter (xiii).

3. Myerhoff and Ruby, "A Crack in the Mirror," 1992, 307. See also Sapir, "Why Cultural Anthropology Needs the Psychiatrist," 1938; Devereux, *From Anxiety to Method in the Behavioral Sciences*, 1967; Nash and Wintrob, "The Emergence of Self-Consciousness in Ethnography," 1972; Honigmann, "The Personal Approach in Cultural Anthropological Research," 1976; Crapanzano, *Tuhami*, 1970; Herdt and Stoller, *Intimate Communications*, 1990.

4. The life history in anthropology is a biographical method distinguished from that in fields such as history and literature by three characteristics: choice of subject (ordinary individuals, rather than public figures, frequently nonliterate, and mostly members of traditional Third World and Fourth World cultures, ethnic minorities, urban subcultures, and various client populations); fieldwork methods involving face-to-face interaction (collaboration with a living subject through interviews that are usually tape-recorded and transcribed, with some use of participant observation and personal documents, such as diaries and historical records); and formal attention to topics of theoretical interest (such as how an individual acquires a cultural, gender, or political identity). See Frank, "Life History," 1996, and Langness and Frank, *Lives*, 1981. Also see Kluckhohn, "The Personal Document in Anthropological Science," 1945.

In the most important work to define the life history method (*Criteria for the Life History*, 1935), psychologist John Dollard proposed a set of evaluative criteria that stressed reconstructing the individual's development in the family from infancy through adulthood, other situations in which specific life events take place, and the wider cultural context. The criteria also include the biologically based factors, or what Dollard called the "organic motors of behavior," that must be shaped and disciplined to make individuals socially competent. In my study of Diane DeVries, I have taken these to encompass her biological drives, her physiological endowment, and the psychodynamics of her development. Dollard's method also demands that the life history material be organized conceptually rather than simply chronologically.

See also Watson and Watson-Franke, *Interpreting Life Histories*, 1985; Bertaux, *Biography and Society*, 1981; Denzin, *Interpretive Biography*, 1989; Angrosino, *Documents of Interaction*, 1989; Agar, "Stories, Background Knowledge, and Themes," 1980; Peacock and Holland, "The Narrated Self: Life Stories in Process," 1993; and the multivolume work *The Narrative Study of Lives* (Josselson and Lieblich, 1993; Lieblich and Josselson, 1994; Josselson and Lieblich 1995; Josselson, 1996; Lieblich and Josselson, 1997). For a brief, updated survey and discussion of life history methods in a range of disciplines, see Frank, "Life Histories in Occupational Therapy Clinical Practice," 1996. There has been an explosion of publications related to life histories and life stories. My failure to mention a particular source should not be taken as a negative assessment of that work.

5.   Frank, "Venus on Wheels," 1981; "Mercy's Children" (ethnographic short story, with theoretical introduction), 1981; "Life History Model of Adaptation to Disability," 1984; "'Becoming the Other,'" 1985; "On Embodiment," 1986; "Beyond Stigma," 1988; and "Myths of Creation," 1996.

6.   In his classic monograph on the life history in anthropology, "The Personal Document in Anthropological Science" (1945), Kluckhohn encourages innovation within the genre to include not only retrospective accounts but also contemporaneous accounts based on participant observation. This study of Diane DeVries is an experiment that combines retrospective and contemporaneous life history approaches with phenomenological reflections and hermeneutic methods of textual analysis.

7.   Starr, *The Transformation of American Medicine,* 1978. Starr uses the concept of "cultural authority" to refer to the public's belief in the efficacy of biomedicine and its interventions. See also the discussion of physician authority and the sick role by Parsons, *The Social System,* 1951, 248–79; Friedson, *The Profession of Medicine,* 1970; Zola, "Medicine as an Institution of Social Control," 1972; Illich, *Medical Nemesis,* 1976; and Conrad and Schneider, *Deviance and Medicalization,* 1992.

8.   See Gritzer and Arluke, *The Making of Rehabilitation,* 1985.

9.   Rickman, "Wilhelm Dilthey," 1967, 405.

10.   Ortner, "Reading America," 1991.

11.   Janet Hoskins reminds me that the traveling to a distant field site is also often a voyage of self-discovery, a way of putting one's own categories into sharp relief. If everyone wanted truly to know herself before trying to understand exotic others, no fieldwork would ever be done. Hoskins also questions whether anthropological research is really about "helping" or simply about trying to understand. I hope that my work is not only valid in its descriptions and interpretations but also useful or helpful.

12.   Two sources, Marxist and phenomenological, are responsible for the insights that even so-called primitive and traditional cultures are not static but dynamic, and that the discipline of anthropology is implicated in the historical processes it studies. On the Marxist side, see the important early article by Gough, "Anthropology: Child of Imperialism," 1968; and Wolf, *Europe and the People without History,* 1982. On the phenomenological side, see Fabian, *Time and the Other,* 1983; and Sanjek, "The Ethnographic Present," 1991. Both approaches put anthropologists and their disciplinary practices into the same frame as ethnographic description and the analysis of cultures.

13.   Myerhoff, *Number Our Days,* 1978, 73–74.

14.   Shostak, "'What the Wind Won't Take Away,'" 1989, 239.

15.   See Swindells, "Liberating the Subject," 1989. Swindells critically examines Marxist-feminist projects to find and liberate the repressed subjectivity of women in history. "Liberating the subject" can have more than one sense. In an

article on ethical aspects of experimentation with human subjects, Mead ("Research with Human Beings," 1969) argued, in contradistinction to the protocols of medical and psychological research, that "anthropological research does not have subjects. We work with informants in an atmosphere of trust and mutual respect" (361).

16.   Langness, *The Life History in Anthropological Science,* 1965.

17.   Langness and Frank, *Lives,* 1.

18.   The life story is defined by Linde (*Life Stories,* 1993):

> A life story consists of all the stories and associated discourse units, such as explanations and chronicles, and the connections between them, told by an individual during the course of his/her lifetime that satisfy the following two criteria:
>
> 1. The stories and associated discourse units contained in the life story have as their primary evaluation a point about the speaker, not a general point about the way the world is.
>
> 2. The stories and associated discourse units have extended reportability; that is, they are tellable and are told and retold over the course of a long period of time (21).

Differences between life histories and life stories are discussed in Frank, "Anthropology and Individual Lives," 1995, and "Life History," 1996.

CHAPTER 2. THE CRISIS OF REPRESENTATION

1.   See Hymes, *Reinventing Anthropology,* 1969. The trend toward critical studies at home in the United States is discussed by Ortner, "Reading America," 1991.

2.   Kirshenblatt-Gimblett, "Foreword," 1992, x.

3.   Based on fieldwork begun in 1972, and published in 1978, Myerhoff's book *Number Our Days* was named one of the ten best social science books for that year by the *New York Times Book Review.* In 1976 a film by the same name was made for KCET public television about Myerhoff's fieldwork. It won an Academy Award for Best Short Subject Documentary the following year.

4.   Kirshenblatt-Gimblett, "Foreword," x.

5.   See Messerschmidt, *Anthropologists at Home in North America,* 1981, and Nakhleh, "On Being a Native Anthropologist," 1979.

6.   Marcus and Fischer, *Anthropology as Cultural Critique,* 1986; Clifford and Marcus, *Writing Culture,* 1986; Clifford, *The Predicament of Culture,* 1988.

7.   See, for example, Cassuto, "Whose Field Is It, Anyway? Disability Studies in the Academy," 1999, for a discussion of this issue.

8.   See, for example, Appadurai, *Modernity at Large,* 1996, and Bhabha, *The Location of Culture,* 1994.

9.   Kaminsky, "Introduction," 1992.

10. Quoted in Frank, "The Ethnographic Films of Barbara G. Myerhoff," 1995, 213. See also Prell, "The Double Frame of Life History in the Work of Barbara Myerhoff," 1989.

11. Personal Narratives Group, "Whose Voice?" 1989, 201. In particular, see the discussion of the "crisis of perspective" and ownership of life history material by Mbilinyi, "'I'd Have Been a Man,'" 1989.

12. Mbilinyi, "'I'd Have Been a Man,'" 223, citing Geiger, "Women's Life Histories, 1986, 336, and Langness, *The Life History in Anthropological Science*, 1965, 4–5.

13. Patai, "U.S. Academics and Third World Women," 1991, 139.

14. Stacey, "Can There be a Feminist Ethnography?" 1991, 113, 114. Kennedy and Davis ("Constructing an Ethnohistory of the Buffalo Lesbian Community," 1996) discuss how they identified and handled an example of role conflict from their study *Boots of Leather, Slippers of Gold*, 1993.

> We began the research by founding the Buffalo Women's Oral History Project as part of a grass-roots movement of gays and lesbians to learn their history. The project had three goals: to research the history of Buffalo's working-class community, to write a book on that history, and to return the research to the community. On many levels the project was a fiction. We never developed a community board with an independent power base in relations to our research. Narrators did not have interest in this degree of responsibility. Although our original intention was to have the project attract, train, and support a number of people interested in lesbian history, in fact it never grew very much. One factor limiting its growth was our concern for writing a book, which meant that we had to focus on analyzing the material rather than on perpetually gathering new and different material. . . . Despite these limitations the existence of the Buffalo Women's Oral History Project was significant in specifying and bringing to consciousness the power relations involved in research. . . . The commitment to give back also oriented us toward sharing the rewards from the project, be they professional, financial, or ego-based. . . . Because lesbian projects do not easily find support and we both had full-time jobs, we put all of our earnings from speaking engagements into such research expenses as transcriptions, trips to archives, and preparation of the final manuscript—and even that did not cover all our expenditures. We also decided to divide the royalties of the project between ourselves (in recognition of the years of hard work of research and writing) and the Buffalo Women's Oral History Project (to be used for projects that better the lives of older lesbians) in recognition of the debt the book owes to the larger lesbian communities that narrators helped to build (176–77).

15. See Rosenwald and Ochberg, *Storied Lives*, 1992.

16. Gubrium and Holstein, "Biographical Work and the New Ethnography," 1995, 46.

17. Gubrium and Holstein, "Biographical Work and the New Ethnography," 46. See Chin, *Doing What Has to Be Done*, 1999 for an outstanding example of multivocality in a life history.

18. See Kluckhohn, "The Personal Document in Anthropological Science," 1945; Langness, *The Life History in Anthropological Science;* Langness and Frank, *Lives*, 1981.

19.   See the discussion of Dyk and Simmons by Kluckhohn, "The Personal Doc-ument in Anthropological Science," 91–100. His call for more information about the conditions in which the data were collected anticipates many of the dialogic or multivocal concerns of contemporary ethnographers. Devereux's book is essentially dialogic in structure and should be considered a precursor to the experimental life history by Crapanzano, *Tuhami,* 1980.

20.   See Dossa, "Critical Anthropology and Life Stories," 1994.

21.   Behar, *Translated Woman,* 1993.

22.   Behar, "The Biography in the Shadow," 1993, 320–42. See also Frank, "Ruth Behar's Biography in the Shadow," 1995.

23.   Ong, "Women Out of China," 1995.

24.   A new wave of work by anthropologists has tried to show that power is not only a top-down phenomenon with repressive results. In her ethnography of workers in a family-owned Tokyo factory, for example, Kondo (*Crafting Selves,* 1990) proposes:

> Rather than relying on notions of a whole subject who can authentically resist power, on a notion of power as simply repressive, and therefore on the assumption that there exists a place beyond power; rather than seeing resistance as a mechanism of social reproduction within a closed system; and rather than subscribing to a view of social action as divisible into neatly separable categories, I would argue for a more complex view of power and human agency. . . . It would require seeing people as decentered, multiple selves, whose lives are shot through with contradictions and creative ten-sions (224).

25.   Ong, "Women Out of China," 353, 354.

26.   This was not a revocation, however, of the permission she had given me to cite her autobiography. Diane and Jim each signed a formal letter of consent in 1989, when a prospective editor at a university press made written permission a condition for publication. The letters authorized my use "of interviews, conver-sations, personal writings such as letters and diaries, clinical records, and field-notes based on participant observations, including but not restricted to previ-ously published materials."

27.   Cadish, "UCLA Project Aids Limbless," 1976.

28.   Michael Farkas, the handsome, rich UCLA student filmmaker, was memo-rialized by Diane in a romantic short story written for a competition sponsored by *Cosmopolitan* magazine in the 1980s. DeVries, "So When I Tell You I Love You . . .," 1981.

29.   See, for example, Okely and Callaway, *Anthropology and Autobiography,* 1992, especially Hendry, "The Paradox of Friendship in the Field," which recounts the effect of perceived power dynamics in action over a twenty-year period between an ethnographer and a friend who later became an informant. See also Kulick and Willson, *Taboo,* 1995, especially Blackwood, "Falling in Love

with an-Other Lesbian," which describes how the effects of inequality were discussed and negotiated in an intimate relationship in the field.

30. Kennedy, with Davis, "Constructing an Ethnohistory," 192.

31. Not a very popular topic in the postcolonial period is the exploitation of researchers by informants, but cases do exist. See, for example, Moreno, "Rape in the Field," 1995.

32. Rosenthal, "Reconstruction of Life Stories," 1993, 62. Rosenthal bases this definition in part on the work of Fischer, *Time and Chronic Illness,* 1982 (also see "Struktur und Funktion erzählter Lebengeschichten," 1978) and Kohli, "Biographical Research in the German Language Area," 1986 (also see "Biography," 1981). There are important conceptual and institutional links between the rigorous phenomenological approach of Rosenthal's group at the University of Kassel and the "grounded theory" approach to ethnography of Anselm Strauss at the University of California, San Francisco. (See Glaser and Strauss, *The Discovery of Grounded Theory,* 1967; and Strauss, *Qualitative Analysis for Social Scientists,* 1987.) Strauss was one of the earliest and best theorists of narrative reconstruction by people whose life courses are disrupted by chronic illness. For a discussion of such "biographical work," see Corbin and Strauss, *Unending Work and Care,* 1988, and "Accompaniments in Chronic Illness," 1987. Also see Becker, *Disrupted Lives,* 1997. I am indebted to Charlotte Heinritz for familiarizing me with Rosenthal's method and its connection to the work of Strauss and his colleagues.

33. Rosenthal's "hermeneutic case reconstruction" method was developed for studies of Nazi collaborators (see Rosenthal, *Die Hitlerjugend-Generation,* 1986). For applications of Rosenthal's method to Holocaust survivors, see Bar-On, *Fear and Hope,* 1995. Also see Heinritz, "The Child in Childhood-Autobiography," 1996, and Frank, "Myths of Creation," 1996. Ironically, lack of interpretation of the life stories collected by anthropologists was a key point of criticism by Dollard, *Criteria for the Life History,* 1935; Kluckhohn, "The Personal Document in Anthropological Science"; and Langness, *The Life History in Anthropological Science.*

34. Rosenthal, "Reconstruction of Life Stories," 61. See Lutkehaus's book *Margaret Mead and the Media.*

35. Several helpful discussions with Nancy Lutkehaus helped me to clarify my definition of cultural biography and prompted me to make more explicit its focus on cultural analysis, especially the power of images.

36. Weltfish, "Franz Boas," 1980, 139–40.

CHAPTER 3. "THERE'S NOTHING ABOUT THE DISABLED WOMAN AND THE DISABLED CULTURE"

1. Malcolm and Rouse, "Thisabled Lives," video, 1995.

2. The independent living and disability rights movements began to emerge in the late 1960s. The landmark Rehabilitation Act of 1973 mandated nondis-

crimination, equal access, and reasonable accommodations for people with disabilities in all federal government programs, and it also applied to nongovernment entities funded by federal contracts and grants. For an overview of the independent living movement's early history, philosophy, and practical objectives, see Crewe and Zola, *Independent Living for Physically Disabled People,* 1983. Also see Charlton, *Nothing About Us Without Us,* 1998, which offers an update on the disability rights movement and puts it in an international perspective.

3.   See Monaghan, "Pioneering Field of Disability Studies," 1998. Some examples of the recent literature in disability studies include Linton, *Claiming Disability,* 1998; Davis, *The Disability Studies Reader,* 1997; Mitchell and Snyder, *The Body and Physical Differences,* 1997; Berubé, *Life As We Know It,* 1996; Thomson, *Extraordinary Bodies,* 1997; and Couser, *Recovering Bodies,* 1997. Whether there is such a thing as "disability culture" in a technical sense is discussed by Barnartt, "Disability Culture or Disability Consciousness?" 1996.

4.   See Kent, "Where There's a Will," 1997. Among the books Kent reviews is Nancy Mairs's *Waist-High in the World,* which continues the probing and irreverent exploration of life as a woman and a writer with multiple sclerosis established in her earlier books: *Plaintext,* 1986; *Carnal Acts,* 1990; and *Remembering the Bone House,* 1989. Mairs's essay "On Being a Cripple" in *Plaintext* has become one of the most influential texts by and about women with disabilities and is discussed by Thomson in "Redrawing the Boundaries of Feminist Disability Studies," 1994.

5.   In Great Britain, Campling, *Images of Ourselves: Women with Disabilities Talking,* appeared in 1981, followed in Canada by Matthews, *Voices from the Shadows: Women with Disabilities Speak Out,* in 1983. Soon after, in the United States, two important collections were issued by feminist presses: Browne, Connors, and Stern, *With the Power of Each Breath: A Disabled Women's Anthology,* 1985, and Saxton and Howe, *With Wings: An Anthology of Literature by and about Women with Disabilities,* 1987.

Saxton and Howe's book was a watershed in the effort to create a disability rights and feminist consciousness: Marcia Saxton had been director of the Boston Self-Help Center, a key organization for the independent living and disability rights movements, and Florence Howe was director of the Feminist Press at the City University of New York.

6.   From Bonnie Sherr Klein, "Finding My Place," Canadian Broadcasting Company, 1992.

7.   Berkowitz, *Disabled Policy,* 1987. See the excellent profile on Heumann's career as an activist, 196–99.

8.   See Charlton, *Nothing About Us Without Us,* 140–41.

9.   The exchange between Pogrebin and Heumann is quoted in Asch and Fine, "Introduction," in *Women with Disabilities,* 1988, 29–30.

10.   Perhaps the most comprehensive update since this volume is the special issue on gender and disability policy by Schriner, Barnartt, and Altman, *Journal of Disability Policy Studies* 8, 1997. Also see Deegan and Brooks, *Women and Disability*, 1985.

11.   Frank, "On Embodiment," 1988, 47.

12.   Occupational science is founded on the observation that routines of meaningful, purposeful activities or "occupations" are as essential to health and well-being as food, shelter, sanitation, and absence of disease. From an occupational perspective, people "are what they do." See Zemke and Clark, *Occupational Science*, 1996. For an example of an occupational history, see also Clark, "Occupation Embedded in a Real Life," 1993. For the analysis of children's development through occupational competence see Reilly, *Play as Exploratory Learning*, 1974, and "Occupational Therapy," 1962.

13.   This discussion of developmental milestones draws upon Challenor, Rangaswamy, and Katz, "Limb Deficiency in Infancy and Childhood," 1982; and Leach, *Your Baby and Child*, 1987.

14.   Interviews with Irene Fields, February 3, 1983, and March 10, 1983.

15.   If this event happened while they lived in Pacific Beach, as Irene remembered it, Diane may have been age two or older. However, there is no reason to assume that Diane's development was delayed.

16.   Diane usually describes her stumps as "arms," as did her mother in the interviews.

17.   Occupations are defined in occupational science as "chunks of daily activity that can be named in the lexicon of the culture. Fishing, grooming, weaving, and dining are all occupations. When we come to understand these occupations within the framework of a human life, we can say 'People are shaped by what they have done, by their daily patterns of occupation.' . . . Thus a person's history of occupation, to some extent, shapes what he or she will become in the future" (Zemke and Clark, *Occupational Science*, vii).

18.   DeVries, "Autobiography," n.d.

19.   Fraiberg, *The Magic Years*, 1959.

20.   Gliedman and Roth (*The Unexpected Minority*, 1980) call for basic descriptions of the childhood of individuals with disabilities to help understand how, within the family, independence and self-respect later in life are developed despite social stigma, discrimination, and the poor fit of social institutions. They ask readers to set aside preconceptions derived from the study of the able-bodied and attempt to discover for the first time "the main constancies, the milestones and 'tasks,' of the handicapped child's development" (69).

21.   DeVries, "Autobiography."

22.   Camp Paivika was founded in 1944 at Tamarack Lodge in Big Bear by the Crippled Children's Society of Los Angeles County, then affiliated with the

Easter Seals Society. In 1946 the camp acquired the site near Crestline, where Diane went for ten summers. This information about Camp Paivika comes from a poster at the First Annual Camp Paivika Alumni Reunion, July 8 and 9, 1989, which I attended with Diane and her husband. A description of Camp Paivika appears in a book by the mother of a child with disabilities (Hamilton, *Borrowed Angel*, 1958, 236–42). I obtained further information about the Crippled Children's Society (CCS) of Southern California from a Background History Sheet, Revised 1993, obtained from its successor, California Children's Services (CCS), Los Angeles. The Crippled Children's Society of Southern California was established in 1926 by the Rotary Clubs. In 1934, the CCS joined the National Easter Seals Organization; the alliance continued until 1971, when CCS withdrew in order to target its funds exclusively for people in Los Angeles County.

23.   Phone report from Lila Beal, M.S.W., to Wilma Gurney, Child Amputee Prosthetics Project, July 30, 1958.

24.   Judy Ferguson, A.C.H., Resident Camp Report, Crippled Children's Society of Los Angeles County, June 19–July 1, 1961. Diane's popularity in camp and at school shows the importance of context to attitudes toward children with amputations among their peers. In research by Centers and Centers ("Peer Group Attitudes toward the Amputee Child," 1963) among children five to twelve years old in regular school classes, rejecting attitudes were more frequently expressed toward children with amputations than toward children without amputations. Mean scores ranked the amputee children as least fun, least liked, and saddest. It should be noted, however, that scores for some individuals with amputations were in the same range as the non-amputees.

25.   At least one other camper also had quadrilateral limb deficiencies and was a patient at CAPP during the years Diane attended Camp Paivika.

26.   Ferguson, Resident Camp Report.

27.   Gingras et al., "Congenital Anomalies of the Limbs," 1964. This study was undertaken by the Rehabilitation Institute of Montreal to gear itself up to treat the cases that occurred in 1962 as a result of the introduction of the sedative thalidomide, which had teratogenic effects. The sample provides a good comparison group for Diane historically and functionally: its members were described as having "more or less severe handicaps," although none had quadrilateral limb deficiencies. Of the forty-one subjects ten were contemporaries of Diane, age twelve to eighteen. The rest were a stratified sample spanning age fourteen months to nineteen years and over.

28.   DeVries, "Autobiography."

29.   DeVries, "Autobiography."

30.   DeVries, "Autobiography."

31.   DeVries, "Autobiography."

32.   Frank, "On Embodiment," 62.

33.   Frank, "On Embodiment," 61.

34.   Frank, "On Embodiment," 48. My expectation that Diane might evaluate her body as a whole forced an alien perspective. She "loved" her arms and breasts but "hated" her back, because of the pain, and her lungs and chest cavity, because of her frequent bouts with asthma. She liked her eyes and nose, but not her mouth and teeth: "When I was young I never smiled . . . because I thought I looked dumb smiling. I got over it. . . . Started showing my teeth because I wanted to laugh and smile." She always keeps her hair cut over her ears to cover the left one, which sticks out: "I've got my Dad's left ear. The right one's normal." Like anyone else I know, Diane scrutinized her body and evaluated it according to normative standards of appearance and function (Frank, "On Embodiment," 48–49).

35.   Frank, "On Embodiment," 63.

36.   Hillyer, "Blueprint for an Alliance," 1989, 10.

37.   Groce, "Review of *Women with Disabilities*," 1994, 112.

38.   Hirsch, "Culture and Disability," 1995, 18.

39.   Charlton, *Nothing About Us Without Us,* 57. Charlton is a former executive vice president of Access Living in Chicago.

40.   Hillyer, *Feminism and Disability,* 1993. Hillyer is founder of the women's studies program at the University of Oklahoma and the mother of a woman with multiple disabilities. Philosopher Susan Wendell (*The Rejected Body,* 1996) presents a thoughtful analysis of Hillyer's work in terms of a feminist ethics of care and introduces arguments by other critics working in this area, such as Jenny Morris, Joan Tronto, and Anne Finger.

41.   Frank, "The Concept of Adaptation," 1996. Also see "Life History Model of Adaptation," 1984.

42.   In 1935, under the New Deal administration of Franklin D. Roosevelt, the federal government entered into partnerships with the states to provide welfare entitlements to aid the needy elderly, dependent children, and the blind. Recipients had to pass a means test. These state-run programs varied widely, depending on the local economy and attitudes toward providing welfare. In 1950, Congress added a new welfare category: aid to the permanently and totally disabled. In 1972, Supplemental Security Income (SSI) was created to replace the old state-run programs. The federal government, which funded and administered the program, now guaranteed a minimum income to recipients, which the states could choose to supplement. The process of declaring someone disabled and thus eligible for welfare was transferred from the state welfare department to the state rehabilitation agency.

In 1956, Social Security Disability Insurance (SSDI) was adopted and a Federal Disability Insurance Trust Fund created for people unable to engage in gainful activity because of a medically demonstrable impairment expected to last at least a year. It was expected to be an improvement over the state workmen's compensations programs, which, like welfare programs prior to 1972, differed greatly from state to state in the benefits provided. SSDI was financed by a tax on employers and employees. See Berkowitz, *Disabled Policy*, 1987.

43.   A certain number of apartments with discounted rents for people with disabilities was mandated by the City of Long Beach when Diane's apartment building was developed. The undiscounted rent for her unit was $750.

44.   This amount was calculated at the rate of $4.32 an hour. IHSS checks come in Diane's name so that she can pay one or more workers.

45.   For example, the Michigan Family Support Subsidy Act of 1983 and the Wisconsin Family Support Program allow for flexible, consumer-driven decisions in the use of cash entitlements to support households with a member with a disability. See Ferguson et al., "Supported Community Life," 1990. Also see Hagner and Marrone, "Empowerment Issues in Services to Individuals with Disabilities," 1995; Nosek, "Personal Assistance Services," 1991; and Simi Litvak, "Financing Personal Assistance Services," 1992.

46.   Frank, "Life History Model of Adaptation," 1984, 644.

47.   Frank, "Life History Model of Adaptation," 644.

48.   DeVries, "Autobiography." Diane reflected on the necessity to gain assistance without her helpers feeling exploited or manipulated: "In its purest form, and with empathetic insight, you are only helping others do what they want to do but are not too sure how to begin."

49.   Scott, *Weapons of the Weak*, 1985, and *Domination and the Arts of Resistance*, 1990. The everyday forms of resistance among Malaysian peasants described by Scott may apply to other "subaltern" groups such as people with disabilities in the United States, most of whom are clients of government systems and live on the economic margin of American society. Scott writes:

> It seemed far more important to understand what we might call *everyday* forms of peasant resistance—the prosaic but constant struggle between the peasantry and those who seek to extract labor, food, taxes, rents, and interest from them. Most of the forms this struggle takes stop well short of collective outright defiance. Here I have in mind the ordinary weapons of relatively powerless groups: foot dragging, dissimulation, false compliance, pilfering, feigned ignorance, slander, arson, sabotage, and so forth. These Brechtian forms of class struggle have certain features in common. They require little or no coordination or planning; they often represent a form of individual self-help; and they typically avoid any direct symbolic confrontation with authority or with elite norms (29).

See also Spivak, "Subaltern Studies," 1996, and "Can the Subaltern Speak?" 1995.

50.   "Help Wanted," *60 Minutes*, October 1979. See also Knowles, "A Woman's Suicide," 1978, and Townsend, "Suicide Spurs Disabled to Ask End to Funds Cutoff," 1978.

51.   Townsend, "Suicide Spurs Disabled."

52. Townsend, "Suicide Spurs Disabled."

53. Thompson's story was brought to the attention of *60 Minutes* by local disability rights activists, led by Douglas Martin, then executive director of the Westside Center for Independent Living (WCIL) in Los Angeles. Martin was interviewed along with Ed Roberts, then director of the state Department of Vocational Rehabilitation, and writer-performer Nancy Becker Kennedy.

54. Originally adopted as a demonstration project in 1980, Section 1619 became a permanent policy in 1986, the Employment Opportunities for Disabled Americans Act (P.L. 99–643), which was signed into law by President Ronald Reagan. The cost effectiveness of the demonstration project and subsequent law has been extremely high. Although the General Accounting Office had estimated that it would cost the federal government about $1 billion a year, by 1986 savings under Section 1619 were about $12 million a year. See WCIL, "Work Incentives Bill Signed by President," 1986; also see Douglas A. Martin, "Overview of Major SSDI and SSI Work Incentives," Testimony before the Senate Subcommittee on Disability Policy, June 26, 1991; and U. S. Department of Health and Human Services, *Red Book on Work Incentives*, 1991.

55. Hillyer, *Feminism and Disability*, 196, citing Goodman, "The Right to Die," 1984.

56. Hahn, "Can Physical Disability Make a Life Not Worth Living?" 1983.

57. Hughes, "Judge Tells Bouvia to Accept Feeding," 1984.

58. Hughes and Miller, "Bouvia Opts for Life, Is Eating," 1984.

59. DeVries, "Autobiography."

CHAPTER 4. DISABILITY IN AMERICAN CULTURE

1. Berkowitz, *Disabled Policy*, 1987. See particularly chapter 6, which includes biographical sketches of Lex Frieden, Judy Heumann, and Ed Roberts, three early activists with severe physical disabilities whose personal efforts to fight discrimination in access to state-funded vocational rehabilitation services, education, and employment led to their becoming major figures in the independent living and disability rights movements. In global perspective, another legacy from this period is the disabilities caused to people in Southeast Asia by the United States military actions during and since the Vietnam War, including new amputations and other injuries by undetected land mines. (See Guest and Bouchet-Saulnier, "International Law and Reality," 1997; and French, "The Political Economy of Injury and Compassion: Amputees on the Thai-Cambodia Border," 1994.) According to statistics from a UNESCO report published in 1995, there are more than 110 million land mines in sixty-four countries. There are 1.5 mines per person in Angola, for example, a country where 120 people a month have become amputees every year since 1978 (Charlton, *Nothing About Us Without Us*, 1998, 45).

2. In 1980, the World Health Organization adopted a set of universal definitions to distinguish the terms *disability, handicap,* and *impairment* that takes into
consideration social contexts. An *impairment* is defined as "any loss or abnormality of psychological, physiological, or anatomical structure or function." *Disability* is defined as "any restriction or lack (resulting from an impairment) of ability
to perform an activity in the manner or within the range considered normal for a
human being." *Handicap* relates to the social consequences of an impairment
(deficiency in the organism) or disability (deficiency in function). It is defined as
"a disadvantage for a given individual, resulting from an impairment or a disability, that limits or prevents the fulfillment of a role that is normal (depending
on age, sex, and social and cultural factors) for that individual" (*International
Classification of Impairments, Disabilities, and Handicaps,* 1980, 27–29). The same
impairment or disability may be evaluated differently in different societies and
settings. In other words, handicap is "socially constructed." See the excellent discussion in Ingstad and Whyte, *Disability and Culture,* 1995.

3. See Berkowitz, *Disabled Policy.* Also see Gritzer and Arluke, *The Making of
Rehabilitation,* 1985. Many of the first social science studies of disability were also
federally funded. A research program to study issues of psychological and social
adjustment was established in 1954 under Mary E. Switzer, the forward-looking
commissioner of the U.S. Vocational Rehabilitation Administration. The first conference of sociologists to be supported by a VRA grant took place in 1965 and
included Thomas Scheff, Eliot Friedson, Saad Nagi, and other key contributors to
the analysis of disability as a form of deviance from normal roles and careers. In
her introduction to the volume, Switzer framed the rationale of the conference,
however, in terms of studying the effects of dependency. See Sussman, *Sociology
and Rehabilitation,* 1966.

4. See DeJong, "Defining and Implementing the Independent Living Concept," 1983. DeJong's article, which originally appeared in 1979, explicitly challenged the "medical model" of disability, citing critics of the medical profession
who have expressed concern that many social problems and life conditions—
including pregnancy and childbirth, alcoholism, homosexuality, death and
dying—have been subjected to unnecessary medical intervention. The best-
known of these is Illich, *Medical Nemesis,* 1976. Also see Zola, "Medicine as an
Institution of Social Control," 1972; Fox, "The Medicalization and Demedicalization of American Society," 1977; and Conrad and Schneider, *Deviance and Medicalization,* 1992. Contrasting the "independent living paradigm" with the "rehabilitation paradigm," DeJong applied the widely influential work of historian of
the natural sciences Thomas Kuhn (*The Structure of Scientific Revolutions,* 1970),
who argued that scientific knowledge does not emerge by the simple accretion of
facts, but within a framework or "paradigm" that defines reality through its
assumptions, technology, and discovery procedures. A new paradigm emerges

only after the following conditions occur: (1) a sufficient number of anomalies arise (events or phenomena that cannot be adequately explained under the existing paradigm), and (2) a new theory appears that explains phenomena previously understood under the old paradigm but also adequately accounts for the anomalies.

5.   The philosophy of the liberal welfare state is fundamental to the independent living movement (ILM), which calls for tax-supported services that include personal assistants, medical insurance (which now covers provision and maintenance of electric wheelchairs, respirators, and other adaptive equipment), and entitlements (income supplements) to guarantee a basic standard of living. Thus, the ILM tends to be allied with left-liberal politics. At the other end of the political spectrum, however, conservatives have been responsive to arguments favoring the disabled that also emphasize self-sufficiency, breaking down barriers to employment so that disabled people can earn their own living in the private sector. Such arguments were the basis for the endorsement of the Americans with Disabilities Act of 1990 by the conservative Bush administration.

6.   See Ingstad and Whyte, *Disability and Culture*. Also see Hanks and Hanks, "The Physically Handicapped in Certain Non-Western Societies, 1948; Scheer and Groce, "Impairment as a Human Constant," 1988; and Groce, "Women with Disabilities in the Developing World," 1997.

7.   Edgerton, *The Cloak of Competence*, 1967. Fred Davis's book *Passage through Crisis*, 1963, is based on extensive interviews with polio survivors, but without participant observation. Like most studies of disability in the United States in the following decades, *The Cloak of Competence* focuses on attempts to adapt or cope with the stigma of being perceived as different from and inferior to others. Ablon's ethnography *Little People in America* (1984) was significant because it began to shift the focus of research to strategies used by people with dwarfism to meet a wide range of challenges not limited to stigma. It was an important model for my research with Diane DeVries. One of the most compelling ethnographies is *Missing Pieces: A Chronicle of Living with a Disability* (1982), by Irving Kenneth Zola, a sociologist and disability rights activist. It is a journal of his week-long stay at a community designed for people with physical disabilities in the Netherlands.

8.   The picture was not unremittingly bleak because Edgerton also noted the presence of "benefactors" in the lives of some of the people in his sample. These included a landlord, employer, or other friend who helped ease the way of an individual with mental retardation by compensating for skills they lacked or providing other resources.

9.   Nicolaisen, "Persons and Nonpersons," 1995. For another example of inclusion, see Talle, "A Child Is a Child," 1995.

10.   See the discussion in Whyte and Ingstad, "Disability and Culture,"1995 contrasting "sociocentric" and "egocentric" concepts of personhood. See also

Geertz, "Person, Time, and Conduct in Bali," 1973, and Shweder and Bourne, "Does the Concept of the Person Vary Cross-Culturally?" 1984.

11.   Groce, "Women with Disabilities."

12.   Fadiman, *The Spirit Catches You and You Fall Down*, 1997. The tender regard of the Lee family for their infant daughter, Lia, whose chronic disabilities claimed an enormous proportion of her family's energy and resources, was not diminished by her extremely compromised functional status. She remained a well-cared for, well-groomed, and well-loved member of the family—in fact, her parents' favorite of their nine surviving children, despite their acknowledgment of and sadness at her lack of cognitive or volitional activity, on the basis of which her doctors labeled her "a vegetable." Fadiman's book presents the clash of sociocentric (Hmong) and egocentric (American) models of personhood.

13.   Fadiman, *The Spirit Catches You*, 77.

14.   See, for example, Geertz, "Religion as a Cultural System," 1973: "The culture concept to which I adhere . . . denotes an historically transmitted pattern of meanings embodied in symbols . . . by means of which men communicate, perpetuate, and develop their knowledge about and attitudes toward life" (89). All the various schools of anthropology from roughly 1890 through the 1950s have been oriented toward considering the "positive forces that integrated cultures and societies and kept them operating systematically" (Voget, "History of Anthropology," 1996, 571). These principally include British social anthropology, American cultural anthropology, and French structuralism. British social anthropology was built upon the idea that a society is like an organism, and consists of interlocking institutions that support the harmony, growth, and perpetuation of social systems. This positive approach to the orderly transmission of rules and norms from generation to generation is known as "structural-functionalism." In the United States, related forms of functionalism became the dominant paradigm for research in all the social sciences in the 1950s, and it is perhaps best known in association with the work of Talcott Parsons, chair of the Department of Sociology at Harvard University.

In contrast to this approach, the American tradition of cultural anthropology founded by German-born and trained Franz Boas, did not view cultures as tightly integrated functional systems but as assemblages of traits encountered through cultural contact or "diffusion." Cultural anthropologists sought to understand, however, the underlying and unconscious psychological patterning by which a people tended to select certain cultural elements over others, giving each culture a distinctive "genius" or style. The American functionalism of Parsons had an important influence upon cultural anthropologists such as Parsons's colleague at Harvard, Clyde Kluckhohn, a student of Navajo culture and a key proponent of life history studies in anthropology, and also the early work of Parsons's student, Clifford Geertz. Functionalism since has been criticized for its totalitarian tendencies by which differences within a culture are understood as deviance from a desired norm rather than as a range of alternative possibilities. Although for those without a strong background in the history of anthropology, the idea of a cultural pattern and core values may be easily assimilated to the idea of a "norm," it is really a different concept generated from another intellectual standpoint.

Since the 1960s, in reaction to the over-emphasis on the rule-bound, harmonious patterning of culture—and also to the depersonalized theories of social organization in French structuralism and certain French Marxist theories—there has been a new focus on the practices of actual individuals in resistance to dominant social discourses and practices. This work has been overwhelmingly influenced by two French scholars, philosopher Michel Foucault and sociologist Pierre Bourdieu. Foucault's work has been most important for theorizing how the rise of modern bureaucratic societies has depended on the standardization of disciplined bodies and the individual internalization of habits of social regulation. See, especially, Foucault, *Discipline and Punish*, 1979. The work of sociologist Pierre Bourdieu has been a key source for theorizing about the production, reproduction, and transformation of cultures through the accrued actions of individual agents in relation to dominant discourses and practices. See Bourdieu, *Outline of a Theory of Practice*, 1977.

15.   See Dirks, Eley, and Ortner, "Introduction," 1994.

16.   Ortner, "Theory in Anthropology Since the Sixties," 1994, 396.

17.   See Goffman, *Stigma*, 1963. The term *stigma* refers to negative characteristics ascribed to an individual because of membership in a social group or category held to be inferior by the dominant group. Goffman refers to three types of stigma: tribal (ethnicity, race, religion, region, class), moral (criminality, prostitution, drug addiction, mental illness), and what he calls ironically "the physical abominations" (physical disability, chronic illness, cosmetic defects, disfigurement). Despite their capacity and willingness to participate normally in society, stigmatized individuals are often barred from education, dating and marriage, employment, and use of public facilities. In Goffman's analysis, the experience of stigma necessarily leads individuals to adopt strategies to cover or hide signs of their difference: that is, to pass for normal by concealing or otherwise managing the presentation of information about themselves.

Goffman's theory of stigma is illuminating, but it also has serious limitations: Goffman's focus on public encounters is one-dimensional. He doesn't explore how people with disabilities deal with stigma over the course of a lifetime and how their families and communities come to deal with it. He also doesn't explore alternative belief systems of people who are the victims of stigma. Thus his theory has the character of a self-fulfilling prophecy, since he presents only cases that support his theory and doesn't explore exceptions and differences. For a fuller discussion, see Frank, "Beyond Stigma," 1988.

18.   See especially the pioneering study by Roger G. Barker (*Adjustment to Physical Handicap and Illness*, 1977 [1953]), sponsored by the Social Sciences Research Council. Barker assembled a team at Stanford University in 1944–1945 to study the social psychology of disability. One of the most useful and best-known books to summarize and apply its perspectives and findings on individual adjustment to disability is Beatrice A. Wright, *Physical Disability: A Psychosocial Approach*, 2d ed., 1983. Barker's team was remarkable for its early incorporation of the minority group and social change models in its theory of adjustment. See the contributions by Lee Meyerson ("Physical Disability as a Social Psychological Problem," "A Fair Employment Act for the Disabled") to a special issue in 1948 of the *Journal of Social Issues* and his retrospective assessment of the *JSI* issue's impact on the field ("The Social Psychology of Physical Disability: 1948 and 1988," 1988).

19.   On the question of sexual expression and reproductive rights for disabled people, see Waxman, "It's Time to Politicize Our Sexual Oppression," 1994; and Finger, *Past Due*, 1990. For an enlightening discussion of reproductive rights by the mother of a woman with mental retardation, see Kaufman, "A Mentally Retarded Daughter Educates Her Mother," 1980. The devaluing of people with congenital disabilities in the United States has included routine sterilization and genocide. See Pernick, *The Black Stork*, 1996, and Proctor, *Racial Hygiene*, 1988.

20.   Kriegel, "Uncle Tom and Tiny Tim," 1969. In a subsequent work, Kriegel (*Falling into Life*, 1991) urges others not to adjust to disability but to "affirm their existence and claim selfhood by pushing beyond those structures and categories their condition has created" (quoted in Couser, *Recovering Bodies*, 1997, 192).

21.   Hahn, "Can Disability Be Beautiful?" 1988. Hahn explores the "subversive sexuality" historically associated with people with disabilities in Western culture.

22.   Hevey, *The Creatures Time Forgot*, 1992.

23.   Frank, "Venus on Wheels," 1981, 165. The quotation is from DeVries, "So When I Tell You I Love You . . . ," an autobiographical short story written in 1980 for a contest sponsored by *Cosmopolitan* magazine. Diane is alluding here to the British author J. R. R. Tolkien's (1892–1973) fantasy adventure novels *The Hobbit* and the epic trilogy *The Lord of the Rings*, which are peopled by endearing creatures called hobbits who are smaller than dwarves.

24.   Although the precise etiology of Diane's limb deficiencies is unknown, they probably resulted from a disturbance of limb formation *in utero* due to any of a number of possible environmental or genetic causes, such as vascular pathogenesis (hemorrhage of the fetal limb buds). In fetal development, the upper and lower limb buds appear during the fourth to fifth week of pregnancy. Ossification of the upper limbs begins to take place in the tenth week, with ossification of the lower extremities starting a few days later. See Warkany, *Congenital Malfor-*

mations, 1971; and Stevenson, Hall, and Goodman, "Limb Deficiencies," 1993. The use of chorionic villus sampling (CVS) and amniocentesis since the 1980s as prenatal diagnostic procedures may be related to an increase in the rates of transverse limb deficiencies (the type Diane has, in which the absence extends across the full width of the limb). See Olney et al., "Chorionic Villus Sampling and Amniocentesis: Recommendations for Prenatal Counseling," 1995.

25.   Frank, "Myths of Creation,"1996, 66. Diane told the story of her birth in an unpublished autobiography, which builds on the story she wrote for *Cosmopolitan* but is recast in light of her Christian conversion. The prologue and first chapter of her autobiography appear in "Myths of Creation" with my analysis using the method of hermeneutic case reconstruction (Rosenthal, "Reconstruction of Life Stories," 1993), which examines the relationship between the lived-through, experienced *life history* and the narrated *life story.*

26.   This was the view of Ambroise Paré (*On Monsters and Marvels*, 1982), who produced one of the first attempts to explain birth defects. Born in the early sixteenth century, Paré was royal surgeon to Charles IV and Henri III of France. His book is an illustrated encyclopedia of curiosities, monstrous human and animal births, bizarre beasts, and natural phenomena. For a contemporary comparison see Bosk, *All God's Mistakes,* 1992.

27.   The thalidomide disaster in the United States and Canada occurred in 1961–62, when the drug was approved for prescription use as a sedative. Many mothers who ingested the drug between the twenty-eighth and forty-second day following conception gave birth to children with multiple limb deficiencies. Typically, the damage was done before the mother even knew she was pregnant. See Roskies, *Abnormality and Normality,* 1972.

Awareness of the thalidomide problem was heightened by the highly publicized case of Sherri Finkbine, a local television personality in Phoenix, Arizona. In 1962 Finkbine, who had been taking thalidomide early in her fifth pregnancy, heard reports of serious birth defects linked to the drug and sought a therapeutic abortion. Unable to get permission from the Arizona courts, Finkbine flew to Sweden for an abortion and was told by her obstetrician that the embryo was so seriously deformed that it would never have survived. Sociologist Kristen Luker (*Abortion and the Politics of Motherhood,* 1984) writes that middle-of-the-road physicians even in the 1960s felt that Finkbine's case presented "an unimpeachable case for abortion" (65). Ironically, the Finkbine case exemplifies tensions within feminism concerning disability rights, because the issue of justifying a woman's choice to have an abortion based on the likelihood that her child will have a disability remains perhaps the most compelling pro-choice argument for most Americans.

Disability activist Judy Heumann articulated the conflict between mainstream feminist assumptions and a disability rights perspective over this issue in an interview in the 1992 radio documentary by Bonnie Sherr Klein. Heumann said:

> I think aborting based on disability is selective abortion. And I don't support it, although I am a pro-choice person. I wouldn't legislate against it, no. But I morally, I really, truly, morally believe its wrong. Women who decide to have children, they're deciding to have *a child*. They don't want to have a child and they wish to have an abortion because they don't want to have a child, I absolutely understand that. But I think a woman has a responsibility to decide whether or not she thinks she can have a disabled child. She can have a child and that child can acquire any one of a number of disabilities. But not wanting to have a child because that child may have a disability is something I personally don't agree with. And that really disturbs me because people really don't think there's anything wrong with that.

For a further discussion of the abortion issue, see Wendell, *The Rejected Body*, 1996, especially chapter 6, "Disability and Feminist Ethics."

The life history of a man born with severe disabilities as a result of thalidomide is sensitively explored in a masters thesis by occupational therapist Steven Townsend (*Declaring One's Personhood*, 1993). Townsend presented selections from articles about Diane DeVries, and from life histories and life stories of other individuals, to prompt his research participant, a black gay man born with quadrilateral limb deficiencies due to thalidomide, to discuss his own experiences comparatively.

28.   Roskies (*Abnormality and Normality*, 1972, 52–53) relates the "bizarre but not uncommon" story of a physician who tried to avoid responsibility and blame for prescribing thalidomide to a woman who afterward gave birth to a limbless child. He maintained to the woman that the deformities were due either to a hereditary defect in her or to her "nervous shock" during the pregnancy.

29.   Frank, "On Embodiment,"1988, 47. Research in medical anthropology suggests that in every society practices for dealing with illnesses and impairments follow from the people's "explanatory model" (i.e., their beliefs about the cause of the illness). Reporting on her research in Botswana, Ingstad ("Mpho ya Modimo—A Gift from God," 1995) documents how people choose among alternative explanatory models to defuse stigma in local situations. Rural Botswana people often locate the origin of disease or disability in witchcraft and the work of spirits (although biomedical explanations are also used, particularly among the professional medical sector). The birth of a child with severe multiple handicaps (*mopakwane*) is believed to be caused by the parents breaking the prohibition on sexual intercourse during the first three months of pregnancy. Parents of such children are considered blameworthy and should be ashamed, but the majority come to terms with the condition and avoid stigma by changing their explanatory model to one of something that "just happened," a residual category that includes conditions that cannot be diagnosed or cured through traditional remedies. Another designation that avoids stigma for parents and the child is *mpho ya*

modimo. This term identifies the child as being a gift from God. The traditional God, Modimo, viewed as having omnipotent power, shows trust in people by presenting them with special challenges, such as a child with a disability. Concerning the concept of the explanatory model, see Kleinman, *Patients and Healers in the Context of Culture,* 1980.

30.   The clippings preserved by Irene Fields focus mostly on the children born with quadrilateral limb deficiencies between 1948 and 1955 near Diane's birthplace: they include two girls born in Texas, Cindy Inman and Eva Jo Wilson, and a boy in Arkansas, Freddie Thomason. In 1948, Freddie Thomason was born without arms and legs in Magnolia, Arkansas, about two hundred miles east of Denison along Route 82 across the Texas-Arkansas border. His was only the second case of quadrilateral limb deficiencies seen by famed orthopedic surgeon Dr. Henry H. Kessler, of the Kessler Institute for Rehabilitation, in West Orange, New Jersey, in thirty years of practice. Dr. Kessler examined Freddie at age one and offered to work with him free of charge. Mrs. Thomason traveled to Kessler with Freddie and was trained in exercises to develop her son's trunk muscles, requiring two forty-five-minute sessions a day. At age two, Freddie returned to Kessler with trunk muscles well enough developed for him to be fitted with short artificial legs and, shortly after, artificial arms. See cover photo, Kessler Institute for Rehabilitation, *Comeback,* 1950; a newsmagazine-style article with photo credit to Acme, "Freddie Stands Up," 1950 (source missing); "Legless Boy, Also Armless at Birth, Stands Up," *New York Herald Tribune,* story dated April 1, 1950; "Love of Entire City to Brighten Birthday of Boy, 4, Born without Arms or Legs," Associated Press story dated March 29, 1952 (source missing).

When Freddie was a year old, the Kiwanis Club of Magnolia started the "Help Freddie Walk" project to raise funds for his physical treatments and education. Over $16,750 had been collected by the time Freddie was age four. Like Diane, Freddie received gifts from well-wishers but reportedly could play independently with just two of them, a toy man on a trapeze and a French harp with a shoulder rest. Freddie had been voted "King of the Company" by a group of U.S. soldiers stationed in Korea. He had a younger brother, apparently normal, and one article stated that "medical science has no explanation for such biological accidents."

In 1953, Cindy Inman was born without legs but with short upper extremity stumps in Sherman, Texas, the nearest town to Diane's birthplace, about ten miles away. Like Freddie Thomason, she was fitted at age two with artificial legs at the Kessler Rehabilitation Institute. In an article from the *Sherman Democrat* (John Frasca, "Church Plans Campaign to Help Baby Born without Arms or Legs," [date missing]), published when Cindy was six months old, a photo caption reads: "'SHE'S OUR BABY'—That's what Mr. and Mrs. Lloyd Inman said when it was suggested that they place the limbless child, Cindy, in an institution." Another article from the *Sherman Democrat* indicates that a group of citizens led by a local minister had started a "See Cindy Walk Drive" that raised fifty-eight hundred dollars for Cindy's rehabilitation ("Cindy, Now Year Old, Has Happy Christmas," [date missing]). Irene also pasted in her album an Associated Press syndicated wire photo, published when Cindy was age two, captioned "Cindy Now Has Legs"(source and date missing).

Finally, in 1955, Eva Jo Wilson was born with quadrilateral limb deficiencies in Lamasco, Texas, a farming community too small to appear on most maps, but twelve miles from Bonham. She had malformations of all four limbs including rudimentary arms, legs, hands, and feet. Bonham is about fifteen miles east of Sherman on Route 82 and about three hours from Magnolia. A fund to "See Eva Jo in School" was started by the congregation of the Lamasco Church of Christ. According to an article in *The Sherman Democrat,* the fund-raisers aimed to raise five to ten thousand dollars for preparatory plastic surgery so that Eva Jo could be sent to the Kessler Rehabilitation Institute, where Cindy Inman of Sherman had been fitted with artificial limbs.

It is tempting, of course, to speculate about possible reasons for births of children with quadrilateral limb deficiencies in this relatively small rural area, as the statistical incidence of quadrilateral limb deficiencies is very low: in one international study, only four infants in almost 10 million births. However, Richard Olney of the Centers for Disease Control has cautioned me about the statistical infeasibility of investigating them. Despite the apparent cluster of rare birth defects in a small area (Thomason, DeVries, Inman, Wilson), there are unfortunately no statistical baselines for the local population nor geographic boundaries through which to establish the abnormal incidence of these closely spaced births. See Rothman, "A Sobering Start for the Cluster Busters' Conference," 1990.

31.   Frank, "Life History Model of Adaptation to Disability," 1984.

32.   Diane's performance in fund-raising events and her media image is described in the concluding chapter of this book.

33.   Frank, "On Embodiment."

34.   Blakeslee, *The Limb-Deficient Child,* 1963. The CAPP staff included orthopedists, pediatricians, medical social workers, prosthetists, engineers, physical therapists, occupational therapists, and consultants in psychiatry and psychology. Their approach was developmental, based on the work of Arnold Gesell in infant and child psychology. The earliest possible fitting of prostheses (such as a passive hand) and consultation with parents within days of the infant's birth were advised so that a child with congenital limb deficiencies would naturally incorporate the devices into her body scheme. Diane's rejection of prostheses was seen by some at CAPP as the result of her having been allowed to improvise and adapt ways of doing things without them. The rationale for CAPP's policy of treating the child as early as possible is described by Blakeslee:

At the birth of a limb-deficient child the parents are almost certain to be extremely disturbed, with a feeling of being totally alone, and with no possible solution to their problem. They urgently need the opportunity—within the first few hours, if possible—to discuss the problem with someone from a child prosthetics center. The medical director and medical social worker have found it well worthwhile to make themselves available for immediate consultation with the parents, even if this requires a trip of a hundred miles or more. Although this may seem like a great deal of trouble to take, especially when the disability is small, it can save many hours, weeks or months of difficult and laborious work later on; it may shorten the many days and nights of frustrated anguish for the parents, and most of all may even make the difference between a successful prosthetic program and a complete failure (4).

35.   Diane's surgeries for terminal humoral overgrowth took place in February 1957 (left), April 1959 (right and left), March 1961 (left), October 1961 (right), April 1962 (left), February 1963 (left), January 1964 (left), and November 1965 (left and right). Orthopedic Summary, Milo B. Brooks, M.D., Medical Director, Child Amputee Prosthetics Project, to Jacquelin Perry, M.D., Rancho Los Amigos Hospital, January 10, 1964, plus undated addendum.

36.   Frank, "On Embodiment," 60.

37.   CAPP General Information Bulletin, September 1971.

38.   Interview with Susan Dustin Clarke, January 17, 1977. Beginning her work at CAPP in February 1974, Clarke was the occupational therapist who worked with Diane when she turned to CAPP for help as a young adult. An early statement of CAPP's goals corroborates Clarke's view of the program: "If the child with an amputation is to function with satisfaction to himself, his family, and his community, he needs not only a well-designed prosthesis, properly fabricated and fitted, but also careful training to achieve skillful and spontaneous use" (Blakeslee, *The Limb-Deficient Child*, viii).

39.   For an outstanding, if poignant, example of conflicting interpretations in social intervention concerning an abused child deprived of ordinary opportunities to learn language, see Curtiss, *Genie*, 1977, and the analysis of the circumstances surrounding her research by Rymer, "Annals of Science," 1992.

40.   Frank, "Beyond Stigma." The life histories of three adults with severe multiple limb deficiencies are compared with regard to choices about using upper and lower prostheses. They include Diane and two men about her age, Charles Jumps and Craig Vick, who were also childhood patients at CAPP.

41.   Frank, "Beyond Stigma," 101.

42.   Hoskins, *Biographical Objects*, 1998. For example, in Melanesian societies, which are characterized by a high degree of sexual polarity and male dominance, the voices of women are typically muted compared to those of men regarding themselves and their place in their cultural tradition. This has made it difficult to elicit informative autobiographical narratives from Melanesian women. Concerning the life history he recorded of an unusually articulate Kalauna woman from a

mountain village on Goodenough Island, Papua New Guinea, Michael W. Young notes that the act of autobiography "masculinized" his informant by obliging her to adopt men's perspectives of her roles in order to account for the events of her life. See Young, "'Our Name is Women,'" 1983. After unsuccessful attempts to elicit women's autobiographies among the Kwaio (Malaita, Solomon Islands) during numerous field trips in the 1960s and 1970s, anthropologist Roger M. Keesing was able, in collaboration with a woman anthropologist, Shelley Schreiner, to elicit surprisingly rich personal narratives from fifteen women. See Keesing, "Kwaio Women Speak,"1985. Keesing notes, however, that most of the material he and Schreiner were able to collect was not, strictly speaking, autobiographical but rather *moral*. That is, the women assumed that their task was "to tell us about women's virtues, their paths to prestige, the ancestral rules governing their lives, and their appropriate roles in relation to the watchful and potentially punitive ancestors, their daughters, and their husbands and affines. Most told us about themselves as commentaries on these more general ideologies about paths and responsibilities and rules of life" (31). Young and Keesing illustrate the importance of the eliciting context, including the relationship established with the life historian, in shaping the narratives they were eventually able to record.

43.   Rosaldo, "The Story of Tukbaw," 1976, quoted in Langness and Frank, *Lives*, 1981, 102.

44.   Bellah et al., *Habits of the Heart*, 1985. There has been an explosion of ethnographic methods in the social sciences and related fields such as social work, psychotherapy, education, nursing, and occupational therapy. The use of first-person interviews is what distinguishes the work of Bellah et al. from the works of social criticism on the same topic by sociologist Richard Sennett, *The Fall of Public Man*, 1974, and historian Christopher Lasch, *The Culture of Narcissism*, 1978. It can be noted that Margaret Mead did not conduct systematic fieldwork or any formal interviews in her book on the American character, *And Keep Your Powder Dry*, 1942. She relied on informal observations and referred to published sources including the now classic sociological studies by Lynd and Lynd (*Middletown*, 1929; *Middletown in Transition*, 1937) and by Warner and Lunt (*The Social Life of a Modern Community*, 1941). For another anthropologically-informed study of aspects of American character, see Marcus and Hall (*Lives in Trust*, 1992). Marcus and Hall focus on the extent to which media constructs the life stories of heirs to great wealth in this country, resulting in biographies that are "multiply authored" by agents and agencies over whom the subjects have little control.

45.   Bellah et al., *Habits of the Heart*, vii.

46.   Bellah et al., *Habits of the Heart*, vii.

47.   On the importance of testimony in the African-American tradition and its distinctive forms, see Gates, *Bearing Witness*, 1991, and *The Signifying Monkey*, 1988; Franklin, *Living Our Stories*, 1995; Braxton, *Black Women Writing Autobiogra-*

phy, 1989; and Bassard, *Spiritual Interrogations*, 1998. Narratives by former slaves were the key literary model for later autobiographies and novels by African Americans. Braxton discusses the importance of women's spiritual autobiographies in the nineteenth century.

48.   A relatively new form of psychotherapy, narrative therapy, takes as its central tenet the view that individuals are the experts on their own lives and that the therapist's role is to facilitate the person's authorship of his or her own life story. Narrative therapy rejects the idea that there is an objective truth and, in particular, aims to liberate the person from belief in dominant discourses and practices that often result in low self-esteem, immobilization, and despair. Narrative therapy rejects the medical model, with its presumption of pathology or deficit, in favor of a more radical political-economic analysis aiming to show how repressive social structures hamper individual growth. The idea is to move the client from the position of a passive or helpless victim to that of an active agent. See White and Epston, *Narrative Means to Therapeutic Ends*, 1990; Freedman and Combs, *Narrative Therapy*, 1996; and Zimmerman and Dickerson, *If Problems Talked*, 1996.

49.   See Appadurai, *Modernity at Large*, 1996, regarding the role of electronic media in the creation of new cultures globally.

50.   See Rainer, *Your Life as Story*, 1997. This excellent guide to the burgeoning genre of the literary memoir, in which autobiographers use the narrative techniques of fiction, may be read also as an exposition of American life story structure. As Rainer points out, the dominant American life story outline is based on the heroic quest (see Campbell, *The Hero with a Thousand Faces*, 1949). However, Rainer suggests, there may be alternatives to the linear model, such as the "quilt" described by Mary Catherine Bateson (*Composing a Life*, 1989). Bateson argues that the linear model of seeking and fulfilling a single unifying goal through a predictable career trajectory no longer holds for the often fragmented and disrupted lives of people today. Using the diverse careers of five professional women as examples, Bateson proposes a methodology of piecing episodes together, as in a collage or patchwork quilt, to see what patterns emerge.

51.   Ginsburg, *Contested Lives*, 1989. See chapter 8, "Interpreting Life Stories," 133–45. Ginsburg points out that these disruptions and life crises are often the result of relatively sudden or severe social changes such as technological innovations, political events, migrations, or economic dislocations. A comparable analysis is presented by Corbin and Strauss (*Unending Work and Care*, 1988), who analyze the "biographical work" that is prompted by the disruptive experience of a chronic illness.

52.   Becker, *Disrupted Lives*, 1997, 15.

53.   In two extremely interesting American memoirs an author tries to supply the missing narrative for a man unable to live up to the elite image that was "normal" to him or to create an appropriate life story. In both cases, the individual

committed suicide. See Trillin, *Remembering Denny*, 1993; and Wolff, *The Duke of Deception*, 1979.

54.   Frank, "Myths of Creation," 1996, 70.

55.   Labov and Waletzky, "Narrative Analysis," 1967. See also Labov, "The Transformation of Experience in Narrative Syntax," 1972; and Polanyi, *Telling the American Life Story*, 1989.

56.   Linde, *Life Stories*, 1993. Linde's work is based on data from English-speaking Americans. For a review of life story research in Europe, see Bertaux and Kohli, "The Life Story Approach," 1984.

57.   Such storytelling does not normally take place as a monologue but is rather a collaborative way of making sense of the world. There is usually a principal teller of the story, but interlocutors help to shape the narrative by interjecting questions, facts, and evaluations. Ochs, Taylor, Rudolph, and Smith ("Storytelling as a Theory-Building Activity," 1992) examine storytelling at dinnertime in English-speaking, white American families. As Diane's text clearly indicates, her autobiography draws on and responds to conversations and family stories. It is, from one point of view, an exercise in theory-building about her life situation.

58.   See Rainer, *Your Life as Story*, 66–67, on the "nine essential story elements." In a sense, Rainer's work applies to a written literature the analysis of folktales by Propp (*Morphology of the Folktale*, 1958 [1928]) that identifies their component parts (i.e., morphemes and motifemes), functions within the tale, and structural relationship to other tales and traditions. Applying a modified Proppian approach, for example, Dundes ("Structural Typology in North American Indian Folktales," 1965) discovered that North American folktales are often organized around a sequence of motifemes involving lack, liquidation of lack, interdiction, violation, consequence, and attempted escape. The basic three-part dramatic structure described by Rainer—a beginning, middle, and end through linear time—was the classical ideal described in Aristotle's *Poetics*. However, the tripartite structure is more generally characteristic of Indo-European cultures, of which the classical Greek is only one (see Dumezil, *Les dieux souverains des indo-européens*, 1977, and Olrik, "Epic Laws of Folk Narrative," 1965 [1909]). Olrik observed that "the greatest law of [Indo-European] folk tradition is concentration on a leading character (*Konzentration um eine Hauptperson*)" (139). Lord Raglan delineated a pattern of twenty-two elements underlying the life stories of folk heroes such as Theseus, Moses, and King Arthur that is organized around ritual themes of birth, initiation, death, and possible incarnation of a god (Raglan, "The Hero of Tradition," 1965, [1934]). Joseph Campbell has argued that there exists a "monomyth," a universal story about the hero's quest that is common to all the world's peoples because it is rooted in a basic human condition—the mystery of life and death, or creation and destruction, that each individual and culture must confront. The tenor of anthropological scholarship during my

lifetime has been to challenge all presumed human universals such as the idea that a certain form of narrative is "natural." Cross-cultural studies show that the structure, style, and assumptions of stories and performances in non-Western cultures sometimes differ considerably from those in Western genres. In his study of Javanese shadow plays (*wayang*), a form of entertainment as popular in Java as the soap opera in America, Alton Becker describes a different set of temporal and causal principles than is found in Western narrative. For example, a plot can begin at any point in time; it has no temporal beginning, middle, or end. What matters is *where* the action takes place. Also, plots turn on coincidences as much or more than on a character's determined actions. See Becker, "Text Building, Epistemology, and Aesthetics in Javanese Shadow Theater," 1979. Also see the discussion by Geertz ("Person, Time, and Conduct in Bali," 1973) of the preference for "absence of climax" in Balinese interactions. Such comparisons allow us to posit the story structure described by Rainer as basically Western (i.e., Indo-European) and, for our purposes, specifically American.

59.   Frank, "Myths of Creation," 67.

60.   Phillips, "Damaged Goods," 1990. Phillips documented narratives of personal experience from twenty women and thirteen men with visible physical disabilities in a Midwestern university town. She found that "three cultural notions about disability dominated the narratives: (1) that society perceives disabled persons to be damaged, defective, and less socially marketable than nondisabled persons; (2) that society believes disabled persons must try harder to overcome obstacles in culture and should strive to achieve normality; and (3) that society attributes to disabled persons a preference to be with their own kind" (850).

CHAPTER 5. HOW TYPICAL OR REPRESENTATIVE (AND OF WHAT) IS THE LIFE OF DIANE DEVRIES?

1.   Mead, "National Character," 1953, 648, emphasis in original.

2.   Goffman, *Stigma*, 1963, 128.

3.   Some suggest that the statistic could be higher than 15 percent, depending on the definition used. See LaPlante, "The Demographics of Disability," 1991.

4.   Congenital limb reduction defects (LRD) are not common, with an overall rate internationally of about 5 in 10,000 births. It is extremely difficult to estimate the prevalence of cases of quadrilateral limb deficiencies exactly like Diane's because of lack of detail in monitoring the various subtypes and combinations of LRD. See Castilla, "Limb Reduction Defects, 1988–1989," 1989, 64. However, according to Mastroiacovo et al. ("Absence of Limbs and Gross Body Wall Defects," 1992) the incidence of tetra-amelia was 0.04 per 100,000—from which the figure of 4 in 10 million births is derived. In a study in British Columbia

between 1952 and 1984, Froster-Iskenius and Baird ("Limb Reduction Defects in Over One Million Consecutive Livebirths," 1989) found an average incidence of LRD of 5.43 per 10,000 live births (or 659 in 1,213,913 consecutive live births); 190 of these cases involved more than one limb. About half the cases (348 of 659) were associated with additional congenital malformations and syndromes. About 13 percent of those with limb deficiencies died within the first year of life, the majority (85 percent) of whom had additional defects.

5.   Esther Williams was a Hollywood actress in musical films of the 1940s and 1950s that featured her abilities as a champion swimmer. Two of her most popular films were *Neptune's Daughter* (1949) and *Easy to Love* (1953). See DeNitto, *Film,* 1985. Diane's allusion to Esther Williams refers to her own experiences as a star in performances to raise funds for the aquatic program for handicapped children that she attended in Long Beach.

6.   See Friedan, *The Feminine Mystique,* 1963.

7.   My discussion of *I Love Lucy* draws on Banner, *Women in Modern America,* 1995; Carabillo, Meuli, and Csida, *Feminist Chronicles, 1953–1993,* 1993; and the videotape "Legends of Comedy," 1992.

8.   The life story of Irene Fields is based on interviews I conducted with her in February and March 1983.

9.   See Banner, *Women in Modern America,* and Taeuber, *Statistical Handbook on Women in America,* 1996, 50.

10.   See Banner, *American Beauty,* 1983. Banner writes that the history of such types or models of physical appearance was "virtually synonymous" (283) with the history of film, beginning with the initial popularity of the movies in the 1910s.

11.   Banner, *American Beauty,* 281.

12.   Banner, *American Beauty,* 283–84.

13.   Banner writes: "Monroe's popularity ensured the triumph of the vogue of dyed blonde hair, which cosmetics companies had been promoting. Sales of hair coloring soared, platinum blondes seemed everywhere. The widespread dyeing of hair to be light blonde indicated women's acceptance of a model of looks and behavior that had them be feminine, sensual, and unintellectual. Women were to seem like children, expressing their adulthood primarily through their sexuality. The 'dumb blonde' who had 'more fun' and whom 'gentlemen preferred' now became the dominant image of beauty for American women" (*American Beauty,* 285).

14.   Mailer, *Marilyn,* 1975, 15.

15.   Diane Fields to Cameron Hall, October 30, 1973, from Diane's medical records, Child Amputee Prosthetics Project, UCLA. The same file shows that Diane was age five, not three, when first treated there.

16.   The Rehabilitation Act of 1973 (PL 93-112) became law on September 26, 1973. For its legislative history, see Scotch, *From Goodwill to Civil Rights,* 1984, and

Berkowitz, *Disabled Policy*, 1987. As defined in Section 504 of the Act, as amended in 1974 (PL 95-602, Section 7), the term *handicapped individual* refers to: "any person who (A) has a physical or mental impairment which substantially limits one or more of such person's major life activities, (B) has a record of such an impairment, or (C) is regarded as having such an impairment."

17.   Jane West, "Introduction—Implementing the Act," 1991, xxi. The Department of Health, Education, and Welfare under the Republican administration of Gerald Ford delayed publishing the proposed regulations for enforcing Section 504 until 1976 (*Federal Register*, vol. 41, no. 96, May 17, 1976, 20296). Regulations were finally signed into law in April 1977 by the Secretary of Health, Education, and Welfare, Joseph Califano, under the Democratic administration of Jimmy Carter. See also Berkowitz, *Disabled Policy*, and Scotch, *From Goodwill to Civil Rights*.

18.   "Meet Ellen Stohl," *Playboy*, 1987.

19.   See Hahn, "The Minority Group Model of Disability," 1994, "Toward a Politics of Disability," 1985, and "The Politics of Physical Difference," 1988.

20.   Engel and Munger ("Rights, Remembrance, and the Reconciliation of Difference," 1996, 11–12) write:

> The ADA represents Congress's most ambitious effort to protect the interests of persons with disabilities and to grant them full membership in American society. The statute aspires to eliminate the "major areas of discrimination faced day-to-day by people with disabilities" (sec. 2(b) (4)). This transformation of "day-to-day" life extends to the employment area, where the statute prohibits discrimination in hiring and failure to provide "reasonable accommodations" to an otherwise qualified individual with a disability (sec. 102(b)). Reasonable accommodations include "making existing facilities . . . readily accessible" and restructuring work and work schedules, acquiring or modifying equipment or devices, exam modifications, and providing readers or interpreters for employees with disabilities (sec. 101 (9)). The ADA mandates such accommodations as long as they do not impose "undue hardship" on an employer—that is "significant difficulty or expense" in light of their nature and cost and the capacity of the employer to provide them (sec. 101 (10)). The employment provisions of the ADA became effective in July 1992 for employers with 25 or more employees and in July 1994 for employers with 15 or more employees. The enforcement provisions of the ADA are the same as those Congress provided under earlier civil rights laws prohibiting discrimination on the basis of race or gender.

As Engel and Munger note, although the Equal Employment Opportunity Commission and the Attorney General of the United States have the power to enforce the ADA, compliance must be initiated by the employer and employee. The employee is expected to raise issues of accommodation and seek intervention by the EEOC or court if his or her employer seems to be out of compliance with the ADA.

21.   See, for example, hooks, *Feminist Theory*, 1984.

22.   See remarks made in 1980 by Donald Galvin, a former director of a state rehabilitation program, quoted by Berkowitz (*Disabled Policy*, 1987, 206–7). He

charged that activists Ed Roberts and Judy Heumann, early directors of the Center for Independent Living in Berkeley, were "living in a white, middle-class dream world" that excluded the poor and the aged. Orthopedic impairments are the most prevalent cause, however, of limitation in an individual's major life activities in the United States, and include impairments due to such conditions as spinal cord injuries, polio, and limb deficiencies. Although limb deficiencies are less common than other impairments, they tend to be more severely disabling. Absence of a leg (or both legs) has been identified as the second highest-ranking cause of major activity limitation for Americans, after mental retardation: Among individuals with chronic conditions, 73.1 percent of individuals with an absence of a leg, or legs, reported at least one major activity limitation, and 39 percent reported that they required help in basic life activities. This was second only to people with mental retardation, for whom major activity limitation was reported for 80 percent. However, only 19.9 percent of people with mental retardation reported needing help in basic life activities or activities of daily living (ADLs). Data are from the National Health Interview Survey, 1983–86. See LaPlante, "The Demographics of Disability," 68.

23.   Diane's immediate family background and environment were solidly white and working-class. Diane's father worked as a carpenter in the construction trade during Southern California's post–World War II boom years. Her family moved from Texas to San Diego, California. From there they moved to the Long Beach area, settling first in Lakewood, one of the new suburban development communities that mushroomed during this period because of favorable lending policies for veterans to obtain mortgages under the GI Bill. Many of these communities had covenants that restricted ownership to white people. In addition, banks and realtors colluded in redlining practices to deny mortgage loans to nonwhites. These policies were sanctioned at the federal level by the Federal Housing Administration (FHA) and Veterans Administration (VA). This is not to suggest that Diane's family was racist, but that its position in the economy and place of residence reflected national policies that reinforced their insulation and privilege, and, therefore, their cultural identity as white. See Davis (*City of Quartz*, 1990) for a discussion of the infamous "Lakewood Plan," which fueled white flight from Los Angeles, between 1954 and 1960, to new suburbs freed from the tax burden for metropolitan services. Regarding institutionalized racism during the mid-1950s in the FHA and VA, see Karen Sacks, "How Did Jews Become White Folks?" 1994. The social class of Diane's family probably would be identified as "lower-middle" according to criteria used by W. Lloyd Warner, *Social Class in America*, 1960, which was originally published in 1949. Warner determines an individual or family's social class based on four "status characteristics": Occupation, Source of Income, House Type, and Dwelling Area. Warner's approach is used here because it makes use of status designations and

popular criteria in American culture during the period under study. As an adult, Diane has achieved the most solid middle-class status among those in her family. For example, she is the only one of her siblings to have finished college and also has earned a graduate degree.

24.   Engel and Munger, "Rights, Remembrance, and the Reconciliation of Difference." Two women, "Sara Lane" and "Jill Golding," were participants in a telephone survey of 180 individuals with disabilities in western New York State, 60 of whom were further interviewed to record their life stories. The authors were interested in "how legal innovations like the ADA become interwoven with the life histories and legal consciousness of individuals who might assert new rights" (12).

25.   Following the sociolinguistic axiom of the "unmarked case," Sara Lane is presumed to be white, like Diane, because the authors make no qualifying remarks about her race or ethnicity. Extrapolating information from the text, she was born in 1955. Sara Lane is unmarried and has one child.

26.   Engel and Munger, "Rights, Remembrance, and the Reconciliation of Difference," 21.

27.   Engel and Munger, "Rights, Remembrance, and the Reconciliation of Difference," 24, 26.

28.   Engel and Munger, "Rights, Remembrance, and the Reconciliation of Difference," 47. One of the tensions in Sara Lane's position is exemplified by her decision not to request flexible hours and permission to work at home under the ADA but to wait until the newspaper guild, a union that represents all employees, makes such a demand for all its members. Flexible hours and working at home would accommodate her physical needs, especially during the added challenge of her recovery from carpal tunnel surgery. Like Diane, one of Sara Lane's main concerns as she ages is whether her body will hold up so that she can continue working.

29.   Louis Harris and Associates, *The ICD Survey of Disabled Americans,* 1986, 19. A national survey of one thousand people with disabilities conducted by telephone in December 1985 found seven out of ten reporting that things had gotten somewhat better (47 percent) or much better (25 percent) for people with disabilities during the past ten years; people with the most severe disabilities (about six out of ten, or 58 percent) were somewhat less likely to feel the improvement. A much larger majority of moderately disabled people (80 percent) and of slightly disabled people (83 percent) felt that things had improved.

30.   Harris and Associates (*ICD Survey,* 2) report: "Disabled Americans have far less education, as a group, than do non-disabled Americans. Forty percent of all disabled persons did not finish high school. This proportion is nearly three times higher than in the non-disabled population, where only 15% of adults have less than a high school education." Anecdotal evidence from women with congenital disabilities who grew up in the 1950s and 1960s suggests that they received fewer

educational opportunities than their male counterparts. See Asch and Fine, "Introduction," 1988.

31. Among unemployed people with disabilities, 78 percent would like to work. Harris and Associates, *ICD Survey*, 4.

32. Harris and Associates (*ICD Survey*, 5) report: "Over twice as many working persons with disabilities report a 1984 household income of $25,000 or more (44%) as did those who don't work (21%). . . . About 6 out of 10 of those out of the labor force (36% of all people with disabilities under the age of 65) receive some sort of income support from either insurance payments or government benefit programs. And the majority of those who receive benefits say that they are the main wage earner in their household."

33. Harris and Associates (*ICD Survey*, 2) report: "Half of all disabled persons (50%) report household incomes for 1984 of $15,000 or less. Among non-disabled Americans, only 25% have household incomes in this bracket."

34. Harris and Associates (*ICD Survey*, 2) report: "An 85% majority of non-disabled people socialize at least once a week with family and friends. Seventy-five percent of all disabled persons say that they socialize at least once a week, but this figure drops to 67% among very severely disabled persons. A 56% majority of all disabled persons say that their disability prevents them from getting around, socializing outside their home, or attending cultural or sports events as much as they would like. This majority rises to 67% among somewhat severely disabled persons, and to 79% among very severely disabled persons."

35. Harris and Associates (*ICD Survey*, 3) report: "Nearly two-thirds of all disabled Americans never went to a movie in the past year. In the full adult population, only 22% said that they had not gone to a movie in the past year. . . . Disabled people are three times more likely than are non-disabled people to never eat in restaurants. Seventeen percent of disabled people never eat in restaurants, compared to 5% of non-disabled people. Only 34% of disabled people eat at a restaurant once a week or more, compared to a 58% majority of non-disabled people."

36. Harris and Associates (*ICD Survey*, 3) report: "Thirteen percent of disabled persons never shop in a grocery store, compared to only 2% of non-disabled persons. About 6 out of 10 disabled persons visit a grocery store at least once a week, while 90% of non-disabled adults shop for food this often."

37. Harris and Associates (*ICD Survey*, 4) report: "Sixty-nine percent of disabled persons say that they are somewhat or very satisfied with life, compared to 90% of non-disabled persons."

38. Harris and Associates (*ICD Survey*, 3–4) report: "A much higher percentage of severely disabled persons believe that their disability has impeded their efforts to reach their potential. Seventy-two percent of very severely disabled persons believe that this is so."

39. See Asch and Fine ("Introduction," 1988, 10):

White disabled men participate [in the labor force] at almost twice the rate of white disabled women (44 percent of men, only 24 percent of women). Ninety percent of non-disabled white males and 64 percent of non-disabled white females participate in the labor force, meaning that they are about half as likely as non-disabled men to work, whereas for white disabled women the gap is even greater, with disabled white women only three-eighths as likely to participate as non-disabled white women. . . . Employed disabled women tend to be tracked in low-wage, service-sector positions. As of 1981, the mean earnings of disabled women fell far below those of disabled men. Including all workers, disabled males averaged $13,863 annually, compared to disabled females, who averaged $5,835.

Some clarification of this picture is offered by Barnartt and Altman ("Predictors of Wages," 1997), who confirm, based on data from 1987, that women with disabilities earn less than men with disabilities. They found that men and women with visual or hearing impairments actually were earning more than their nondisabled, same-sex peers (106 percent and 109 percent respectively). But within these categories, women with disabilities earned less than 60 percent of the income of men with disabilities. Men with mobility impairments or multiple impairments were earning less (about 85 percent) income than their nondisabled male peers. But, again, women in these impairment categories earned around 60 percent of the income of their male counterparts. The authors conclude that the poorer economic status of women with disabilities reflects trends in the general population of sex segregation and wage discrimination based on gender, rather than disability.

40.   Baldwin, "Gender Differences in Social Security Disability Decisions," 1997.

41.   Diane reflected on her experiences of discrimination as a person with a disability and as a woman: "It's the first time I've come face to face with discrimination," Diane said. "I never felt that before. My life has been rough. I've had to fight and struggle. But I've never really been discriminated against to my face. If I was put down at all in college, I felt it was because I'm a woman. I remember something Jim said when I graduated: 'Now you've got to go out in the real world and see how they treat you.' He was right. It hit hard." All quotes are verbatim, recorded in field notes of July to November 1990.

42.   To add to Diane's frustration and desperation during this episode, all services provided by the State of California were suspended when Governor George Deukmejian refused to sign the new annual budget as presented by the legislature. Not only was the Department of Fair Housing and Employment shut down, but Diane's IHSS checks, which she needed to pay her attendant, also stopped coming.

43.   Fiore, "Disabled Worker Claims Job Bias," 1990, and Hinch, "Disabled Woman Fired, Comes Back Fighting," 1990.

44.   See Bogdan, *Freak Show*, 1988; Thomson, *Extraordinary Bodies*, 1997; Gilman, *Difference and Pathology*, 1985, and *The Jew's Body*, 1991; and Harrowitz and Hyams, *Jews and Gender*, 1995.

45.   See Rickman, "Wilhelm Dilthey," 1967. *Verstehen* (understanding) was introduced by Dilthey (1833–1911) as an indispensable part of the methods appropriate to the social sciences (*Geisteswissenschaften,* or human studies), as differentiated from the natural sciences. The goal of the natural sciences is explanation, he asserted, whereas the goal of the social sciences is understanding. The legacy of Dilthey's philosophy of life (*Philosophie des Lebens*) remains alive in the social sciences in the 1990s, with their increased interdisciplinarity, attention to temporality, focus on meaning, and renewed concern with the individual's agency in society. For Dilthey, *Das Verstehen* meant, specifically, "the comprehension of some mental content—an idea, an intention, or a feeling—manifested in empirically given expressions such as words or gestures" (405). In other words, *Verstehen* is the method that allows us to understand "the meaning that human beings perceive in, or attribute to, a single situation or their whole lives."

Dilthey's theory of understanding became the basis of Max Weber's sociology, which continues to exert a strong influence on mainstream sociology and which also provides the theoretical foundation for the interpretative anthropology of Clifford Geertz. See Winch, "Max Weber," 1967, and Gadamer, *Truth and Method,* 1975 [1960], specifically his critique of Dilthey in the section "Dilthey's Entanglement in the Impasses of Historicism," 193–234. Gadamer makes clear the radicalism of the central tendency of Dilthey's historicism—a movement away from the prior Hegelian positing of a transcendental spirit and rational unfolding of history, and toward an appreciation of history as a temporally unfolding expression of nothing but itself. At the same time, Gadamer argues that Dilthey's reliance on Romantic hermeneutics, with its idea of achieving understanding by relating the parts to a whole (based on the model of understanding a text) resulted in his historicism retaining a problematic commitment to some kind of transcendental or objective spirit in history. Gadamer's criticism should not affect my use of Dilthey's historicist approach, since I am not attempting a systematic philosophy of history. But the following point does apply.

Citing the philosopher O. F. Bollnow, Gadamer remarks that Dilthey did not adequately explore the concept of power as an objective force. I have added an analysis of power. In fact, not to do so is almost an impossibility for an anthropologist in the United States in the 1990s, given the impact of: historical studies by philosopher Michel Foucault that focus precisely on a reconceptualization of power; the widespread use by social scientists of the concept of hegemony as expressed in the writings of neo-Marxist Antonio Gramsci; and the spread of other neo-Marxist analyses, known as cultural studies, through the work of Raymond Williams, Stuart Hall, and others. See Dirks, Eley, and Ortner, "Introduction," 1994.

Finally, there is support in Dilthey's philosophy for critical standpoint theories, which are generally regarded as a much later contribution of Marxist feminism and feminist sociology, but which probably can be traced, with Dilthey's philosophy, to Hegel. See Hartsock, "The Feminist Standpoint," 1987; and Smith, "Women's Perspective as a Radical Critique of Sociology," 1990. A very good discussion and criticism of standpoint theories in relation to Marxism and feminism is presented by Donovan (*Feminist Theory*, 1992, chapter 8). Donovan notes that standpoint theorists have been criticized for essentializing women or covering up important differences among them. Dilthey's philosophy lends itself less to such typifications, I think, than Weber's sociology. I do not intend Diane's case to represent "disabled women" as a class. My goal, instead, is to describe Diane's life as a woman with a disability in relation to the dominant cultural discourses and social practices affecting people with disabilities in the United States during her lifetime. Obviously, there will be many commonalities between Diane's life and those of others with disabilities, men and women. However, classes may have multiple standpoints and many philosophers no longer presume that even the transcendental subject (in this case, the "I" of Diane) is unified. Therefore, I make no all-encompassing claim for Diane's life history in terms of statistical representativeness (positivism), a disabled standpoint or class consciousness (Marxism), or an ideal type (Weberian sociology), but only limited claims for its interpretative validity in specified contexts. I hope that readers will recognize this circumscription to be a theoretical and methodological strength of the study, not a weakness.

46.   See Donovan, *Feminist Theory*, 1992, 1–30; and Brenner, "The Best of Times, the Worst of Times," 1996.

47.   Brenner ("The Best of Times") writes:

> Liberal feminism rests on the strand of liberalism that looks primarily to the regulatory arm of the state to ensure free and fair competition. . . . A politics which focuses exclusively on discriminatory treatment is inevitably class and race biased because it ignores women's differential resources for competing in the market. Liberal feminists do not necessarily support an expanded welfare state. A survey of women voters displeased by the defeat of the ERA (i.e., feminists of some sort) found that women from high-income families and white women were more likely than women from lower-income families and black women to think that too much was spent on welfare and food stamps and that government ought not to guarantee jobs (30–31).

48.   Brenner, "The Best of Times," 30.

49.   See Daines and Seddon, "Confronting Austerity," 1993; and Charlton, *Nothing About Us Without Us*, 1998. Obviously, Diane DeVries enjoys generally far greater status and economic security than most women with disabilities in the Third World. Nevertheless, even in the United States, women who are poor are more likely to be disabled, and women who are disabled are more likely to be poor (Asch and Fine, "Introduction"; Baldwin, "Gender Differences in Social Security Disability Decisions," 1997).

50.   Toulmin, "Occupation, Employment and Human Welfare," 1995.

51.   See Piven, "Women and the State," 1987, regarding such structural contra-dictions despite the generally empowering opportunities for women created by expansion of the welfare state.

52.   With Judith Butler (*Gender Trouble*, 1990), I think that individual identities cannot be understood without prior reference to gender. In Diane's case, it is nec-essary also to understand her gender as conditioned by her disability. Butler writes: "It would be wrong to think that the discussion of 'identity' ought to pro-ceed prior to a discussion of gender identity for the simple reason that 'persons' only become intelligible through becoming gendered in conformity with recog-nizable standards of gender intelligibility" (16).

53.   Donovan, *Feminist Theory*, 1992, 31.

54.   Moi, *Sexual/Textual Politics*, 1985, 21–22.

55.   Donovan, *Feminist Theory*, 141. Radical feminists argue that male supremacy and the subjugation of women are the source and model for all forms of oppression in society.

56.   Gill, "Questioning Continuum," 1994, 43, 49.

57.   The binary character of such a formulation has been increasingly chal-lenged since the late 1970s, particularly with the English translation of works by Lyotard (*The Postmodern Condition*, 1984 [1979]) and Derrida (*Of Grammatology*, 1976 [1967]). A helpful explanation of Derrida's concept of *différance*, a critique of binary logic, is presented by Moi (*Sexual/Textual Politics*, 1985):

> For Derrida, meaning (signification) is not produced in the static closure of the binary opposition. Rather it is achieved through the "free play of the signifier." One way of illustrating Derrida's arguments at this point is to use Saussure's concept of the *phoneme*, defined as the smallest differential—and therefore signifying—unit in the language. The phoneme can in no way be said to achieve signification through binary opposition alone. In itself the phoneme /b/ does not signify anything at all. If we had only one phoneme, there would be no meaning and no language. /b/ only signifies in so far as it is perceived to be *different* from say /k/ or /h/. Thus /bat/:/kat/:/hat/ are all perceived to be different words with different meanings in English. The argu-ment is that /b/ signifies only through a process that effectively *defers* its meaning on to other differential elements in language. In a sense it is the *other* phonemes that enable us to determine the meaning of /b/. For Derrida, signification is produced pre-cisely through this kind of open-ended play between the presence of one signifier and the absence of others. . . . As we have seen, the interplay between presence and absence that produces meaning is posited as one of *deferral*: meaning is never truly present, but is only constructed through the potentially endless process of referring to other, absent signifiers (105–6).

This move breaks down the idea that subject and class positions are closed, uni-fied, and completely specifiable. Yet, as various critics have pointed out, such a move threatens to subvert the political efforts of subordinated groups at exactly the moment in history when they have begun to gain a degree of power and a voice in the academy. This argument is made forcefully by hooks ("Postmodern Blackness," 1990):

Should we not be suspicious of postmodern critiques of the "subject" when they surface at a historical moment when many subjugated people feel themselves coming to a voice for the first time. . . . An adequate response to this concern is to critique essentialism while emphasizing the significance of "the authority of experience." There is a radical difference between a repudiation of the idea that there is a black "essence" and recognition of the way black identity has been specifically constituted in the experience of exile and struggle (28–29).

A similar analysis, concerning gender politics, is made by Bordo, "Feminism, Postmodernism, and Gender Skepticism," 1993.

58.   Gill, "Questioning Continuum," 1994, 43–44.

59.   Practices used by a cohort of white women to develop an antiracist consciousness are described by Frankenberg, *White Women, Race Matters*, 1993. I thank Steve Kurzman for pointing out the connection to me, through Frankenberg's work, between the construction of ablism and racism. And I thank Harlan Hahn for suggesting in an earlier draft that I emphasize this insight.

60.   Behar, *The Vulnerable Observer*, 1996.

61.   See Visweswaran, *Fictions of Feminist Ethnography*, 1994. Visweswaran claims shifting identities, temporality, and silence as tools of feminist ethnography. In her critique of experimental ethnographies to date, Visweswaran writes:

I suggest that polyphony and multiple voicings are not a solution to the vexed problems of power and authority, and that we should be attentive to silence as a marker of women's agency. I argued that a feminist ethnography cannot assume the willingness of women to talk and maintained that "one avenue open to it is to investigate when and why women do talk; to assess the strictures placed on their speech; the avenues of creativity they have appropriated; the degrees of freedom they possess." Perhaps then, a feminist ethnography can take the silences among women as the central site for the analysis of power between them (51).

CHAPTER 6. "THE BIOGRAPHY IN THE SHADOW" MEETS "VENUS ON WHEELS"

1.   Rousseau, *The Confessions*, 1954, 17. Known to us as a philosopher and author, Rousseau (1712–1778) had been at various stages of his life an engraver's apprentice, footman, seminarist, music teacher, and private tutor. Among his best known works are *Émile* and *The Social Contract*, both published in 1762. The *Confessions*, completed in 1770 and published posthumously, in 1781, covered the first fifty-three years of his life.

2.   Augustine, *The Confessions of Saint Augustine*, 1961. *The Confessions*, written in A.D. 397, is a conversion story often considered to be the prototype for all subsequent Western autobiography. Augustine's story is itself modeled on the story of Paul's conversion in the New Testament.

3.   Rousseau, *The Confessions*, 17.

4.   Olney, *Metaphors of Self*, 1972. See also Olney, *Memory and Narrative*, 1999.

5.   Van Den Berg, *The Changing Nature of Man*, 1954.

6.   See Schafer, *Retelling a Life*, 1992, and *The Analytic Attitude*, 1983. See also Bruner, *Acts of Meaning*, 1990; Sarbin, *Narrative Psychology*, 1986; Spence, *Narrative Truth and Historical Truth*, 1982; Polkinghorne, *Narrative Knowing and the Human Sciences*, 1988; Rosenwald and Ochberg, *Storied Lives*, 1992; White and Epston, *Narrative Means to Therapeutic Ends*, 1990; Freedman and Combs, *Narrative Therapy*, 1996; and Zimmerman and Dickerson, *If Problems Talked*, 1996. Ethnographic and life history research in the South Pacific supports the view that the "self" as we know it is a narrative convention (see above chapter 3). A focus on the co-construction of life stories and the self through discourse in families and other institutions, or with psychotherapists or ethnographers, is important to an anthropological, as compared to literary, understanding of the self in relation to culture. Linde (*Life Stories*, 1993) begins to theorize the links between narratives of self and social discourses. In particular, see chapter 6, "Coherence Systems," 163–91, and chapter 7, "Common Sense and Its History," 192–218. An excellent example of autobiography understood in relation to a dominant cultural narrative appears in Harding, "The Afterlife of Stories," 1992. Also see Linden, *Making Stories, Making Selves*, 1993, for an analysis of conflicting narrative perspectives on a core set of life history events.

7.   See Sanjek, *Fieldnotes*, 1990, especially Ottenberg, "Thirty Years of Fieldnotes."

8.   I refer to the argument that action can be "read" like a text. See Ricoeur, "The Model of the Text," 1981 [1971]. Many postmodern critics also use the word *inscription* in the way that anthropologists like myself use the word *construction*.

9.   Frank, "Finding the Common Denominator," 1979, 85. A key source is the pioneering, psychoanalytically influenced work of anthropologist George Devereux (*From Anxiety to Method in the Social Sciences*, 1967), who drew on thirty years of observations to illustrate how investigators' personal reactions (countertransference) to their subject matter affect their formulations of research problems and methods.

10.   Frank, " 'Becoming the Other,' " 1985.

11.   Moi, *Sexual/Textual Politics*, 1985, 43–45.

12.   Moi, *Sexual/Textual Politics*, 44.

13.   Several reviewers had this unfortunate reaction to the last chapter of Ruth Behar's *Translated Woman* (1993), a beautifully written life history of a Mexican marketing woman, in which the author attempts to locate herself in the feminist, autobiographical mode. For a discussion, see Frank, "Ruth Behar's Biography in the Shadow," 1995.

14.   Hoskins, personal communication, spring 1998.

15.   See Gilder, Thompson, Slack, and Radcliffe, "Amputations, Body Image, and Perceptual Distortion," 1954. On the basis of a wide review of literature in

the social sciences and humanities, Hahn ("Can Disability Be Beautiful?" 1988) claims that perceptions of disability provoke two types of responses in nondisabled people: *existential anxiety* (fears about loss of function) and *aesthetic anxiety* (fears about disfigurement).

16.   Cadish, "UCLA Project Aids Limbless," 1976, 1.

17.   Roskies, *Abnormality and Normality,* 1972, 284.

18.   Weiss, *Conditional Love,* 1994, 261.

19.   DeVries, "Autobiography."

20.   In his charter work, *Ideas: General Introduction to Pure Phenomenology,* 1913, Husserl (1859–1938) recommended a number of procedures including "bracketing," the suspension of beliefs and prejudices about an object, to encounter fully how the object is constituted in consciousness. Bracketing results in two kinds of "reductions": the *eidetic reduction* is a description of the pure generalities or pure possibilities of an object, apart from empirical examples of the thing. Such descriptions constitute the realm of general essences or "ideas" (in Greek, *eidos*). The *phenomenological reduction,* in contrast, refers to the objects encountered empirically. It confronts the concrete reality of the everyday world, and attempts to describe the ultimate presuppositions of the things we experience. In Husserl's phenomenology the objects given in consciousness (phenomena) are constructed; they are always "consciousness-of-an-object" and never purely objective. It follows that phenomenological experiences can differ because experiences are *intentional,* meaning that a person must turn toward an object in order to perceive it. See Spiegelberg, *The Phenomenological Movement,* 1976, and Kockelmans, *Phenomenology,* 1967. Gaining an "essential" perception of mental objects became a troubled area for later philosophers such as Emmanuel Levinas and Jacques Derrida, who use phenomenological and other methods to demarcate difference rather than sameness.

21.   Bachelard, *The Psychoanalysis of Fire,* 1964. Bachelard advised that, when dealing with the inert world, it is necessary to restrain our enthusiasm and repress our personal feelings, but not so when dealing with "our equals," fellow human beings. Then our method "should be based on sympathy" (1).

22.   See Frank, *Venus on Wheels,* 1981. I adopted the term *crips* that Diane learned and used at Rancho Los Amigos Hospital.

23.   Hermeneutics refers to specific procedures for interpreting the meaning of texts which, since Dilthey, have been used also to understand history and social action. The hermeneutic circle is virtually unending, although at some point meanings usually become clear enough for practical purposes. See Kockelmans, "Toward an Interpretative or Hermeneutic Social Science," 1976.

24.   Gadamer, *Truth and Method,* 1975 [1960]. Gadamer criticizes enlightenment hermeneutics, in which the belief in reason necessitates the rejection of all beliefs based in traditional authority. He founds his critique on the temporally based

hermeneutics of Martin Heidegger (1889–1976). See Heidegger, *Being and Time*, 1962 [1927]. I argue that some of an interpreter's preunderstandings are irreducibly personal. This is where my phenomenology overlaps with psychoanalysis. For an application of Gadamer's work to life history methods, see Watson and Watson-Franke, *Interpreting Life Histories*, 1985. Another approach to the problem of preunderstandings was taken by phenomenologist Max Scheler in his work on the "idols of self-knowledge," that is, the sources of illusion in self-understanding. See Spiegelberg, *The Phenomenological Movement*, 1976, 243–44.

25.   The most comprehensive statement of the usefulness of psychoanalysis for anthropological research is by Herdt and Stoller, *Intimate Communications*, 1990. However, there is a rich background to their argument. See Sapir, "Why Cultural Anthropology Needs the Psychiatrist,"1938, and Devereux, *From Anxiety to Method*.

26.   Although Diane was not in psychotherapy during most of the time covered by our collaboration, she experienced at least two episodes of severe depression and suicidal feelings, during which she was hospitalized and received medication. The first episode, in 1989, occurred in reaction to the breakup of her marriage to Jim DeVries; the second, in 1994, in reaction to several losses, including the death from AIDS of her much-loved client Christopher and the breakup of her relationship with her boyfriend Dave.

27.   Edith Stein (1891–1942) was one of the last students of Edmund Husserl and was his assistant (*Privatdozent*) at the University of Freiburg. In her first full-length book, *On the Problem of Empathy*, 1970 [1917], Stein used Husserl's methods to achieve an eidetic reduction of the phenomenon of empathy. Advancement of Stein's academic career in the German university system was stymied in 1932 by sexism and anti-Semitism. Having been born into a Jewish merchant family in Breslau, Stein converted to Catholicism in 1933 and became a Carmelite nun. During the Nazi period, she was deported from a haven to which she had been sent, in the Netherlands, to the death camp at Auschwitz, where she perished. Known as Sister Teresa Benedicta of the Cross, Stein was beatified as a martyr by the Roman Catholic Church in 1987. As a result of a miracle that occurred in New York City in 1987, in which a fatally ill toddler, Benedicta McCarthy, was saved through prayers to her namesake, the Vatican has declared Sister Teresa Benedicta a saint. See Baseheart, "Edith Stein's Philosophy of Woman and of Women's Education," 1996; also Goodstein, "Pope Intends to Canonize German Nun as Saint," 1997, and Dart, "Sainthood for Jewish Convert Stirs Debate," 1998. For an official biography of Stein by a fellow member of the Carmelite order, see Herbstrith, *Edith Stein, A Biography*, 1985. Also see Stein, *Life in a Jewish Family*, 1986, her unfinished autobiography through the year 1916.

28.   Stein, *On the Problem of Empathy*, 98–99. The phenomenon of empathy was also investigated by Max Scheler (1874–1928), Stein's older colleague. In his book

The Nature of Sympathy, 1973 [1912, with several subsequent revisions], a study of love and hate, Scheler identified four types of empathy or "fellow-feeling." He argued that empathy is not mediated by symbols but is a direct apprehension of the other's state, the position first taken by Edith Stein. However, Scheler does not admit comparisons with oneself and analogies (as in the question, "How would it be if that had happened to me?") as part of genuine empathy. I argue that empathic imagination is necessarily part of biographical understanding, not only for life historians but also for other biographers, readers of biographies, and participants in everyday life. (See Runyan, "Alternative Accounts of Lives," 1980, on the tendency of writers to perceive, select, and imagine facts about Shakespeare's life that resemble the facts of their own lives.) Stein's discussion of the more complex states of empathy allows use of one's imagination to feel into the other's situation. The work on empathy by Scheler and Stein was fairly orthodox in terms of using Husserl's early methods, which focused on immediate apperceptions, but later Husserl increasingly looked toward imagination as a valid source of phenomenological knowledge. Kockelmans ("Essences and Eidetic Reduction"—Introduction," 1967) writes: "It is of some importance to notice that in the beginning, Husserl seemed to adopt the point of view that ideation takes place on the basis of the particular experience of an individual of a certain class. Later we see an increasingly important role assigned to the imagination, until ultimately Husserl saw the imagination as the essential factor in the revealing of the essences of things" (81–82).

29.　Frank, "On Embodiment," 65. In Greek mythology, Venus is the goddess of love. Her Roman name is not Diana but Aphrodite. Diana, whose Greek name is Artemis, is goddess of the hunt, of chastity, and of the moon. Note also that I, too, made a "mistake" by imagining the Venus de Milo as lacking legs when, in fact, the statue's lower limbs are merely draped or covered. In my study of Diane's life, I have tried to reconcile factual discrepancies as much as possible by cross-checking sources. What is most important for understanding Diane, however, are her interpretations, including her adoption of a powerful metaphor by which she identifies with the goddess of love.

30.　There are other modes. For example, Diane has described herself as someone who could *become* crippled by scoliosis (see above chapter 2). At times it has been Diane's asthma that has disabled her. At low points in her life, Diane occasionally expresses self-denigrating feelings about being a "crip."

31.　Valentine ("The Relative Reliability of Men and Women in Intuitive Judgments of Character," 1929) examined the prevailing belief that women are more intuitive than men by performing an experiment that exposed both groups to information about an individual previously unknown to them. He concluded that women are "not superior to men" in forming accurate judgments about other people, once men "give their minds to the task."

32.   Dallery ("The Politics of Writing [The] Body," 1989) identifies empathy as a devalued trait ascribed to women that supports male hegemony. In a critique of the concept of androgyny, she argues: "The so-called masculine traits—for example, rationality, objectivity, autonomy—are precisely those historically based on the suppression of woman's body, desire and difference. On the other side, the so-called feminine or nurturing traits—for example, empathy, caring, emotional responsiveness—are the epiphenomenon of structures of male domination and suppression, the virtues of the oppressed" (65). Her point is that the so-called feminine traits are not necessary or essential to being female. Rather, they are socially constructed but made to seem natural.

33.   See Gilligan, *In a Different Voice*, 1982. Gilligan's work on moral development corrects the masculinist bias in the theory of Kohlberg, *The Philosophy of Moral Development*, 1981. She shows that girls, more than boys, tend to find solutions to moral dilemmas based on empathic reasoning rather than abstract principles. In Kohlberg's hierarchical model, this tendency places females at a lower stage of moral development than their male peers.

34.   Spivak, *The Post-Colonial Critic*, 1990, 121. According to Raymond Williams (*Keywords*, 1983), the term *hegemonic* is:

> not limited to matters of direct political control but seeks to describe a more general predominance which includes, as one of its key features, a particular way of seeing the world and human nature and relationships. It is different in this sense from the notion of 'world-view', in that the ways of seeing the world and ourselves and others are not just intellectual but political facts, expressed over a range from institutions to relationships and consciousness. It is also different from *ideology* in that it is seen to depend for its hold not only on its expression of the interests of a ruling class but also on its acceptance as 'normal reality' or 'commonsense' by those in practice subordinated to it (145).

Williams points out that the overthrow of a specific hegemony can only be done "by creating an alternative hegemony—a new predominant practice and consciousness" (145). The achievements of the independent living and disability rights movement are counterhegemonic to the rehabilitation paradigm and to many prior commonsense views of disability in the culture; they are also increasingly constitutive of a new hegemony in that new laws (the Rehabilitation Act of 1973; the Americans with Disabilities Act of 1990) impose negative sanctions for acts of discrimination against people with disabilities and thus promote alternative practices and consciousness.

35.   Kleinman, *The Illness Narratives*, 1988.

36.   See Minow, *Making All the Difference*, 1990. Minow uses the phrase "the dilemma of difference" to refer to the inadvertent stigmatization that occurs when socially constructed differences such as race and disability are highlighted in order to remedy discrimination. In an example taken from a novel, Minow points out that one woman's "process of empathizing and identifying with" another woman who is absent should be recognized as "something that obvi-

ously takes work, not as the natural result of something that all women always feel toward one another" (220).

37.   Minow, *Making All the Difference*, 113. For a critique of false empathy by a legal scholar, see Delgado, "Rodrigo's Eleventh Chronicle," 1997.

38.   *Cultural anthropology* is one of the four fields (cultural anthropology, physical anthropology, archaeology, and linguistics) established as the domain of academic anthropology in the United States about a century ago. *Social anthropology* is the comparable field of study established in Britain. There are important differences between the two fields, which have had long, complex, and sometimes interlocking trajectories. Cultural anthropology, associated with Franz Boas (1858–1942), focuses on: (1) understanding the beliefs and values (or worldview) of indigenous peoples and nations and how they are passed and transformed from generation to generation; and (2) tracing the patterns and processes by which specific elements of cultures, or culture traits, are distributed geographically and adapted to new environments. The somewhat disjunctive relationship between these areas of concern was a mark of the tension in German philosophy in Boas's time over differences in the grounds for establishing truth or knowledge in the natural sciences and the social sciences. British social anthropology, associated with Bronislaw Malinowski (1884–1942) and A. R. Radcliffe-Brown (1881–1955), focuses on: (1) the development of social institutions (such as kinship, religion, politics, and economics) to meet the organic and spiritual needs of human beings; and (2) the organization and structural cohesion of a society as a whole through the functioning of its institutions. British social anthropology was strongly influenced by French positivism as expressed in the philosophy of August Comte (1798–1857) and the sociology of Émile Durkheim (1858–1917). For an interesting and readable history examining the complex relationships between cultural anthropology and social anthropology, see Kuper, *The Invention of Primitive Society*, 1988; and also Vincent, *Anthropology and Politics*, 1990.

39.   See Frank, "Jews, Multiculturalism, and Boasian Anthropology," 1997.

40.   This dual inheritance continues to pose problems for the discipline of anthropology that surface periodically in debates about whether anthropology belongs to the humanities or the sciences. For a classic statement of this problem, see Redfield, "Relations of Anthropology to the Social Sciences and to the Humanities," 1953. Cultural anthropology's present swing toward narrative and interpretation reflects the current hegemony of advocates for the humanistic side of the discipline. This was not always the case and may not remain so.

41.   Gillispie, *The Edge of Objectivity*, 1960, 321.

42.   See Stocking, "Introduction," 1974. Stocking points out that Boas's training and scientific outlook embodied the contemporary tensions in German thought between idealism and materialism. Stocking emphasizes that Boas was influenced as much by the methodology of the natural sciences as by historicism. In

Boas's work, the tensions persist without undermining either methodology; he used both according to the problem at hand. See Stocking, "From Physics to Ethnology," 1968, and Bunzl, "Franz Boas and the Humboldtian Tradition," 1996.

43.   Lowie, "Empathy, or 'Seeing from Within,'" 1960. Lowie taught at the Department of Anthropology at the University of California, Berkeley.

44.   See Lowie, "Franz Boas," 1937.

45.   See Finn, "Ella Cara Deloria and Mourning Dove," 1995. Finn's article shows Deloria's relationship with Boas to be fraught with "the complexities and contradictions expressed by many 'native' women anthropologists" (137). Finn argues that Boas valued Deloria more as an informant than as a scholar in her own right and that he did not sufficiently appreciate the significance to her of kinship relations (including the implications to her of adopting the fictive kin relation that "Papa Franz" had with his female students; Deloria called him, more formally and respectfully, "Father Franz"). Finn's comparison of the experiences of Ella Deloria, a Sioux, and Mourning Dove, a Salish informant for the ethnographer Lucullus McWhorter, highlights their resistance to the imposition of their patrons' European and American perspectives:

> Like Boas, McWhorter was obsessed with determining the veracity of his key informant's accounts. . . . I suggest that both Mourning Dove and Deloria understood that ethnographic truth was partial, perspectival, and embedded in social and material relations of power and obligation. . . . At times Mourning Dove and Deloria voiced strong challenges to their mentors and to the stance of the Anglo ethnographer. . . . Deloria, in a letter to Boas, more bluntly states, "To go at it like a white man, for me, an Indian, is to throw up an immediate barrier between myself and the people" (140).

Also see Beatrice Medicine, "Ella Cara Deloria, 1888–1971," 1989.

46.   Lowie, "Franz Boas," 133. Lowie attributes Boas's training of European-American women (Elsie Clews Parsons, Ruth Benedict, Ruth Bunzel, Gladys Reichard, Erna Gunther, Margaret Mead, Gene Weltfish, and Ruth Underhill) to "the same urge to see aboriginal mentality in all its phases" (134). He writes: "Since primitive peoples often draw a sharp line between the sexes socially, a male observer is automatically shut out from the native wife's or mother's activities. A woman anthropologist, on the other hand, may naturally share in feminine occupations that would expose a man to ridicule" (134). For the contributions of these women to anthropology, see Gacs, Khan, McIntyre, and Weinberg, *Women Anthropologists*, 1989, and Behar and Gordon, *Women Writing Culture*, 1995.

47.   Benedict, *Patterns of Culture*, 1959 [1934], and *The Chrysanthemum and the Sword*, 1946.

48.   Benedict, "Anthropology and the Humanities," 1959, 469.

49.   Mead, "Preface," 1958, 5. Mintz writes: "The investigator must do his best to make clear what he thinks *he* is like so that readers may better judge his inter-

pretation of the life of another" ("Comment on the Study of Life History," 1973, 200).

50. The neutral, objective style of conventional ethnographic writing obscures the fact that the anthropologist's collecting and interpreting information about people's lives has a profoundly personal dimension. Crapanzano (*Tuhami*, 1980) writes: "Ever since my first experience in field work—it was with Haitians in New York City, for a course with Margaret Mead—I have been deeply concerned with the anthropologist's impress on the material he collects and his presentation of it. Anthropologists have been inclined to proclaim neutrality and even invisibility in their field work: certainly they have tended to efface themselves in their descriptive ethnographies. I have come to believe that in doing so they have acted in what Jean-Paul Sartre would call bad faith and have presented an inaccurate picture of ethnography and what it can reveal. I do not mean to imply insincerity or prevarication on the part of the individual anthropologist: I want only to call attention to a culturally constituted bias, a scotoma or blind spot, within the anthropological gaze" (ix). I find Crapanzano to be much stronger theoretically than practically on the issue of self-reflection. *Tuhami* contains almost no self-analysis, only occasional self-disclosure. Crapanzano's attraction to, choice to work with, and construction of a marginal and disturbed individual, Tuhami, seem underanalyzed despite the author's commitment to placing his self-understanding in the ethnographic frame.

51. Geertz, "From the Native's Point of View," 1976.

52. Although Geertz does not cite any sources on empathy, his conceptualization would follow that of Max Scheler, who describes empathy mainly as the direct apprehension or sharing of another's state, unmediated by symbols. Scheler also includes "emotional identification," a more complex form of empathy that is similar, I think, to Freud's concept of identification—that is, an emotional tie to a figure, especially one's parent of the same sex, who serves as a model for oneself (cf. Sigmund Freud, *Group Psychology and the Analysis of the Ego*, 1960, 46–53). Like Dilthey, Edith Stein goes further, to include an individual imaginatively stepping into the center of another's consciousness by orienting to the same objects.

53. Malinowski, *A Diary in the Strict Sense of the Term*, 1967.

54. Geertz, "From the Native's Point of View," 226.

55. Bohannan and Glazer, "Bronislaw Malinowski, 1884–1942," 1988, 272.

56. Geertz, *Works and Lives*, 1988, 9–10.

57. Krieger, "An Anthropologist and a Mystery Writer," 1991. Krieger compares Geertz's biographical approach with that of Carolyn Heilbrun (*Writing a Woman's Life*, 1988).

58. All quotations from Geertz, "Us/Not Us" in this paragraph are cited by Krieger, "An Anthropologist and a Mystery Writer," 59.

59.   The psychology of object relations, for example, concerns the development of the self as distinct from the m(other), as in the work of Melanie Klein, John Bowlby, D. W. Winnicott, and others. See Buckley, *Essential Papers on Object Relations*, 1986. Heinz Kohut (*The Restoration of the Self*, 1977) deals with empathy and narcissism as polarities that may, in my opinion, be seen as aspects of the same mirroring phenomenon; and Flax, "Lacan and Winnicott," 1990. Daniel N. Stern (*The Interpersonal World of the Infant*, 1985) explores the importance of mirroring by the mother for the infant's development of self, although he prefers to call it "affect attunement." It is also important to consider the possible protocultural phylogenetic roots of empathy and mirroring. For example, Ekman, Friesen, and Ellsworth (*Emotion in the Human Face*, 1972) argue that empathy is a panhuman phenomenon because of the universality of the facial expressions accompanying the primary emotions. This supposed universality has been challenged by ethologists and cross-cultural psychologists. Although it may be possible to "read" another's bodily emotions at a gross level, contextual experience and dialogue are generally needed to access and validate meanings.

CHAPTER 7. I-WITNESSING DIANE'S "I"

1.   Clifford, "On Ethnographic Authority," 1988; and Geertz, "I-Witnessing: Malinowski's Children," 1988. See also Van Maanen, *Tales of the Field*, 1988.

2.   Geertz, "I-Witnessing," 78, 79.

3.   Joan W. Scott ("Experience," 1992) criticizes the increasingly common use in the human sciences of the concept of "experience" as a foundation for knowledge. Like Judith Grant ("I Feel Therefore I Am," 1987), she argues that an appeal to the experience of women as a source of information about "women," for example, fails to problematize how the category *woman* is historically constructed through discourse so that certain individuals are included and others excluded. Scott's goal is to de-essentialize and denaturalize such categories as *man, woman, black, white, heterosexual,* or *homosexual* that are conventionally treated as given characteristics of individuals. Instead, she urges that we examine how discourses and practices historically construct particular kinds of individuals into particular kinds of subjects (male, female, etc.). To follow Scott, we would need to consider how Diane's experiences are historically based on discourses and practices that position and construct her as, for example, a woman or a disabled subject. I have tried to do this in chapters 4 and 5.

4.   See Ebron and Tsing, "In Dialogue?" 1995. The authors reframe minority discourses by breaking down borders between otherwise marginalized positions through dialogue. This reframing is useful at other sites of exclusion, such as in this ethnography, where the silence that conventionally protects the anthropologist/

author is broken to allow: (1) some deconstruction of my position as a detached "expert" whose experience, *because* it is seen as constructed, is of ultimately more interest, importance, and value than that of the "native," whose experience is seen as raw data belonging to a prior and now-past stage of the research; and (2) some placement of both anthropologist and native within the world system of concrete exchange, with all its asymmetry and contradictions. Insights such as these have been core to Clifford's project ("On Ethnographic Authority" and "Introduction: Partial Truths," 1986), in which he has argued for experimentation in writing texts to restore the suppressed dialogic dimension to anthropology. The turn to dialogue is supported by the arguments of Kevin Dwyer (*Moroccan Dialogues,* 1982) and Dennis Tedlock ("The Analogical Tradition and the Emergence of a Dialogical Anthropology," 1983) and by an important early work by Joseph Casagrande (*In the Company of Man,* 1960) in which anthropologists describe their relationships with key informants. Rabinow ("Representations are Social Facts,"1986) suggests that even Clifford does not take seriously enough the problem of the social referentiality of our textual mediations. I follow Rabinow in this regard.

5.   In "I-Witnessing" Geertz analyzes in detail two ethnographic works based exclusively on a fieldwork relationship with a single informant: Crapanzano, *Tuhami,* 1970, and Dwyer, *Moroccan Dialogues,* 1982. Geertz's exclusive interest in literary text-building (what happens literally on the page) screens out concrete interactions based on the mirror phenomenon because attention is solely on the formal position of anthropologist/author. The analysis lends a kind of solipsism to these works that may or may not actually be present, but in which the "native" appears—in Geertz's representation, at least—to be rather passively engaged in the research process and whose presence is reduced to that of material ("data") for textualization. The results are disquieting. According to Geertz, the imagery of these "'author-saturated,' supersaturated even, anthropological texts in which the self the text creates and the self that creates the text are represented as being very near to identical" is of "estrangement, hypocrisy, helplessness, domination, disillusion" (97). In a footnote, Geertz refers to dialogic and reflexive works in which this mood is not present. One of these, Myerhoff's *Number Our Days* (1978), is precisely about the active self-constructive work of the "natives" in relation to the anthropologist/author's simultaneous self-construction. When conflicting interests impinge on the ethnography itself, Myerhoff analyzes and deals with them face-to-face (cf. "Surviving Stories: Reflections on *Number Our Days,*" 1992) and her informants, in turn, display a lively agency.

6.   Crapanzano, *Tuhami,* 1980, x–xi.

7.   Finitude was the fundamental insight of Heidegger's interpretation of human existence in *Being and Time,* that of our being-toward-death. This insight into the temporality of "our" human situation is further conditioned by Western

concepts of death and personhood. See Frank, "Finding the Common Denominator," 1979.

8.   Field notes, March 26, 1989.

9.   The topic of longstanding friendships between women with and without disabilities has been explored ethnographically and reflexively in the study by Pendleton, "Establishment and Sustainment of Friendships of Women with Physical Disability," 1998. A phenomenological study of best friends by Becker ("Friendship between Women," 1987), for example, offers the definition:

> Friendship is a loving relationship that develops in a shared world created between the friends. For women, friendship consists of an evolving dialogue based on attributes of care, sharing, commitment, freedom, respect, trust, and equality. It is a relationship that enables each woman to be engaged in her own pursuits, her friend's experiences and her other relationships. As such, friendship provides a context for each woman becoming herself, personally and interpersonally (65).

Goldberg ("Women's Friendships—Women's Groups," 1990), a psychotherapist, proposes another definition:

> Friendship is the feeling of being understood and of understanding, a quality almost beyond empathy, of feeling into another even without words, watching another woman's struggles or joys and knowing intimately how she feels. It is allowing oneself to merge and separate, to depend and be depended on despite fears of losing others, of fusion, or of loss of self. Not just a friend in need but a friend who can support strength, achievements and joys despite feelings of envy, jealousy and competition, to affirm and be affirmed. Someone who can help us regain our objective, observing ego not only through confrontation and trust or emotional release but also through the healing of laughter. Learning to share and trust, to have something private and special to feel connected to others and not alone (398).

As Pendleton points out, these definitions stress the psychology of friendship while overlooking the occupational dimensions—i.e. what the friends do together and why these activities matter to them. The research relationship between Diane and me was not initially or primarily intended as a friendship. But it was a relationship with a distinctive set of occupations that demanded mutual commitment, required that we establish trust, involved caring and confrontation, and generated a special sense of connection. Over time, elements of friendship were developed, although not always with the same freedom and equality expected in the ideal of a friendship existing solely for its own sake.

See also Fisher and Galler ("Friendship and Fairness,"1988), who studied their own friendship dyad as a woman with a disability and one without, and also interviewed women with disabilities about their experiences in making and keeping nondisabled friends.

10.   Frank, "Detailed History of the Tribe's Land Tenure," 1980.

11.   Frank, "Crafts Production and Resistance to Domination in the Late 20th Century," 1996.

12.   Anyone who questions the fierce politics of biographical representation should read the account by Janet Malcolm ("The Silent Woman," 1993) of her efforts to research and write about the life of poet Sylvia Plath.

13.   See Hand, "Introduction," 1989; and Manning, "The Challenge of Ethics as First Philosophy," 1993.

14.   The philosophy of Levinas (1906–1995), which has been described in his own phrase as one of being "ordered toward the face of the other," may be seen as a translation of Jewish ethics and ontology into a secular Western philosophical agenda. See Levinas, "Essence and Disinterestedness," 1996 [1974].

15.   See Levinas, "Substitution," 1996 [1968]. At the same time, one must be prepared to see one's ethical obligation as unavoidable and oneself as irreplaceable in the face-to-face relation; that is to say, no one else may substitute for one's own ethical obligation. It seems to me that there is a hidden epistemology in Levinas's ethics that depends on the mirroring phenomenon I described in the previous chapter. That is, one must first recognize the Other as a fellow being toward whom one is obligated. It may seem evident today that Levinas means *any* man, or even *any* woman, but do the same ethical obligations adhere to those who are cognitively or profoundly physically different? Disability is often a dividing line for who will count as a candidate for ethical treatment. Among those sent to the ovens by the Nazis, along with the Jews, were people with disabilities. Even earlier, in Europe and the United States, people with disabilities had been candidates for racial cleansing through forced sterilization and euthanasia. See Pernick, *The Black Stork,* 1996; and Proctor, "The Destruction of Lives Not Worth Living," 1995. Note that because of her high "cognitive competence" (i.e. capacity for reason and speech), Diane does not appear to present a radical test case for ethical obligation, even though her functional challenges remain severe. This was not so clear at Diane's birth, however, before she could speak, which makes her autobiographical account of birth and infancy so compelling. In cases of severe mental impairment, including minors and infants, does Levinas still say that he is a substitute for the Other? To contemplate this question is why philosophy needs social science and why Levinas needs Diane DeVries. See also the discussion of Levinas's ethics in Bauman ("The Elusive Universality," 1993).

16.   See Crapanzano, "The Life History in Anthropological Field Work," 1977. Crapanzano refers to the alienating *"prise de conscience"* that may occur as a result of the objectification of a person's life into various textual forms, such as case history, life history, or biography. The first evidence I had of Diane's experiencing such a jolt to her awareness is described above in chapter 6. An article by Robert Stoller ("Patients' Responses to Their Own Case Reports," 1988) indicates nuanced responses by patients to their case histories, including very positive responses as well as very negative ones. In every case, however, the document provoked strong feelings that needed working through.

17.   Harris and Wideman, "The Construction of Gender and Disability in Early Attachment," 1988.

18.   I felt that I had a transference to Diane of certain aspects of my relationship with my mother, although my identification with Diane and attraction to the project of documenting her life has other sources, too. Related to my mother was the feeling that Diane seemed to be denying me the right to voice my own version of our relationship and, therefore, to have my own experience. Of course Diane could not deny this to me, and I could understand very well her objections to the paper I had written. After all, I had *chosen* the role of empathic listener with Diane, while it was demanded by my mother as a condition of getting her attention. This dilemma was described in Alice Miller's book, *The Drama of the Gifted Child* (1981), which captured a great deal of my childhood experience. Miller describes the situation of an emotionally sensitive child who is expected to use her talents to provide an empathic audience or mirror for a narcissistic parent. Waiting to hear from Diane, I found myself resenting having to second-guess what her silence meant. In my fieldnotes, I wrote that "this kind of active use of self to construct another's world no longer interests me as much as it did at the start of our project." This shift in my motivation probably signaled the successful conclusion of my project with Diane as a form of self-therapy, although the project remained alive in other aspects. The failure of my relationship with my psychoanalyst around this time can be seen as another version of the problem described above, in which it appeared that my version of reality had to be subordinated to hers in order for the relationship to survive. My paper for the Norway conference can be seen as my "acting out" the conflict with my analyst. Too deterministic an interpretation should be avoided, since if Diane had substantially agreed with what I had written, there would be no need to account retrospectively for the breach.

19.   Pachter, "The Biographer Himself," 1979.

20.   Qualitative researchers are increasingly reporting tensions in their relationships with informants. I believe that this is a sign not that standards of professionalism are declining but that we are willing to face more honestly the complexity of such relationships. See, for example, Bloom, "Locked in Uneasy Sisterhood," 1997. Also see Josselson, *Ethics and Process in The Narrative Study of Lives,* 1996, and the Personal Narratives Group, *Interpreting Women's Lives,* 1989, especially the essays by Marks, "The Context of Personal Narrative"; Mbilinyi, " 'I'd Have Been a Man' "; Shostak, " 'What the Wind Won't Take Away' "; and Prell, "The Double Frame of Life History in the Work of Barbara Myerhoff." Also see Kulick and Willson, *Taboo,* 1995, and Lewin and Leap, *Out in the Field,* 1996.

21.   Letter from Diane DeVries to Gelya Frank, August 27, 1992.

22.   Frank, "Myths of Creation," 1996.

23.   Field notes, June 30, 1993.

24.   See Powdermaker, *Stranger and Friend,* 1966, which set a high standard for honest and compassionate self-examination concerning the complex emotions and ethical dilemmas of fieldwork.

25.   Transcript of meeting, November 24, 1992. In our videotaped interview by Carolyn Rouse, in spring 1995, Diane described her confronting me over the Norway paper as the point at which she gained power in our relationship, whereas previously she had felt "intimidated," beginning in 1976 with my being her TA. Although I was indeed a teaching assistant in the lecture course, Diane was not assigned to my discussion section, and I was not responsible for giving her a grade. This points to the real potential for the inflation of researchers' power when they are perceived as authority figures.

26.   Graff, "Co-optation," 1989.

27.   Gadamer, *Truth and Method,* 1975 [1960], 223. Here Gadamer is discussing Heidegger's solution to certain inadequacies of Dilthey and Husserl in dealing with the problem of intersubjectivity. In particular, Heidegger drew on the fragmentary writings of the philosopher Graf Yorck, who in turn drew on the phenomenology of life as described by Georg W. F. Hegel (1770–1831). Gadamer also uses the term *application* to get at the way that a text opens to and merges with its "other" in the world. See also Ricoeur, "Appropriation," 1981.

28.   See Williams, "René Descartes," 1967. Descartes's (1596–1650) *Discourse on Method* was published in 1637. Toulmin (*Cosmopolis,* 1990) places Descartes's thought in a historicist and biographical context.

29.   Sartre, *Saint Genet,* 1963 [1952], 592. Note that Sartre's (1905–1980) existentialism is a branch of the phenomenological movement (Spiegelberg, *The Phenomenological Movement,* 1976).

30.   Olney, *Metaphors of Self,* 1972, vii. Olney acknowledges the influence of Georges Gusdorf's work, particularly an article originally published in 1956 that Olney later translated ("Conditions and Limits of Autobiography," 1980). Gusdorf noted that the urge to recollect and narrate one's own life was not a universal human phenomenon, but a product of particular cultural and historical conditions. He further emphasized the nonidentity of the narrator with his or her narration, which, although a double of the narrator, is nevertheless a constructed self-image only. It may be said that Olney's literary focus in autobiography concerned that constructed self-image, whereas Gusdorf leaned more psychologically and sociologically toward elaborating the sources of ambiguity and incoherence against which an autobiography is created.

31.   Fox-Genovese ("Claims of a Common Culture, or, Whose Autobiography?" 1991) argues against the presumed universality of the unitary (male) subject of Western civilization and for the need to replace it. In her words, the Western canon "assumes individualism as defined by men . . . to represent the

purpose and embodiment of civilization" (171), but it is "an individualism designed for the benefit of the few, universalist rhetoric notwithstanding" (187). See also Friedman, "Women's Autobiographical Selves," 1988; and Smith, "The Universal Subject, Female Embodiment, and the Consolidation of Autobiography," 1993. The alternative ways in which selves have been constructed in autobiographical writings by women in diverse cultural traditions and sociohistorical contexts have been discussed by Benstock, *The Private Self,* 1988; Braxton, *Black Women Writing Autobiography,* 1989; Brodzki and Schenk, *Life/Lines,* 1988; Jelinek, *Women's Autobiography,* 1980, and *The Tradition of Women's Autobiography,* 1986; Personal Narratives Group, *Interpreting Women's Lives,* 1989; Smith, *Subjectivity, Identity, and the Body,* 1993; Stanley, *The Auto/biographical I,* 1992; and Stanton, *The Female Autograph,* 1984. Braxton expresses feminist concerns to discover an expanded and more interdependent "self" when she writes: "Black women's autobiography is also an occasion for viewing the individual in relation to those others with whom she shares emotional, philosophical, and spiritual affinities, as well as political realities" (9). She also argues persuasively for looking to other kinds of sources and texts for the autobiographical "Afra-American" self than within the confines of the conventional genre of autobiography.

CHAPTER 8. THE WOMEN IN DIANE'S BODY

1.   I play on the title of Emily Martin's book *The Woman in the Body,* 1987, an ethnography of American women's experiences of menstruation, pregnancy, and birth according to race and class. Martin emphasizes the influence of material conditions on women's experiences of supposedly natural and universal biological functions.

2.   Benstock, *The Private Self,* 18, 19.

3.   For a cultural analysis of this theme based in the intergenerational exchange practices of a non-Western society see Hoskins, *The Play of Time,* 1993.

4.   The opening scenario of this book, with me viewing Diane in the lecture hall, can be analyzed as a form of scopophilia (Mulvey, "Visual Pleasure and Narrative Cinema," 1985). Like the critics discussed earlier in this book of the transcendental male subject in philosophy, Mulvey describes male visual pleasure as the controlling pleasure in cinema. She identifies two forms: scopophilic pleasure linked to sexual attraction (voyeurism) and to narcissistic identification (introjection of ideal egos). Although feminist alternatives to Mulvey's perspective have been proposed, her insights remain important. Concerning voyeurism, she writes:

> Originally, in his *Three Essays on Sexuality,* Freud isolated scopophilia as one of the component instincts of sexuality which exist as drives quite independently of the erotogenic zones. At this point he associated scopohilia with taking other people as

objects, subjecting them to a controlling and curious gaze. His particular examples center around the voyeuristic activities of children, their desire to see and make sure of the private and the forbidden (curiosity about other people's genital and bodily functions, about the presence or absence of the penis and, retrospectively, about the primal scene. . . . Although the instinct is modified by other factors, in particular the constitution of the ego, it continues to exist as the erotic basis for pleasure in looking at another person as object (307).

Hélène Cixous ("The Newly Born Woman," 1981, 95, quoted by Dallery, "The Politics of Writing (The) Body," 1989, 55) argues against the *specular* in the psychoanalytic theories of Freud and Lacan, which depend on exteriority—that is, the body as *seen* by self and other, which she calls: "A voyeur's theory, of course."

5.   This theme, evoking the "dark" side of the Enlightenment, is examined by Horkheimer and Adorno, *Dialectic of Enlightenment,* 1972 [1944]. For a more recent exposition of related ideas, see Morrison, *Playing in the Dark,* 1990, particularly her discussion of "the historical connection between the Enlightenment and the institution of slavery—the rights of man and his enslavement" (42).

6.   See Derrida, "Violence and Metaphysics," 1978. Also see Levinas, *Otherwise than Being, or Beyond Essence,* 1991.

7.   See Spivak, "Translator's Preface," 1976. For discussions of the political implications of Derridean deconstruction for feminism, particularly the deconstruction of the (female) subject, see Grosz, "Ontology and Equivocation," 1997, and Kamuf, "Deconstruction and Feminism," 1997.

8.   Geertz, "Thick Description," 1973. Geertz's interpretative anthropology depends on the ethnographer writing "thick description"—description so rich that outside interpreters can get a sense of the layers of meaning insiders would use to negotiate the situations described. My debt to Geertz's interpretative anthropology should be obvious. I mean simply that even a thick description remains a description only, not a life.

9.   Derrida, "Deconstruction and the Other," 1984, quoted in Grosz, "Ontology and Equivocation," 99.

10.   Giddens, *Modernity and Self-Identity,* 1991.

11.   Gergen, *The Saturated Self,* 1991.

12.   Lyotard, *The Postmodern Condition,* 1984 [1979].

13.   Jameson, "Foreword," 1984, viii, ix.

14.   These are the old problems of reliability and validity that were addressed with extreme thoroughness by Gordon Allport, *The Use of Personal Documents in Psychological Science,* 1942. Most qualitative researchers have not completely abandoned the criterion of reliability, but the notion of validity has become even more important than before, and new definitions have been proposed. For an excellent overview see Krefting, "Rigor in Qualitative Research," 1991. Also see Mishler, *Research Interviewing,* 1986, and "Validation in Inquiry-Guided Research," 1990; and Hammersley, *Reading Ethnographic Research,* 1990.

15.   See Clifford and Marcus, *Writing Culture,* 1986; Marcus and Fischer, *Anthropology as Cultural Critique,* 1986; and, for a perspective on anthropology's colonial past, Gough, "Anthropology: Child of Imperialism," 1968.

16.   Lila Abu-Lughod (*Writing Women's Worlds,* 1993) uses stories to "write against culture," seeking to avoid descriptions of non-Westerners that are static, exoticized, and overgeneralized. Also see Behar and Gordon, *Women Writing Culture,* 1995. "Writing against the grain" is the term used by Faye V. Harrison ("Writing against the Grain," 1995) to talk about the production of narratives by women and members of ethnic minorities that are devalued in the academic mainstream. See also Finn, "Ella Cara Deloria and Mourning Dove," 1995, which is discussed in chapter 6.

17.   This insight was probably first realized anthropologically by Marcel Maus, writing on the concept of *habitus,* which since has been elaborated on by Bourdieu, *Outline of a Theory of Practice,* 1977. In the United States, medical anthropologists have led the way to a renewed interest in the body. See Scheper-Hughes and Lock, "The Mindful Body," 1987; Scheper-Hughes, "Embodied Knowledge," 1994; DiGiacomo, "Metaphor as Illness," 1992; Frank, "On Embodiment," 1986; and Csordas, *Embodiment and Experience,* 1994.

18.   I have in mind Gershom Scholem and Walter Benjamin's linguistic and materialist elaborations on the Kabbalistic theory of God's creation through an act not of proliferation but of self-contraction (in Hebrew, *tzimtzum*). See Handelman, *Fragments of Redemption,* 1991.

19.   Spiegelberg, "The Phenomenological Philosophy of Maurice Merleau-Ponty (1908–1961)," in *The Phenomenological Movement,* 1976.

20.   Interview transcript, October 21, 1976.

21.   Tape-recorded interview, 1976, quoted in Frank, "On Embodiment," 1988, 43.

22.   Frank, "On Embodiment," 50.

23.   Frank, "On Embodiment," 50.

24.   Mattingly, *Healing Dramas and Clinical Plots,* 1998.

25.   Frank, "On Embodiment," 51.

26.   Frank, "On Embodiment," 43.

27.   With Drew Leder (*The Absent Body,* 1990), I question the dualistic distinction in philosophy, and embedded in the German language, between *Korper* (the physical body) and *Leib* (the living body). Leder's phenomenology of the body is an extension of the work of Merleau-Ponty, which was cut off by the earlier philosopher's untimely death. Following Merleau-Ponty's interest in perception and motility, Leder describes how the horizon of human experience and action partly depends on aspects of embodiment that are impersonal and often beyond our awareness (such as the autonomous rhythms of breathing and circulation, digestion, sleep, the corpse). These are among the various forms of "experiential absence," which include the "ecstatic body" (having one's awareness centered

outside one's body), the "recessive body" (having only limited awareness and sensation of the processes of the internal organs), and the "dys-appearing" body (experiences of the body that are self-alienating, in part because others cannot perceive or understand them, as in the case of pain). Presence/absence, in Leder's analysis, as in the views of his predecessors, is crucially related to the "gaze" or sense of sight—that is, how the body appears to oneself (first-person point of view) and to others (third-person point of view). (Note the similarity to Freud and Lacan in Cixous's critique above, note 4.) In the case of Diane DeVries, the medical gaze and my own layperson's gaze are not well prepared to deal with the ambiguities of Diane's body, and the resultant tendency is to impose a definitive, normalizing language. For a discussion of the "medical gaze" see Foucault, *The Birth of the Clinic*, 1973 [1963], and DelVecchio-Good and Good, "Learning Medicine," 1993.

28.   Michael pressed Diane to have Pasqual, her former boyfriend with quadriplegia, whom she met as a teenager at Rancho, play himself in the film. He insisted on recreating intimate scenes between Diane and Pasqual. Neither Diane nor Pasqual was comfortable with this decision. While videotaping them on a UCLA sound stage, Michael asked Pasqual to show more emotion.

"What's the matter," Michael probed. "Didn't you once feel for Diane?"

"Yes," Pasqual responded. "But it's hard to do it knowing that it's just for the film and will be over."

"Go up and touch her, kiss her," Michael urged.

Later Diane expressed her outrage that Michael wanted to film a love scene in bed.

"You were in love with him. You carried his baby," Michael replied.

"But you don't have to *show* it," Diane protested.

"Did you talk to Pasqual about this? I'll do it, but I doubt if Pasqual will do it. I know him and he's not going to make love with me in front of people or pretend to."

Diane complained to me that Michael had completely changed the direction of the film since it started: "It used to be, 'Here's a girl who has all these problems and look how far she's come.' Now it's a Pasqual and Diane love story." Field notes, November 17, 1976.

CHAPTER 9. CONCLUSION: TRULY YOUR DIANE

1.   Werner and Smith, *Vulnerable but Invincible*, 1982, and *Overcoming the Odds*, 1992. Also see Nichol, *Longitudinal Studies in Child Psychology and Psychiatry*, 1985; and Fine, "Resilience and Human Adaptability," 1991.

2.   The dialogue between Diane and her father is quoted from DeVries, "Autobiography," n.d.

3.   This informal interview occurred on January 26, 1977, while I was being accompanied by Susan Clarke, Diane's occupational therapist at CAPP, through the corridors of the facility to photocopy Diane's medical records from CAPP and Rancho Los Amigos. Dr. Brooks told me he was not too disappointed that Diane had decided not to use prostheses. But he was critical because she had gained a great deal of weight (which he saw as the result of her living with her boyfriend), a choice that he felt left her little means of gratifying herself except with food and sex. Nevertheless, Dr. Brooks expected Diane to have a more fulfilling life and possibly to make a greater contribution than other former patients who may have appeared more brilliant and career-driven. He thought it was unlikely that Diane would be able to obtain a service position because she lacked arms, but he thought she might become a writer.

4.   Yoshio Setoguchi, medical director, Child Amputee Prosthetics Project, to Mrs. Margaret Peeples, UCLA Medical Center Auxiliary, University of California Medical Center, March 25, 1975.

5.   Irene Fields wrote the date, August 4, 1953. The source is missing.

6.   Harris, "Pair of Red Shoes Tiny Girl's Dream," 1954.

7.   For an insightful and amusing semiotic analysis of blondness and its implications about personality and character in North American culture, see McCracken, *Big Hair*, 1995.

8.   See also Oliver Williams, "Friends Seek Funds to Give Little Girl Plastic Legs" [source and date missing, probably 1956]. Kiwanis is a worldwide organization founded in 1915, in Detroit, Michigan, whose purpose is "Service to Youth and the Elderly, to Community and Nation." Kiwanis International is made up of eighty-seven hundred clubs with more than 330,000 members (290,014 men and 38,792 women) in eighty-three nations and geographic areas. Source: Letter with enclosures from Ellen Hardin, administrative secretary, Member Services Department, Kiwanis International, Indianapolis, Indiana, August 11, 1993. Kiwanis raised money for the rehabilitation of other children with quadrilateral limb deficiencies born near Diane's birthplace of Denison, Texas, including Freddie Thomason and Cindy Inman. Prostheses can be made and sold commercially without a medical prescription. Diane's first artificial limbs were made commercially by a prosthetist in San Diego and no physician was regularly associated with her case. Source: Letter from R. F. Chittenden, M.D., Newport Beach, to Miss Ogg and Mrs. Dunigan, Prosthesis Clinic, Department of Pediatrics, UCLA School of Medicine, Los Angeles, February 20, 1955.

9.   "Teenage March of Dimes Dance" [source and date missing, probably 1961]. On January 3, 1938, President Franklin Delano Roosevelt established the National Foundation for Infantile Paralysis, a private voluntary organization. Comedian Eddie Cantor coined the phrase "March of Dimes," which became synonymous with the foundation. The March of Dimes (MOD) supported

research including the discovery by Dr. Jonas Salk in 1953 of a killed-virus vaccine for polio. In 1958, MOD expanded its focus to include the prevention and treatment of birth defects, with an emphasis on genetics. In 1979, the name of the foundation was officially changed to March of Dimes Birth Defects Foundation. Source: "March of Dimes Milestones," pamphlet published by the March of Dimes Birth Defects Foundation, National Headquarters, Communications Department, White Plains, NY, 1988.

10.   "At Kick-off Luncheon" [source and date missing, probably 1963].

11.   "All Aboard for Camp," *The Los Angeles Examiner* [date missing].

12.   Shrine is a philanthropic organization, founded in New York City in 1872 by two Freemasons, that has established and supported facilities for children with physical disabilities and critical injuries. Its official name, Ancient Arabic Order of the Nobles of the Mystic Shrine (A.A.O.N.M.S.), is an acronym for the words "A Mason." The organization is composed solely of men who are thirty-second-degree Scottish Rite Masons or Knights Templar York Rite Masons, and there are currently about 690,000 members in North America. In 1922, a membership of more than 350,000 committed itself to the philanthropic mission of establishing a Shriners Hospital for Crippled Children in Shreveport, Louisiana, which provided free orthopedic treatment to minors with physical disabilities from families otherwise unable to pay. In the 1960s, the Shrine began funding laboratory research that could be applied to orthopedics. During the 1980s, Shriners Hospitals expanded their prosthetic services by founding regional programs. Consequently, in 1987, the Los Angeles Shriners Hospital "adopted" the Child Amputee Prosthetics Project (CAPP). Source: *A Short History of the Ancient Arabic Order of the Nobles of the Mystic Shrine,* Shrine General Offices, Tampa, FL, 1992, and related brochures, "Who Are the Shriners and What Is the Shrine?" and "20 Questions, 1992–1993: The Shrine of North America and Shriners Hospitals for Crippled Children."

13.   Vera Williams, "Armless, Legless Swimmer Stars in Handicapped Children's Aqua Show" [source and date missing, possibly 1963]. According to Diane, she was thirteen rather than twelve years old at this, her last performance.

14.   Clifford, "Introduction: Partial Truths,"1986.

15.   Mintz, "The Sensation of Moving, While Standing Still," 1989.

16.   Mintz, "The Sensation of Moving, While Standing Still," 786.

17.   Dwyer, *Moroccan Dialogues,* 1982.

18.   Dossa, "Critical Anthropology and Life Stories," 1994, 350.

19.   Stoller, "Patients' Responses to Their Own Case Reports," 1988, 389, 391.

20.   Dollard, *Criteria for the Life History,* 1935, 8.

21.   Herdt and Stoller, *Intimate Communications,* 1990, 49.

22.   See, for example, Fiedler, *Freaks,* 1978.

23.   Bogdan, *Freak Show,* 1988, 1.

24.   The writer went on to mirror her unclarified emotions about her own sister, who had a disability:

> Please do not misconstrue this letter and think that I am suggesting that you put Diane in the Circus or anything like that, I was thinking how much she could learn from this girl, in my own family we had a sad case, my young sister was horribly crippled from Multiple Sclerosis and in a wheel chair for many years, she was kept at home for years and she got into such a rut, thinking she was the only one so afflicted, I begged my brother-in-law to take her to a clinic where she would see many cases of M.S. and see others much worse off than she, we did end up at a wonderful clinic in Tacoma where there were 300 such cases and it did give her morale a big boost, sorry to say she was too far gone to be helped and she passed away in 1952, of course that isn't what Diane needs, she looks so healthy but I am sure that when she is older, it would be wonderful for her to meet other people who have the same problem as she has and I couldn't help but to write to you and offer what knowledge I have. If you are ever out this way I would be very pleased to have you call on me, I think Diane is just precious and would like to send her a little gift, does she like dolls or what would she like?

25.   DeVries, "Autobiography."

26.   DeVries, "Autobiography."

27.   White, *Barriers to Employment and the Adaptive Strategies Used to Overcome Them*, 1998.

28.   Louis Harris and Associates, *The ICD Survey of Disabled Americans*, 1986, 14. People in the survey were less likely to consider themselves disabled who were younger, less severely disabled, and younger when their disability was acquired.

29.   Stone, *The Disabled State*, 1984.

30.   Ablon, *Little People in America*, 1984.

31.   Braun, "Graduating from UCLA the Hard Way," 1987, 3.

32.   Abu-Lughod, *Writing Women's Worlds*, 1993. Some methodological recommendations to apply the concept of "tactical humanism" to ethnography are suggested by Knauft, "Pushing Anthropology Past the Posts," 1994.

Bibliography

Ablon, Joan.
   1984. *Little People in America*. New York: Praeger.

Abu-Lughod, Lila.
   1993. *Writing Women's Worlds: Bedouin Stories*. Berkeley: University of California Press.

Allport, Gordon.
   1942. *The Use of Personal Documents in Psychological Science*. New York: Social Science Research Council.

Appadurai, Arjun.
   1996. *Modernity at Large: Cultural Dimensions of Globalization*. Minneapolis: University of Minnesota Press.

Asch, Adrienne, and Michelle Fine.
   1988. "Introduction: Beyond Pedestals." In *Women with Disabilities: Essays in Psychology, Culture, and Politics,* ed. M. Fine and A. Asch, 1–37. Philadelphia: Temple University Press.

Augustine, Saint.

1961 *The Confessions of Saint Augustine.* Translated by E. B. Pusey. New York: Collier Books.

Bachelard, Gaston.

1964. *The Psychoanalysis of Fire.* Translated by A. C. M. Ross. Boston: Beacon Press.

Baldwin, Marjorie L.

1997. "Gender Differences in Social Security Disability Decisions." *Journal of Disability Policy Studies* 8:25–50.

Banner, Lois W.

1983. *American Beauty.* New York: Alfred A. Knopf.

1995. *Women in Modern America: A Brief History.* 3d ed. Fort Worth: Harcourt Brace College Publishers.

Barker, Roger G.

1977 [1953]. *Adjustment to Physical Handicap and Illness: A Survey of the Social Psychology of Physique and Disability.* Milwood, NY: Kraus Reprint Co.

Barnartt, Sharon N.

1996. "Disability Culture or Disability Consciousness?" *Journal of Disability Policy Studies* 7:1–19.

Barnartt, Sharon N., and Barbara M. Altman.

1997. "Predictors of Wages: Comparisons by Gender and Type of Impairment." *Journal of Disability Policy Studies* 8:51–74.

Bar-On, Dan.

1995. *Fear and Hope: Three Generations of the Holocaust.* Cambridge: Harvard University Press.

Baseheart, Mary Catharine.

1996. "Edith Stein's Philosophy of Woman and of Women's Education." In *Hypatia's Daughters: Fifteen Hundred Years of Women Philosophers,* ed. L. Lopez McAlister, 267–79. Bloomington: Indiana University Press.

Bassard, Katherine Clay.

1998. *Spiritual Interrogations: Culture, Gender, and Community in Early African American Women's Writings.* Princeton: Princeton University Press.

Bateson, Mary Catherine.

1989. *Composing a Life.* New York: Penguin Books.

Bauman, Zygmunt.

1993. "The Elusive Universality." In *Postmodern Ethics,* 37–61. Oxford: Blackwell.

Becker, Alton.
  1979. "Text Building, Epistemology, and Aesthetics in Javanese Shadow Theater." In *The Imagination of Reality,* ed. A. Becker and A. Yengoyan, 211–43.
  New Jersey: Ablex.

Becker, Carol S.
  1987. "Friendship between Women: A Phenomenological Study of Best
  Friends." *Journal of Phenomenological Psychology* 18:59–72.

Becker, Gay.
  1997. *Disrupted Lives: How People Create Meaning in a Chaotic World.* Berkeley:
  University of California Press.

Behar, Ruth.
  1993. "The Biography in the Shadow." In *Translated Woman: Crossing the Border with Esperanza's Story,* 320–42. Boston: Beacon Press.

  1993. *Translated Woman: Crossing the Border with Esperanza's Story.* Boston:
  Beacon Press.

  1996. *The Vulnerable Observer: Anthropology That Breaks Your Heart.* Boston:
  Beacon Press.

Behar, Ruth, and Deborah A. Gordon, eds.
  1995. *Women Writing Culture.* Berkeley: University of California Press.

Bellah, Robert N., Richard Madsen, William M. Sullivan, Ann Swidler, and
Steven M. Tipton.
  1985. *Habits of the Heart: Individualism and Commitment in American Life.*
  Berkeley: University of California Press.

Benedict, Ruth.
  1959 [1934]. *Patterns of Culture.* Boston: Houghton Mifflin.

  1946. *The Chrysanthemum and the Sword: Patterns of Japanese Culture.* Boston:
  Houghton Mifflin.

  1959. Anthropology and the Humanities." In *An Anthropologist at Work: Writings of Ruth Benedict,* ed. Margaret Mead, 459–70. Boston: Houghton Mifflin.

Benstock, Shari, ed.
  1988. *The Private Self: Theory and Practice of Women's Autobiographical Writings.*
  Chapel Hill: University of North Carolina Press.

Berkowitz, Edward D.
  1987. *Disabled Policy: America's Programs for the Handicapped.* Cambridge:
  Cambridge University Press.

Bertaux, Daniel, ed.
  1981. *Biography and Society: The Life History Approach in the Social Sciences.*
  Beverly Hills: Sage.

Bertaux, Daniel, and Martin Kohli.
   1984. The Life Story Approach: A Continental View." *Annual Review of Sociology* 10:215–37.

Berubé, Michael.
   1996. *Life As We Know It.* New York: Pantheon.

Bhabha, Homi K.
   1994. *The Location of Culture.* London: Routledge.

Blackwood, Evelyn.
   1995. Falling in Love with an-Other Lesbian: Reflections on Identity in Fieldwork." In *Taboo: Sex, Identity and Erotic Subjectivity in Anthropological Fieldwork,* ed. D. Kulick and M. Willson, 51–75. London: Routledge.

Blakeslee, Berton, ed.
   1963. *The Limb-Deficient Child.* Berkeley: University of California Press.

Bloom, Leslie Rebecca.
   1997. "Locked in Uneasy Sisterhood: Reflections on Feminist Methodology and Research Relations." *Anthropology and Education Quarterly* 28:111–22.

Bogdan, Robert.
   1988. *Freak Show: Presenting Human Oddities for Amusement and Profit.* Chicago: University of Chicago Press.

Bohannan, Paul, and Mark Glazer.
   1988. "Bronislaw Malinowski, 1884–1942." In *High Points in Anthropology,* 2d ed., 272–75. New York: McGraw-Hill.

Bordo, Susan.
   1993. "Feminism, Postmodernism, and Gender Skepticism." In *Unbearable Weight: Feminism, Western Culture, and the Body,* 215–43. Berkeley: University of California Press.

Bosk, Charles L.
   1992. *All God's Mistakes: Genetic Counseling in a Pediatric Hospital.* Chicago: University of Chicago Press.

Bourdieu, Pierre.
   1977 [1972]. *Outline of a Theory of Practice.* Translated by R. Nice. Cambridge: Cambridge University Press.

Braun, Stephen.
   1987. "Graduating from UCLA the Hard Way." *Los Angeles Times,* June 15, part I, 3.

Braxton, Joanne M.
   1989. *Black Women Writing Autobiography: A Tradition within a Tradition.* Philadelphia: Temple University Press.

Brenner, Johanna.
1996. "The Best of Times, the Worst of Times: Feminism in the United States." *Mapping the Women's Movement: Feminist Politics and Social Transformation in the North,* ed. M. Threlfall, 17–72. London: Verso.

Brodzki, Bella, and Celeste Schenk, eds.
1988. *Life/Lines: Theorizing Women's Autobiography.* Ithaca: Cornell University Press.

Brown, Karen McCarthy.
1991. *Mama Lola: A Vodou Priestess in Brooklyn.* Berkeley: University of California Press.

Browne, Susan E., Debra Connors, and Nanci Stern, eds.
1985. *With the Power of Each Breath: A Disabled Women's Anthology.* Pittsburgh and San Francisco: Cleis Press.
Bruner, Jerome.
1990. *Acts of Meaning.* Cambridge: Harvard University Press.

Buckley, Peter, ed.
1986. *Essential Papers on Object Relations.* New York: New York University Press.

Bunzl, Matti.
1996. "Franz Boas and the Humboldtian Tradition: From *Volksgeist* and *Nationalcharakter* to an Anthropological Concept of Culture." In *Volksgeist as Method and Ethic: Essays on Boasian Ethnography and the German Anthropological Tradition,* ed. G. W. Stocking Jr., 17–78. Madison: University of Wisconsin Press.

Butler, Judith.
1990. *Gender Trouble: Feminism and the Subversion of Identity.* New York: Routledge.

Cadish, Barry.
1976. "UCLA Project Aids Limbless." *Daily Bruin,* April 15, 1.

Campbell, Joseph.
1949. *The Hero with a Thousand Faces.* Princeton: Princeton University Press.

Campling, Jo, ed.
1981. *Images of Ourselves: Women with Disabilities Talking.* London: Routledge and Kegan Paul.

Carabillo, Toni, Judith Meuli, and June Bundy Csida.
1993. *Feminist Chronicles, 1953–1993.* Los Angeles: Women's Graphics.

Casagrande, Joseph B., ed.
1960. *In the Company of Man: Twenty Portraits by Anthropologists.* New York: Harper and Brothers Publishers.

Cassuto, Leonard.
    1999. "Whose Field Is It Anyway? Disability Studies in the Academy." *Chronicle of Higher Education*, March 19, A60.

Castilla, Eduardo.
    1992. "Limb Reduction Defects, 1988–1989." In *International Clearinghouse for Birth Defects Monitoring Systems*, Annual Report, 64–70. Rome: International Centre for Birth Defects.

Centers, Louise, and Richard Centers.
    1963. "Peer Group Attitudes toward the Amputee Child." *Journal of Social Psychology* 61:27–132.

Challenor, Yasoma B., Leela Rangaswamy, and Jacob F. Katz.
    1982. "Limb Deficiency in Infancy and Childhood." In *The Child with Disabling Illness: Principles of Rehabilitation*, ed. J. A. Downey and N. L. Low, 409–47. New York: Raven Press.

Charlton, James I.
    1998. *Nothing About Us Without Us: Disability Oppression and Empowerment*. Berkeley: University of California Press.

Chin, Soo-Young.
    1999. *Doing What Has to Be Done: The Life Narrative of Dora Yum Kim*. Philadelphia: Temple University Press.

Cixous, Hélène.
    1981. "The Newly Born Woman." In *New French Feminisms*, ed. E. Marks and I. de Courtivron. New York: Schocken.

Clark, Florence.
    1993. "Occupation Embedded in a Real Life: Interweaving Occupational Science and Occupational Therapy." *American Journal of Occupational Therapy* 47:1067–78.

Clifford, James.
    1988 [1983]. "On Ethnographic Authority." In *The Predicament of Culture: Twentieth-Century Ethnography, Literature, and Art*, 21–54. Cambridge: Harvard University Press.

    1986. "Introduction: Partial Truths." In *Writing Culture: The Poetics and Politics of Ethnography*, ed. J. Clifford and G. E. Marcus, 1–26. Berkeley: University of California Press.

    1988. *The Predicament of Culture: Twentieth-Century Ethnography, Literature, and Art*. Cambridge: Harvard University Press.

Clifford, James, and George E. Marcus, eds.
    1986. *Writing Culture: The Poetics and Politics of Ethnography*. Berkeley: University of California Press.

Conrad, Peter, and Joseph W. Schneider.
  1992. *Deviance and Medicalization: From Badness to Sickness*. Rev. ed. Philadelphia: Temple University Press.

Corbin, Juliet M., and Anselm Strauss.
  1987. "Accompaniments in Chronic Illness: Changes in Body, Self, Biography, and Biographical Time." In *Research in the Sociology of Health Care*, ed. J. Roth and P. Conrad, 6:249–81. Greenwich, CT: JAI.

  1988. *Unending Work and Care: Managing Chronic Illness at Home*. San Francisco: Jossey-Bass.

Couser, G. Thomas.
  1997. *Recovering Bodies: Illness, Disability, and Life Writing*. Madison: University of Wisconsin Press.

Crapanzano, Vincent.
  1977. "The Life History in Anthropological Field Work." *Anthropology and Humanism Quarterly* 2:3–7.

  1980. *Tuhami: Portrait of a Moroccan*. Chicago: University of Chicago Press.

Crewe, Nancy M., and Irving Kenneth Zola, eds.
  1983. *Independent Living for Physically Disabled People*. San Francisco: Jossey-Bass.

Csordas, Thomas J., ed.
  1994. *Embodiment and Experience: The Existential Ground of Culture and Self*. Cambridge: Cambridge University Press.

Curtiss, Susan.
  1977. *Genie: A Psycholinguistic Study of a Modern-Day "Wild Child."* San Diego: Academic Press.

Daines, Victoria, and David Seddon.
  1993. "Confronting Austerity: Responses to Economic Reform." In *Women's Lives and Public Policy: The International Experience*, ed. M. Turshen and B. Holcomb, 3–32. Westport, CT: Greenwood Press.

Dallery, Arleen B.
  1989. "The Politics of Writing (the) Body." In *Gender/Body/Knowledge: Feminist Reconstructions of Being and Knowing*, ed. A. M. Jaggar and S. R. Bordo, 52–67. New Brunswick, NJ: Rutgers University Press.

Dart, John.
  1998. "Sainthood for Jewish Convert Stirs Debate." *Los Angeles Times*, October 10, B4.

Davis, Fred.
  1963. *Passage through Crisis*. Indianapolis: Bobbs-Merrill.

Davis, Lennard J., ed.

1997. *The Disability Studies Reader.* New York: Routledge.

Davis, Mike.

1990. *City of Quartz: Excavating the Future in Los Angeles.* New York: Vintage Books.

Deegan, Mary Jo, and Nancy A. Brooks, ed.

1985. *Women and Disability: The Double Handicap.* New Brunswick, NJ: Transaction Books.

DeJong, Gerben.

1983 [1979]. "Defining and Implementing the Independent Living Concept." In *Independent Living for Physically Disabled People,* ed. N. Crewe and I. Zola, 4–27. San Francisco: Jossey-Bass.

Delgado, Richard.

1997. "Rodrigo's Eleventh Chronicle: Empathy and False Empathy." In *Critical White Studies: Looking behind the Mirror,* ed. R. Delgado and J. Stephancic, 614–18. Philadelphia: Temple University Press.

DelVecchio-Good, Mary-Jo, and Byron Good.

1993. "Learning Medicine: The Construction of Medical Knowledge at Harvard Medical School." In *Knowledge, Power, and Practice: The Anthropology of Medicine and Everyday Life,* ed. S. Lindenbaum and M. Lock, 91–107. Berkeley: University of California Press.

DeNitto, Dennis.

1985. *Film: Form and Feeling.* New York: Harper and Row.

Denzin, Norman K.

1989. *Interpretive Biography.* Newbury Park, CA: Sage.

Derrida, Jacques.

1976 [1967]. *Of Grammatology.* Translated by G. C. Spivak. Baltimore: Johns Hopkins University Press.

1978. "Violence and Metaphysics: An Essay on the Thought of Emmanuel Levinas." In *Writing and Difference.* Translated by A. Bass, 79–153. Chicago: University of Chicago Press.

1984. "Deconstruction and the Other." In *Dialogues with Contemporary Continental Thinkers—The Phenomenological Heritage: Paul Ricoeur, Emmanuel Levinas, Herbert Marcuse, Stanislas Breton, Jacques Derrida.* Translated by R. Kearney, 105–26. Manchester: Manchester University Press.

Devereux, George.

1951. *Reality and Dream: Psychotherapy of a Plains Indian.* New York: International Universities Press.

1967. *From Anxiety to Method in the Behavioral Sciences.* The Hague: Mouton.

DeVries, Diane.
   1981. "So When I Tell You I Love You . . . " In G. Frank, "Venus on Wheels: The Life History of a Congenital Amputee." Appendix B, 193–211. Ph.D. diss., University of California, Los Angeles.

   n.d. "The Autobiography of Diane DeVries."

DiGiacomo, Susan M.
   1992. "Metaphor as Illness: Postmodern Dilemmas in the Representation of Body, Mind and Disorder." *Medical Anthropology* 14:109–37.

Dirks, Nicholas B., Geoff Eley, and Sherry B. Ortner.
   1994. "Introduction." In *Culture/Power/History: A Reader in Contemporary Social Theory*, ed. N. B. Dirks, G. Eley, and S. B. Ortner, 3–45. Princeton: Princeton University Press.

Dollard, John.
   1935. *Criteria for the Life History, with an Analysis of Six Notable Documents.* New Haven: Yale University Press.

Donovan, Josephine.
   1992. *Feminist Theory: The Intellectual Traditions of American Feminism.* New expanded ed. New York: Continuum.

Dossa, Parin A.
   1994. "Critical Anthropology and Life Stories: Case Study of Elderly Ismaili Canadians." *Journal of Cross-Cultural Gerontology* 9:335–54.

Dumezil, Georges.
   1977. *Les dieux souverains des indo-européens.* Paris: Gallimard.

Dundes, Alan.
   1965. "Structural Typology in North American Indian Folktales." In *The Study of Folklore*, ed. A. Dundes, 206–18. Englewood Cliffs, NJ: Prentice-Hall.

Dwyer, Kevin.
   1982. *Moroccan Dialogues: Anthropology in Question.* Baltimore: Johns Hopkins University Press.

Dyk, Walter.
   1938. *Son of Old Man Hat: A Navaho Autobiography Recorded by Walter Dyk.* New York: Harcourt.

Ebron, Paulla, and Anna Lowenhaupt Tsing.
   1995. "In Dialogue? Reading across Minority Discourses." In *Women Writing Culture*, ed. R. Behar and D. A. Gordon, 390–412. Berkeley: University of California Press.

Edgerton, Robert B.
   1967. *The Cloak of Competence: Stigma in the Lives of the Mentally Retarded.* Berkeley: University of California Press.

Ekman, Paul, Wallace V. Friesen, and Phoebe Ellsworth.
   1972. *Emotion in the Human Face: Guidelines for Research and an Integration of Findings.* Elmsford, New York: Pergamon.

Engel, David M., and Frank W. Munger.
   1996. "Rights, Remembrance, and the Reconciliation of Difference." *Law and Society Review* 30:7–53.

Fabian, Johannes.
   1983. *Time and the Other: How Anthropology Makes Its Object.* New York: Columbia University Press.

Fadiman, Anne.
   1997. *The Spirit Catches You and You Fall Down: A Hmong Child, Her American Doctors, and the Collision of Two Cultures.* New York: Farrar, Straus, and Giroux.

Ferguson, Philip, Michael Hibbard, James Leinen, and Sandra Schaff.
   1990. "Supported Community Life: Disability Policy and the Renewal of Mediating Structures." *Journal of Disability Policy Studies* 1:9–35.

Fiedler, Leslie.
   1978. *Freaks: Myths and Images of the Secret Self.* New York: Simon and Schuster.

Fine, Michelle, and Adrienne Asch.
   1988. "Disability beyond Stigma: Social Interaction, Discrimination, and Activism." *Journal of Social Issues* 44, no. 1:3–22.

Fine, Michelle, and Adrienne Asch., eds.
   1988. *Women with Disabilities: Essays in Psychology, Culture, and Politics.* Philadelphia: Temple University Press.

Fine, Susan B.
   1991. "Resilience and Human Adaptability: Who Rises Above Adversity?" *American Journal of Occupational Therapy* 45:494–503.

Finger, Anne.
   1990. *Past Due: A Story of Disability, Pregnancy and Birth.* Seattle, WA: Seal Press.

Finn, Janet L.
   1995. "Ella Cara Deloria and Mourning Dove: Writing for Cultures, Writing against the Grain." In *Women Writing Culture,* ed. R. Behar and D. A. Gordon, 131–47. Berkeley: University of California Press.

Fiore, Faye.
   1990. "Disabled Worker Claims Job Bias." *Los Angeles Times,* August 23, J5.

Fisher, Berenice, and Roberta Galler.
   1988. "Friendship and Fairness: How Disability Affects Friendship between Women." In *Women with Disabilities: Essays in Psychology, Culture, and Politics,* ed. M. Fine and A. Asch, 172–94. Philadelphia: Temple University Press.

Fischer, W.

1978. *"Struktur und Funktion erzählter Lebengeschichten"* (Structure and function of narrated life histories). In *Soziologie des Lebenslaufs,* ed. M. Kohli, 311–36. Darmstadt: Luchterhand.

1982. "Time and Chronic Illness: A Study on Social Constitution of Temporality." Habilitation thesis, University of California, Berkeley.

Flax, Jane.

1990. "Lacan and Winnicott: Splitting and Regression in Psychoanalytic Theory." In *Thinking Fragments: Psychoanalysis, Feminism, and Postmodernism in the Contemporary West,* 89–132. Berkeley: University of California Press.

Foucault, Michel.

1973 [1963]. *The Birth of the Clinic: An Archaeology of Medical Perception.* Translated by A. M. Sheridan Smith. New York: Random House.

1979 [1975]. *Discipline and Punish: The Birth of the Prison.* Translated by A. Sheridan. New York: Vintage Books.

Fox, Renée C.

1977. "The Medicalization and Demedicalization of American Society." In *Doing Better and Feeling Worse: Health in the United States,* ed. J. Knowles, 9–22. New York: W. W. Norton.

Fox-Genovese, Elizabeth.

1991. "Claims of a Common Culture, or, Whose Autobiography?" In *Feminism without Illusions: A Critique of Individualism,* 167–98. Chapel Hill: University of North Carolina Press.

Fraiberg, Selma H.

1959. *The Magic Years: Understanding and Handling the Problems of Early Childhood.* New York: Charles Scribner's Sons.

Frank, Gelya.

1979. "Finding the Common Denominator: A Phenomenological Critique of Life History Method." *Ethos* 7:68–94.

1980. "Detailed History of the Tribe's Land Tenure." In *Restoration of Tule River Indian Reservation Lands.* Hearing before the United States Senate Select Committee on Indian Affairs 96, 1 of S.1998, February 5, 74–141. Washington, DC: United States Government Printing Office.

1981. "Mercy's Children." *Anthropology and Humanism Quarterly* 6:8–12.

1981. "Venus on Wheels: The Life History of a Congenital Amputee." Ph.D. diss., University of California, Los Angeles.

1984. "Life History Model of Adaptation to Disability: The Case of a 'Congenital Amputee.'" *Social Science and Medicine* 19:639–45.

1985. "'Becoming the Other': Empathy and Biographical Interpretation." *Biography* 8:189–210.

1986. "On Embodiment: A Case Study of Congenital Limb Deficiency in American Culture." *Culture, Medicine and Psychiatry* 10:189–219. Reprinted in *Women with Disabilities: Essays in Psychology, Culture, and Politics,* ed. M. Fine and A. Asch (Philadelphia: Temple University Press, 1988), 41–71.

1988. "Beyond Stigma: Visibility and Self-Empowerment of Persons with Congenital Limb Deficiencies." *Journal of Social Issues* 44:95–115.

1995. "Anthropology and Individual Lives: The Story of the Life History and the History of the Life Story." *American Anthropologist* 97:145–48.

1995. "The Ethnographic Films of Barbara G. Myerhoff: Anthropology, Feminism, and the Politics of Jewish Identity." In *Women Writing Culture,* ed. R. Behar and D. A. Gordon, 207–32. Berkeley: University of California Press.

1995. "Ruth Behar's Biography in the Shadow: A Review of Reviews." *American Anthropologist* 97:357–59.

1996. "The Concept of Adaptation as a Foundation for Occupational Science Research." In *Occupational Science: The Evolving Discipline,* ed. R. Zemke and F. Clark, 47–55. Philadelphia: F. A. Davis.

1996. "Crafts Production and Resistance to Domination in the Late 20th Century." *Journal of Occupational Science: Australia* 3:56–64.

1996. "Life Histories in Occupational Therapy Clinical Practice." *American Journal of Occupational Therapy* 50:251–64.

1996. "Life History." In *Encyclopedia of Cultural Anthropology,* vol. 2, ed. D. Levinson and M. Ember, 705–8. New York: Henry Holt.

1996. "Myths of Creation: Construction of Self in an Autobiographical Account of Birth and Infancy." In *Imagined Childhoods: Self and Society in Autobiographical Accounts,* ed. M. Gullestad, 63–90. Oslo: Scandinavian University Press.

1997. "Jews, Multiculturalism, and Boasian Anthropology." *American Anthropologist* 99:731–45.

Frankenberg, Ruth.
1993. *White Women, Race Matters: The Social Construction of Whiteness.* Minneapolis: University of Minnesota Press.

Franklin, V. P.
1995. *Living Our Stories, Telling Our Truths: Autobiography and the Making of the African-American Intellectual Tradition.* New York: Scribner.

Freedman, Jill, and Gene Combs.
1996. *Narrative Therapy: The Social Construction of Preferred Realities.* New York: W. W. Norton.

French, Lindsay.
1994. "The Political Economy of Injury and Compassion: Amputees on the Thai-Cambodia Border." In *Embodiment and Experience: The Existential Ground of Culture and Self,* ed. T. J. Csordas, 69–99. Cambridge: Cambridge University Press.

Freud, Sigmund.
1960. [1922] *Group Psychology and the Analysis of the Ego.* Translated by J. Strachey. New York: Bantam Books.

Friedan, Betty.
1963. *The Feminine Mystique.* New York: W. W. Norton.

Friedman, Susan Stanford.
1988. "Women's Autobiographical Selves." In *The Private Self: Theory and Practice of Women's Autobiographical Writings,* ed. S. Benstock, 34–62. Chapel Hill: University of North Carolina Press.

Friedson, Eliot.
1970. *The Profession of Medicine.* New York: Dodd, Mead.

Froster-Iskenius, Ursula G., and Patricia A. Baird.
1989. "Limb Reduction Defects in Over One Million Consecutive Livebirths." *Teratology* 39:127–35.

Gacs, Ute, Aisha Khan, Jerrie McIntyre, and Ruth Weinberg, eds.
1989. *Women Anthropologists: Selected Biographies.* Urbana: University of Illinois Press.

Gadamer, Hans-Georg.
1975 [1960]. *Truth and Method.* New York: Seabury Press.

Gates, Henry Louis, Jr.
1988. *The Signifying Monkey: A Theory of African-American Literary Criticism.* New York: Oxford University Press.

1991. *Bearing Witness: Selections from African American Autobiography in the Twentieth Century.* New York: Pantheon Books.

Geertz, Clifford.
1973. "Person, Time, and Conduct in Bali." In *The Interpretation of Cultures: Selected Essays,* 360–411. New York: Basic Books.

1973. "Religion as a Cultural System." In *The Interpretation of Cultures: Selected Essays,* 87–125. New York: Basic Books.

1973. "Thick Description: Toward an Interpretive Theory of Culture." In *The Interpretation of Cultures: Selected Essays*, 3–30. New York: Basic Books.

1976. "From the Native's Point of View: On the Nature of Anthropological Understanding." In *Meaning in Anthropology*, ed. K. H. Basso and H. A. Selby. Albuquerque: University of New Mexico Press. Reprinted in *Interpretive Social Science: A Reader*, ed. P. Rabinow and W. M. Sullivan (Berkeley: University of California Press, 1979), 225–241.

1988. "I-Witnessing: Malinowski's Children." In *Works and Lives: The Anthropologist as Author*, 73–101. Stanford: Stanford University Press.

1988. "Us/Not-Us: Benedict's Travels." In *Works and Lives: The Anthropologist as Author*, 102–28. Stanford: Stanford University Press.

1988. *Works and Lives: The Anthropologist as Author*. Stanford: Stanford University Press.

Geiger, Susan N. G.
1986. "Women's Life Histories: Method and Content." *Signs* 11:334–51.

Gergen, Kenneth J.
1991. *The Saturated Self: Dilemmas of Identity in Contemporary Life*. New York: Basic Books.

Giddens, Anthony.
1991. *Modernity and Self-Identity: Self and Society in the Late Modern Age*. Stanford: Stanford University Press.

Gilder, R. S., V. Thompson, C. W. Slack, and K. B. Radcliffe.
1954. "Amputations, Body Image, and Perceptual Distortion: A Preliminary Study." U.S. Navy Medical Research Institute Report, no. 12, 587–600.

Gill, Carol J.
1994. "Questioning Continuum." In *The Ragged Edge: The Disability Experience from the Pages of the First Fifteen Years of the Disability Rag*, ed. B. Shaw, 42–49. Louisville, KY: Advocado Press.

Gilligan, Carol.
1982. *In a Different Voice: Psychological Theory and Women's Development*. Cambridge: Harvard University Press.

Gillispie, C. C.
1960. *The Edge of Objectivity*. Princeton: Princeton University Press.

Gilman, Sander L.
1985. *Difference and Pathology: Stereotypes of Sexuality, Race and Madness*. Ithaca: Cornell University Press.

1991. *The Jew's Body*. New York: Routledge.

Gingras, G., M. Mongeau, P. Moreault, M. Dupuis, B. Hebert, and C. Corriveau.
1964. "Congenital Anomalies of the Limbs, part II: Psychological and Educational Aspects." *Canadian Medical Association Journal* 91:115–19.

Ginsburg, Faye D.
1989. *Contested Lives: The Abortion Debate in an American Community.* Berkeley: University of California Press.

Glaser, Barney, and Anselm L. Strauss.
1967. *The Discovery of Grounded Theory: Strategies for Qualitative Research.* Chicago: Aldine.

Gliedman, John, and William Roth.
1980. *The Unexpected Minority: Handicapped Children in America.* New York: Harcourt Brace Jovanovich.

Goffman, Erving.
1963. *Stigma: Notes on The Management of Spoiled Identity.* Englewood Cliffs, NJ: Prentice-Hall.

Goldberg, M. C.
1990. "Women's Friendships—Women's Groups." *Psychiatric Annals* 20: 398–401.

Golfus, Billy, and David E. Simpson.
1994. *When Billy Broke His Head And Other Tales of Wonder.* Boston: Fanlight Productions. Film and video.

Goodman, Ellen
1984."The Right to Die" (syndicated column). *Oklahoma Observer,* Jan. 10, p. 16.

Goodstein, Laurie.
1997. "Pope Intends to Canonize German Nun as Saint." *Los Angeles Times,* May 31, B4.

Gough, Kathleen.
1968. "Anthropology: Child of Imperialism." *Monthly Review* 19:12–27.

Graff, Gerald.
1989. "Co-optation." In *The New Historicism,* ed. H. Aram Veeser, 168–81. New York: Routledge.

Gramsci, Antonio.
1971. *Selections from the Prison Notebooks.* Translated by Q. Hoare and G. N. Smith. London: Lawrence and Wishart.

Grant, Judith.
1987. "I Feel, Therefore I Am: A Critique of Female Experience as the Basis for a Feminist Epistemology." *Women and Politics* 7:99–114.

Gritzer, Glenn, and Arnold Arluke.
 1985. *The Making of Rehabilitation: A Political Economy of Medical Specialization, 1890–1980.* Berkeley: University of California Press.

Groce, Nora E.
 1994. "Book Review: *Women with Disabilities* by M. Fine and A. Asch, eds." *Journal of Disability Policy Studies* 5:111–14.

 1997. "Women with Disabilities in the Developing World: Arenas for Policy Revision and Programmatic Change." *Journal of Disability Policy Studies* 8:177–93.

Grosz, Elizabeth.
 1997. "Ontology and Equivocation: Derrida's Politics of Sexual Difference." In *Feminist Interpretations of Jacques Derrida,* ed. N. J. Holland, 73–102. University Park: Pennsylvania State University Press.

Gubrium, Jaber F., and James A. Holstein.
 1995. "Biographical Work and New Ethnography." In *The Narrative Study of Lives,* vol. 3: *Interpreting Experience,* ed. R. Josselson and A. Lieblich, 45–58. Thousand Oaks: Sage.

Guest, Iain, and Françoise Bouchet-Saulnier.
 1997. "International Law and Reality: The Protection Gap." In *World in Crisis: The Politics of Survival at the End of the 20th Century,* ed. Médecins sans frontières/Doctors without Borders. London: Routledge.

Gusdorf, Georges.
 1980 [1956]. "Conditions and Limits of Autobiography." In *Autobiography: Essays Theoretical and Critical,* ed. J. Olney, 28–48. Princeton: Princeton University Press.

Hagner, David, and Joseph Marrone.
 1995. "Empowerment Issues in Services to Individuals with Disabilities." *Journal of Disability Policy Studies* 6:17–36.

Hahn, Harlan.
 1983. "Can Physical Disability Make a Life Not Worth Living?" *Los Angeles Times,* December 9, part II, 7.

 1985. "Toward a Politics of Disability: Definitions, Disciplines, and Policies." *Social Science Journal* 22:87–105.

 1988. "Can Disability Be Beautiful?" *Social Policy* 18:26–32.

 1988. "The Politics of Physical Difference: Disability and Discrimination." *Journal of Social Issues* 44:39–47.

 1994. "The Minority Group Model of Disability: Implications for Medical Sociology." *Research in the Sociology of Health Care* 11:3–24.

Hamilton, Marguerite.
1958. *Borrowed Angel.* Garden City, NJ: Hanover House.

Hammersley, Martin.
1990. *Reading Ethnographic Research: A Critical Guide.* London: Longman.

Hand, Séan.
1989. "Introduction." In *The Levinas Reader,* ed. S. Hand, 1–8. Oxford: Blackwell.

Handelman, Susan A.
1991. *Fragments of Redemption: Jewish Thought and Literary Theory in Benjamin, Scholem, and Levinas.* Bloomington: University of Indiana Press.

Hanks, J., and L. M. Hanks.
1948. "The Physically Handicapped in Certain Non-Western Societies." *Journal of Social Issues* 4:11–19.

Harding, Susan.
1992. "The Afterlife of Stories: Genesis of a Man of God." In *Storied Lives: The Cultural Politics of Self-Understanding,* ed. G. C. Rosenwald and R. L. Ochberg, 60–75. New Haven: Yale University Press.

Harris, Adrienne, and Dana Wideman.
1988. "The Construction of Gender and Disability in Early Attachment." In *Women with Disabilities: Essays in Psychology, Culture, and Politics,* ed. M. Fine and A. Asch, 115–38. Philadelphia: Temple University Press.

Harris, Don.
1954. "Pair of Red Shoes Tiny Girl's Dream." *Evening Tribune* (San Diego, California), August 9, A12.

Harris, Louis, and Associates.
1986. *The ICD Survey of Disabled Americans: Bringing Disabled Americans into the Mainstream.* Conducted for the International Center for the Disabled, in cooperation with the National Council on the Handicapped. New York: Louis Harris and Associates.

Harrison, Faye V.
1995. "Writing against the Grain: Cultural Politics of Difference in the Work of Alice Walker." In *Women Writing Culture,* ed. R. Behar and D. A. Gordon, 233–45. Berkeley: University of California Press.

Harrowitz, Nancy A., and Barbara Hyams, eds.
1995. *Jews and Gender: Responses to Otto Weininger.* Philadelphia: Temple University Press.

Hartsock, Nancy C. M.
1987. "The Feminist Standpoint: Developing the Ground for a Specifically Feminist Historical Materialism." In *Feminism and Methodology: Social Science Issues,* ed. S. Harding, 157–80. Bloomington: Indiana University Press.

Heidegger, Martin.
  1962 [1927]. *Being and Time.* Translated by J. Macquarrie and E. Robinson. New York: Harper and Row.

Heilbrun, Carolyn.
  1988. *Writing a Woman's Life.* New York: W. W. Norton.

Heinritz, Charlotte.
  1996. "The Child in Childhood-Autobiography: Secret or Mystery?" In *Imagined Childhoods: Self and Society in Autobiographical Accounts,* ed. M. Gullestad, 179–99. Oslo: Scandinavian University Press.

Herbstrith, Waltraud.
  1985. *Edith Stein: A Biography.* New York: Harper and Row.

Herdt, Gilbert, and Robert J. Stoller.
  1990. *Intimate Communications: Erotics and the Study of Culture.* New York: Columbia University Press.

Hevey, David.
  1992. *The Creatures Time Forgot: Photography and Disability Imagery.* New York: Routledge.

Hillyer, Barbara.
  1989. "Blueprint for an Alliance." *Women's Review of Books* 6, no. 6 (March): 10.

  1993. *Feminism and Disability.* Norman: University of Oklahoma Press.

Hinch, Robin.
  1990. "Disabled Woman Fired, Comes Back Fighting." *Long Beach Press-Telegram,* August 24, E1.

Hirsch, Karen.
  1995. "Culture and Disability: The Role of Oral History." *Oral History Review* 22:1–27.

Honigmann, John J.
  1976. "The Personal Approach in Cultural Anthropological Research." *Current Anthropology* 17:243–61.

hooks, bell.
  1984. *Feminist Theory: From Margin to Center.* Boston: South End Press.

  1990. "Postmodern Blackness." In *Yearning: Race, Gender, and Cultural Politics.* Boston: South End Press.

Horkheimer, Max, and Theodor W. Adorno.
  1972 [1944]. *Dialectic of Enlightenment.* Translated by J. Cumming. New York: Herder and Herder.

Hoskins, Janet.

1993. *The Play of Time: Kodi Perspectives on Calendars, History, and Exchange.* Berkeley: University of California Press.

1998. *Biographical Objects: How Things Tell the Stories of People's Lives.* New York: Routledge.

Husserl, Edmund.

1962 [1913]. *Ideas: General Introduction to Pure Phenomenology.* Translated by W. R. Boyce Gibson. New York: Collier.

Hymes, Dell, ed.

1974 [1969]. *Reinventing Anthropology.* New York: Vintage Books.

Illich, Ivan.

1976. *Medical Nemesis.* New York: Pantheon Books.

Ingstad, Benedicte.

1995. "Mpho ya Modimo—A Gift from God: Perspectives on 'Attitudes' toward Disabled Persons." In *Disability and Culture,* ed. B. Ingstad and S. R. Whyte, 246–63. Berkeley: University of California Press.

Ingstad, Benedicte, and Susan Reynolds Whyte, eds.

1995. *Disability and Culture.* Berkeley: University of California Press.

Jameson, Fredric.

1984. "Foreword." In J.-F. Lyotard, *The Postmodern Condition: A Report on Knowledge.* Translated by G. Bennington and B. Massumi, vii–xxi. Minneapolis: University of Minnesota Press.

Jelinek, Estelle C., ed.

1980. *Women's Autobiography: Essays in Criticism.* Bloomington: Indiana University Press.

1986. *The Tradition of Women's Autobiography: From Antiquity to the Present.* Boston: Twayne Publishers.

Josselson, Ruthellen, ed.

1996. *Ethics and Process in the Narrative Study of Lives.* Vol. 4 of *The Narrative Study of Lives.* Thousand Oaks: Sage.

Josselson, Ruthellen, and Amia Lieblich, eds.

1993. *The Narrative Study of Lives.* Vol. 1. Thousand Oaks: Sage.

1995. *Interpreting Experience.* Vol. 3 of *The Narrative Study of Lives.* Thousand Oaks: Sage.

Kaminsky, Marc.

1992. "Introduction." In B. Myerhoff, *Remembered Lives: The Work of Ritual, Storytelling, and Growing Older,* 1–97. Ann Arbor: University of Michigan Press.

Kamuf, Peggy.
1997. "Deconstruction and Feminism: A Repetition." In *Feminist Interpretations of Jacques Derrida*, ed. N. J. Holland, 103–26. University Park: Pennsylvania State University Press.

Kaufman, Sandra Z.
1980. "A Mentally Retarded Daughter Educates her Mother." *The Exceptional Parent* (December): 17–22.

Keesing, Roger M.
1985. "Kwaio Women Speak: The Micropolitics of Autobiography in a Solomon Island Society." *American Anthropologist* 87:27–39.
Kennedy, Elizabeth Lapovsky, and Madeline Davis.

1993. *Boots of Leather, Slippers of Gold: The History of a Lesbian Community.* New York: Routledge.

Kennedy, Elizabeth Lapovsky, with Madeline Davis.
1996. "Constructing an Ethnohistory of the Buffalo Lesbian Community: Reflexivity, Dialogue, and Politics." In *Out in the Field: Reflections of Lesbian and Gay Anthropologists,* ed. E. Lewin and W. L. Leap, 171–99. Urbana: University of Illinois Press

Kent, Debra.
1987. "In Search of Liberation." In *With Wings: An Anthology of Literature by and about Women with Disabilities,* ed. M. Saxton and F. Howe, 82–83. New York: The Feminist Press at the City University of New York.

1997. "Where There's a Will." *Women's Review of Books* 14:8–9.

Kirshenblatt-Gimblett, Barbara.
1992. "Foreword." In B. Myerhoff, *Remembered Lives: The Work of Ritual, Storytelling, and Growing Older,* ed. M. Kaminsky, ix–xiv. Ann Arbor: University of Michigan Press.

Klein, Bonnie Sherr.
1992. "Finding My Place: A Journey into the World of Disability." Canadian Broadcasting Company. Radio documentary.

Kleinman, Arthur.
1980. *Patients and Healers in the Context of Culture: An Exploration of the Borderland between Anthropology, Medicine, and Psychiatry.* Berkeley: University of California Press.

1988. *The Illness Narratives: Suffering, Healing, and the Human Condition.* New York: Basic Books.

Kluckhohn, Clyde.
1945. "The Personal Document in Anthropological Science." In *The Use of Personal Documents in History, Anthropology, and Sociology,* ed. L. Gottschalk,

C. Kluckhohn, and R. Angell, 78–193. New York: Social Science Research Council.

Knauft, Bruce M.

1994. "Pushing Anthropology Past the Posts: Critical Notes on Cultural Anthropology and Cultural Studies as Influenced by Postmodernism and Existentialism." *Critique of Anthropology* 14:117–52.

Knowles, Robert.

1978. "A Woman's Suicide: 'Thanks for Being the Straw that Broke the Camel's Back.'" *Los Angeles Herald Examiner,* March 8, 1.

Kockelmans, Joseph J., ed.

1967. *Phenomenology: The Philosophy of Edmund Husserl and Its Interpretation.* Garden City, NY: Doubleday.

1967. "Essences and Eidetic Reduction—Introduction." In *Phenomenology: The Philosophy of Edmund Husserl and Its Interpretation,* 80–82. Garden City, NY: Doubleday.

1976. "Toward an Interpretative or Hermeneutic Social Science." *Graduate Faculty Philosophical Journal* 5:73–96.

Kohlberg, Lawrence.

1981. *The Philosophy of Moral Development.* San Francisco: Harper and Row.

Kohli, Martin.

1981. "Biography: Account, Text, Method." In *Biography and Society: The Life History Approach in the Social Sciences,* ed. D. Bertaux, 61–75. Beverly Hills: Sage.

1986. "Biographical Research in the German Language Area." In *A Commemorative Book in Honor of Florian Znaniecki on the Centenary of His Birth,* ed. Z. Dulczewski, 91–110. Poznan: Naukowe.

Kohut, Heinz.

1977. *The Restoration of the Self.* New York: International Universities Press.

Kondo, Dorinne K.

1990. *Crafting Selves: Power, Gender, and Discourses of Identity in a Japanese Workplace.* Chicago: University of Chicago Press.

Krefting, Laura.

1991. "Rigor in Qualitative Research: The Assessment of Trustworthiness." *American Journal of Occupational Therapy* 45:214–22.

Kriegel, Leonard.

1969. "Uncle Tom and Tiny Tim: Some Reflections on the Cripple as Negro." *American Scholar* (summer): 412–30.

Krieger, Susan.
    1991. "An Anthropologist and a Mystery Writer." In *Social Science and the Self: Personal Essays on an Art Form,* 56–64. New Brunswick, NJ: Rutgers University Press.

Kuhn, Thomas.
    1962. *The Structure of Scientific Revolutions.* Chicago: University of Chicago Press.

Kulick, Don, and Margaret Willson, eds.
    1995. *Taboo: Sex, Identity, and Erotic Subjectivity in Anthropological Fieldwork.* London: Routledge.

Kuper, Adam.
    1988. *The Invention of Primitive Society: Transformations of an Illusion.* London: Routledge.

Labov, William.
    1972. "The Transformation of Experience in Narrative Syntax." In *Language in the Inner City,* 354–96. Philadelphia: University of Pennsylvania Press.

Labov, William, and Joshua Waletzky.
    1967. "Narrative Analysis: Oral Versions of Personal Experience." In *Essays on the Verbal and Visual Arts,* ed. June Helm, 12–44. San Francisco: American Ethnological Society.

Langness, L. L.
    1965. *The Life History in Anthropological Science.* New York: Holt, Rinehart and Winston.

Langness, L. L., and Gelya Frank.
    1981. *Lives: An Anthropological Approach to Biography.* Novato, CA: Chandler and Sharp.

LaPlante, Mitchell P.
    1991. "The Demographics of Disability." In *The Americans with Disabilities Act: From Policy to Practice,* ed. J. West, 55–77. New York: Milbank Memorial Fund.

Lasch, Christopher.
    1978. *The Culture of Narcissism: American Life in an Age of Diminishing Expectations.* New York: W. W. Norton.

Leach, Penelope.
    1987. *Your Baby and Child: From Birth to Age Five.* New York: Alfred A. Knopf.

Leder, Drew.
    1990. *The Absent Body.* Chicago: University of Chicago Press.

Levinas, Emmanuel.
  1996 [1968]. "Substitution." In *Emmanuel Levinas: Basic Philosophical Writings*, ed. A. T. Peperzak, S. Critchley, and R. Bernasconi, 79–95. Bloomington: Indiana University Press.

  1991 [1974]. *Otherwise than Being, or Beyond Essence*. Translated by A. Lingis. Dordrecht: Kluwer Academic Publishers.

  1996 [1974]. "Essence and Disinterestedness." In *Emmanuel Levinas: Basic Philosophical Writings*, ed. A. T. Peperzak, S. Critchley, and R. Bernasconi, 111–27. Bloomington: Indiana University Press.

Lewin, Ellen, and William L. Leap, eds.
  1996. *Out in the Field: Reflections of Lesbian and Gay Anthropologists*. Urbana: University of Illinois Press.

Lewis, Oscar.
  1961. *Children of Sánchez: Autobiography of a Mexican Family*. New York: Random House.

Lieblich, Amia, and Ruthellen Josselson, eds.
  1994. *Exploring Identity and Gender*. Vol. 2 of *The Narrative Study of Lives*. Thousand Oaks: Sage.

  1997. *The Narrative Study of Lives*. Vol. 5. Thousand Oaks: Sage.

Linde, Charlotte.
  1993. *Life Stories: The Creation of Coherence*. New York: Oxford University Press.

Linden, R. Ruth.
  1993. *Making Stories, Making Selves: Feminist Reflections on the Holocaust*. Columbus: Ohio State University Press.

Linton, Simi.
  1998. *Claiming Disability: Knowledge and Identity*. New York: New York University Press.

Litvak, Simi.
  1992. "Financing Personal Assistance Services: Federal and State Legislative and Revenue-Enhancing Options." *Journal of Disability Policy Studies* 3:93–102.

Lowie, Robert H.
  1937. "Franz Boas." In *The History of Ethnological Theory*, 128–55. New York: Holt, Rinehart and Winston.

  1960. "Empathy, or 'Seeing from Within.'" In *Culture in History: Essays in Honor of Paul Radin*, ed. S. Diamond, 145–59. New York: Columbia University Press.

Luker, Kristen.
1984. *Abortion and the Politics of Motherhood.* Berkeley: University of California Press.

Lutkehaus, Nancy C.
Forthcoming. *Margaret Mead and the Media: Anthropology and the Rise and Fall of a Contested Symbol.* Princeton: Princeton University Press.

Lynd, Robert S., and Helen M. Lynd.
1929. *Middletown: A Study in Contemporary American Culture.* New York: Harcourt, Brace.

1937. *Middletown in Transition: A Study in Cultural Conflicts.* New York: Harcourt, Brace.

Lyotard, Jean-François.
1984 [1979]. *The Postmodern Condition: A Report on Knowledge.* Translated by G. Bennington and B. Massumi. Minneapolis: University of Minnesota Press.

McCracken, Grant.
1995. *Big Hair: A Journey into the Transformation of Self.* Woodstock, NJ: Overlook Press.

McLuhan, Marshall.
1964. *Understanding Media: The Extensions of Man.* New York: Signet.

Mailer, Norman.
1975. *Marilyn: A Biography.* New York: Warner Books.

Mairs, Nancy.
1986. *Plaintext: Essays.* Tucson: University of Arizona Press.

1987. "On Being a Cripple." In *With Wings: An Anthology of Literature by and about Women with Disabilities,* ed. M. Saxton and F. Howe, 118–27. New York: The Feminist Press.

1989. *Remembering the Bone House: An Erotics of Place and Space.* New York: Harper and Row.

1990. *Carnal Acts: Essays.* New York: Harper.

1996. *Waist-High in the World: A Life Among the Nondisabled.* Boston: Beacon Press.

Malcolm, Barbara, and Carolyn Rouse.
1995. "Thisabled Lives: The Twenty-Year Collaboration of Diane DeVries and Gelya Frank." Video.

Malcolm, Janet.
1993. "The Silent Woman." *New Yorker,* August 23 and 30.

Malinowski, Bronislaw.
   1967. *A Diary in the Strict Sense of the Term.* New York: Harcourt, Brace, and World.

Manning, Robert John Sheffler.
   1993. "The Challenge of Ethics as First Philosophy." In *Interpreting Otherwise than Heidegger: Emmanuel Levinas's Ethics as First Philosophy,* 88–135. Pittsburgh: Duquesne University Press.

Marcus, George E., and Michael M. J. Fischer.
   1986. *Anthropology as Cultural Critique: An Experimental Moment in the Human Sciences.* Chicago: University of Chicago Press.

Marcus, George E., and Peter D. Hall.
   1992. *Lives in Trust: The Fortunes of Dynastic Families in Late Twentieth Century America.* Boulder: Westview Press.

Marks, Shula.
   1989. "The Context of Personal Narrative: Reflections on '*Not Either an Experimental Doll'—The Separate Worlds of Three South African Women.*" In *Interpreting Women's Lives: Feminist Theory and Personal Narratives,* ed. Personal Narratives Group, 39–58. Bloomington: Indiana University Press.

Martin, Douglas A.
   1991. "Overview of Major SSDI and SSI Work Incentives." Testimony before the Senate Subcommittee on Disability Policy, June 26.

Martin, Emily.
   1987. *The Woman in the Body.* Boston: Beacon Press.

Mastroiacovo, Pierpaolo, Bengt Källen, Lisbeth B. Knudsen, Paul A. L. Lancaster, Eduardo E. Castilla, Osvaldo Mutchinick, and Elisabeth Robert.
   1992. "Absence of Limbs and Gross Body Wall Defects: An Epidemiological Study of Related Rare Malformation Conditions." *Teratology* 46:455–64.

Matthews, Gwyneth Ferguson.
   1983. *Voices from the Shadows: Women with Disabilities Speak Out.* Toronto: Women's Press.

Mattingly, Cheryl.
   1998. *Healing Dramas and Clinical Plots.* Cambridge: Cambridge University Press.

Mbilinyi, Marjorie.
   1989. "'I'd Have Been a Man': Politics and the Labor Process in Producing Personal Narratives." In *Interpreting Women's Lives: Feminist Theory and Personal Narratives,* ed. Personal Narratives Group, 204–27. Bloomington: Indiana University Press.

Mead, Margaret.

1942. *And Keep Your Powder Dry: An Anthropologist Looks at America*. New York: William Morrow.

1953. "National Character." In *Anthropology Today*, ed. A. L. Kroeber, 642–67. Chicago: University of Chicago Press.

1958. "Preface." In M. G. Carstairs, *The Twice-Born: A Study of a Community of High-Caste Hindus*. Bloomington: Indiana University Press.

1969. "Research with Human Beings: A Model Derived from Anthropological Field Practice." *Daedalus* 98: 361–86.

Medicine, Beatrice.

1989. "Ella Cara Deloria, 1888–1971." In *Women Anthropologists: Selected Biographies*, ed. U. Gacs, A. Khan, J. McIntyre, and R. Weinberg, 45–50. Urbana: University of Illinois Press.

"Meet Ellen Stohl."

1987. *Playboy* (July): 68–74.

Messerschmidt, Donald A., ed.

1981. *Anthropologists at Home in North America: Methods and Issues in the Study of One's Own Society*. Cambridge: Cambridge University Press.

Meyerson, Lee.

1948. "A Fair Employment Act for the Disabled." *Journal of Social Issues* 4, no. 4:107–9.

1948. "Physical Disability as a Social Psychological Problem." *Journal of Social Issues* 4, no. 4:2–9.

Miller, Alice.

1981. *The Drama of the Gifted Child: The Search for the True Self*. New York: Basic Books.

Minow, Martha.

1990. *Making All the Difference: Inclusion, Exclusion, and American Law*. Ithaca: Cornell University Press.

Mintz, Sidney W.

1960. *Worker in the Cane: A Puerto Rican Life History*. New York: W. W. Norton.

1973. "Comment on 'The Study of Life History: Gandhi,' by David G. Mandelbaum." *Current Anthropology* 14:200.

1989. "The Sensation of Moving, While Standing Still." *American Ethnologist* 16:786–96.

Mishler, Elliot G.

1986. *Research Interviewing: Context and Narrative*. Cambridge: Harvard University Press.

1990. "Validation in Inquiry-Guided Research: The Role of
Exemplars in Narrative Studies." *Harvard Educational Review* 60:415–42.

Mitchell, David T., and Sharon L. Snyder.
1997. *The Body and Physical Differences: Discourses of Disability.* Ann Arbor:
University of Michigan Press.

Moi, Toril.
1985. *Sexual/Textual Politics: Feminist Literary Theory.* New York: Routledge.

Monaghan, Peter.
1998. "Pioneering Field of Disability Studies Challenges Established
Approaches and Attitudes." *Chronicle of Higher Education* 44, January 23,
A15–16.

Moreno, Eva.
1995. "Rape in the Field: Reflections from a Survivor." In *Taboo: Sex, Identity,
and Erotic Subjectivity in Anthropological Fieldwork,* ed. D. Kulick and M. Willson, 219–50. London: Routledge.

Morrison, Toni.
1990. *Playing in the Dark: Whiteness and the Literary Imagination.* Cambridge:
Harvard University Press.

Mulvey, Laura.
1985. "Visual Pleasure and Narrative Cinema." In *Movies and Methods,* ed. B.
Nichols, 303–15. Berkeley: University of California Press.

Myerhoff, Barbara.
1974. *Peyote Hunt: The Sacred Journey of the Huichol Indians.* Ithaca: Cornell
University Press.

1978. *Number Our Days.* New York: Dutton.

1992. *Remembered Lives: The Work of Ritual, Storytelling, and Growing Older,* ed.
M. Kaminsky. Ann Arbor: University of Michigan Press.

1992. "Surviving Stories: Reflections on *Number Our Days.*" In *Remembered
Lives: The Work of Ritual, Storytelling, and Growing Older,* 277–304. Ann Arbor:
University of Michigan Press.

Myerhoff, Barbara, and Jay Ruby.
1992 [1982]. "A Crack in the Mirror: Reflexive Perspectives in Anthropology." In B. Myerhoff, *Remembered Lives: The Work of Ritual, Storytelling, and
Growing Older,* 307–40. Ann Arbor: University of Michigan Press.

Nakhleh, Khalil.
1979. "On Being a Native Anthropologist." In *The Politics of Anthropology:
From Colonialism and Sexism toward a View from Below,* ed. G. Huizer and B.
Mannheim. Paris: Mouton.

Nash, Dennison, and Ronald Wintrob.
    1972. "The Emergence of Self-Consciousness in Ethnography." *Current Anthropology* 13:527–42.

Nichol, A. R.
    1985. *Longitudinal Studies in Child Psychology and Psychiatry: Practical Lessons from Research Experience.* New York: John Wiley and Sons.

Nicolaisen, Ida.
    1995. "Persons and Nonpersons: Disability and Personhood among the Punan Bah of Central Borneo." In *Disability and Culture,* ed. B. Ingstad and S. R. Whyte, 47–48. Berkeley: University of California Press.

Nosek, Margaret A.
    1991. "Personal Assistance Services: A Review of the Literature and Analysis of Policy Implications." *Journal of Disability Policy Studies* 2:1–17.

Ochs, Elinor, Carolyn Taylor, Dina Rudolph, and Ruth Smith.
    1992. "Storytelling as a Theory-Building Activity." *Discourse Processes* 15:37–72.

Okely, Judith, and Helen Callaway, eds.
    1992. *Anthropology and Autobiography.* London and New York: Routledge.

Olney, James.
    1972. *Metaphors of Self: The Meaning of Autobiography.* Princeton: Princeton University Press.

    1999. *Memory and Narrative: The Weave of Life-Writing.* Chicago: University of Chicago Press.

Olney, Richard S., Cynthia A. Moore, Muin J. Khoury, J. David Erickson, Larry D. Edmonds, Lorenzo D. Botto, and Hani K. Atrash.
    1995. "Chorionic Villus Sampling and Amniocentesis: Recommendations for Prenatal Counseling." *Morbidity and Mortality Weekly Report* 44 (RR-9), July 21. Atlanta: Centers for Disease Control.

Olrik, Axel.
    1965 [1909]. "Epic Laws of Folk Narrative." In *The Study of Folklore,* ed. A. Dundes, 129–41. Englewood Cliffs, NJ: Prentice-Hall.

Ong, Aihwa.
    1995. "Women out of China: Traveling Tales and Traveling Theories in Post-colonial Feminism." In *Women Writing Culture,* ed. R. Behar and D. A. Gordon, 350–72. Berkeley: University of California Press.

Ortner, Sherry B.
    1991. "Reading America: Preliminary Notes on Class and Culture." In *Recapturing Anthropology: Working in the Present,* ed. R. G. Fox, 163–90. Santa Fe: School of American Research Press.

1994. "Theory in Anthropology Since the Sixties." In *Culture/Power/ History: A Reader in Contemporary Social Theory*, ed. N. B. Dirks, G. Eley, and S. B. Ortner, 372–411. Princeton: Princeton University Press.

Ottenberg, Simon.

1990. "Thirty Years of Fieldnotes: Changing Relationships to the Text." In *Fieldnotes: The Makings of Anthropology*, ed. R. Sanjek, 139–59. Ithaca: Cornell University Press.

Pachter, Marc.

1979. "The Biographer Himself: An Introduction." In *Telling Lives: The Biographer's Art*, ed. M. Pachter, 2–15.Washington, DC: New Republic Books/Smithsonian Institution.

Paré, Ambroise.

1982. *On Monsters and Marvels*. Translated by J. L. Pallister. Chicago: University of Chicago Press.

Parsons, Talcott.

1951. *The Social System*. New York: Free Press.

Patai, Daphne.

1991. "U.S. Academics and Third World Women: Is Ethical Research Possible?" In *Women's Words: The Feminist Practice of Oral History*, ed. S. B. Gluck and D. Patai, 137–53. New York: Routledge.

Pendleton, Heidi McHugh.

1998. "Establishment and Sustainment of Friendships of Women with Physical Disability: The Role of Participation in Occupation." Ph.D. diss., University of Southern California.

Pernick, Martin S.

1996. *The Black Stork: Eugenics and the Death of "Defective" Babies in American Medicine and Motion Pictures since 1915*. New York: Oxford University Press.

Personal Narratives Group (Joy Webster Barbre, Amy Farrell, Shirley Nelson Garner, Susan Geiger, Ruth-Ellen Boetcher Joeres, Susan M.-A. Lyons, Mary Jo Maynes, Pamela Mittlefehldt, Riv-Ellen Prell, and Virginia Steinhagen), eds.

1989. *Interpreting Women's Lives: Feminist Theory and Personal Narratives*. Bloomington: Indiana University Press.

1989. "Whose Voice?" In *Interpreting Women's Lives: Feminist Theory and Personal Narratives*, ed. Personal Narratives Group, 201–3. Bloomington: Indiana University Press.

Phillips, Marilyn J.

1990. "Damaged Goods: Oral Narratives of the Experience of Disability in American Culture." *Social Science and Medicine* 30:849–57.

Piven, Frances Fox.
    1987. "Women and the State: Ideology, Power, and the Welfare State." In
    Families and Work, ed. N. Gerstel and H. E. Gross, 512–19. Philadelphia: Tem-
    ple University Press.

Polanyi, Livia.
    1989. *Telling the American Life Story: A Structural and Cultural Analysis of Con-
    versational Storytelling*. Cambridge: MIT Press.

Polkinghorne, Donald E.
    1988. *Narrative Knowing and the Human Sciences*. Albany: State University of
    New York Press.

Powdermaker, Hortense.
    1966. *Stranger and Friend: The Way of an Anthropologist*. New York: W. W. Norton.

Prell, Riv-Ellen.
    1989. "The Double Frame of Life History in the Work of Barbara Myerhoff."
    In *Interpreting Women's Lives: Feminist Theory and Personal Narratives*, ed. Per-
    sonal Narratives Group, 241–58. Bloomington: Indiana University Press.

Proctor, Robert N.
    1988. *Racial Hygiene: Medicine under the Nazis*. Cambridge: Harvard Univer-
    sity Press.

Rabinow, Paul.
    1986. "Representations Are Social Facts." In *Writing Culture: The Poetics and
    Politics of Ethnography*, ed. J. Clifford and G. E. Marcus, 234–66. Berkeley:
    University of California Press.

Raglan, Lord.
    1965 [1934]. "The Hero of Tradition." In *The Study of Folklore*, ed. A. Dundes,
    142–57. Englewood Cliffs, NJ: Prentice-Hall.

Rainer, Tristine.
    1997. *Your Life as Story: Writing the New Autobiography*. New York: Jeremy P.
    Tarcher/Putnam.

Reader's Digest.
    1992. *Legends of Comedy: TV Comedy Classics of the '50s and '60s*. Pleasantville,
    NY: Reader's Digest Association. Video.

Redfield, Robert.
    1953. "Relations of Anthropology to the Social Sciences and to the Humani-
    ties." In *Anthropology Today: An Encyclopedic Inventory*, ed. A. L. Kroeber,
    728–38. Chicago: University of Chicago Press.

Reilly, Mary.
    1962. "Occupational Therapy Can Be One of the Great Ideas of 20th Century
    Medicine." *American Journal of Occupational Therapy* 16:1–9.

Reilly, Mary, ed.
1974. *Play as Exploratory Learning: Studies of Curiosity Behavior.* Beverly Hills: Sage.

Rickman, H.P.
1967. "Wilhelm Dilthey." In *The Encyclopedia of Philosophy,* vol. 2, ed. P. Edwards, 403–7. New York: Macmillan.

Ricoeur, Paul.
1981 [1971]. "Appropriation." In *Hermeneutics and the Human Sciences: Essays on Language, Action, and Interpretation,* ed. and trans. J. B. Thompson, 182–93. Cambridge: Cambridge University Press.

1981 [1971]. "The Model of the Text: Meaningful Action Considered as Text." In *Hermeneutics and the Human Sciences: Essays on Language, Action and Interpretation,* ed. and trans. J. B. Thompson, 197–221. Cambridge: Cambridge University Press.

Rosaldo, Renato.
1976. "The Story of Tukbaw: 'They Listen as He Orates.'" In *The Biographical Process: Studies in the History and Psychology of Religion,* ed. F. Reynolds and D. Capps, 121–51. The Hague: Mouton.

Rosenthal, Gabriele, ed.
1986. *Die Hitlerjugend-Generation.* Essen: Blaue Eule.

1993. "Reconstruction of Life Stories: Principles of Selection in Generating Stories for Narrative Biographical Interviews." In *The Narrative Study of Lives,* vol. 1, ed. R. Josselson and A. Lieblich, 59–91. Newbury Park: Sage.

Rosenwald, George C., and Richard L. Ochberg.
1992. *Storied Lives: The Cultural Politics of Self-Understanding.* New Haven: Yale University Press.

Roskies, Ethel.
1972. *Abnormality and Normality: The Mothering of Thalidomide Children.* Ithaca: Cornell University Press.

Rothman, Kenneth J.
1990. "Keynote Presentation: A Sobering Start for the Cluster Buster's Conference." *American Journal of Epidemiology* 132:S6–13.

Rousseau, Jean-Jacques.
1954 [1781]. *The Confessions.* Translated by J. M. Cohen. Harmondsworth: Penguin.

Runyan, William McKinley.
1980. "Alternative Accounts of Lives: An Argument for Epistemological Relativism." *Biography* 3, no. 3:209–24.

Rymer, Russ.
  1992. "Annals of Science: A Silent Childhood." Parts 1 and 2. *New Yorker,*
  April 13, 41–81; April 20, 43–77.

Sacks, Karen.
  1994. "How Did Jews Become White Folks?" In *Race*, ed. S. Gregory and R.
  Sanjek, 78–102. New Brunswick, NJ: Rutgers University Press.

Sanjek, Roger.
  1990. *Fieldnotes: The Makings of Anthropology.* Ithaca: Cornell University Press.

  1991. "The Ethnographic Present." *Man* 26:609–28.

Sapir, Edward.
  1938. "Why Cultural Anthropology Needs the Psychiatrist." *Psychiatry*
  1:7–12.

Sarbin, Theodore R., ed.
  1986. *Narrative Psychology: The Storied Nature of Human Conduct.* New York:
  Praeger.

Sartre, Jean-Paul.
  1963 [1952]. *Saint Genet: Actor and Martyr.* New York: New American Library.

Saxton, Marcia, and Florence Howe, eds.
  1987. *With Wings: An Anthology of Literature by and about Women with Disabilities.* New York: The Feminist Press at the City University of New York.

Schafer, Roy.
  1983. *The Analytic Attitude.* New York: Basic Books.

  1992. *Retelling a Life: Narration and Dialogue in Psychoanalysis.* New York:
  Basic Books.

Scheer, Jessica, and Nora Groce.
  1988. "Impairment as a Human Constant: Cross-Cultural and Historical Perspectives on Variation." *Journal of Social Issues* 44:23–37.

Scheler, Max.
  1973 [1912]. *The Nature of Sympathy.* Translated by P. Heath. London: Routledge and Kegan Paul.

Scheper-Hughes, Nancy.
  1994. "Embodied Knowledge: Thinking with the Body in Critical Medical
  Anthropology." In *Assessing Cultural Anthropology*, ed. R. Borofsky, 229–42.
  New York: McGraw-Hill.

Scheper-Hughes, Nancy, and Margaret M. Lock.
  1987. "The Mindful Body: A Prolegomenon to Future Work in Medical Anthropology." *Medical Anthropology Quarterly*, n.s., 1, no. 1:6–41.

Schriner, Kay Fletcher, Sharon N. Barnartt, and Barbara M. Altman, eds.
  1997. *Journal of Disability Policy Studies* 8. Special Issue on Gender and Disability Policy.

Scotch, Richard K.
  1984. *From Goodwill to Civil Rights.* Philadelphia: Temple University Press.

Scott, James C.
  1985. *Weapons of the Weak: Everyday Forms of Peasant Resistance.* New Haven: Yale University Press.

  1990. *Domination and the Arts of Resistance: Hidden Transcripts.* New Haven: Yale University Press.

Scott, Joan W.
  1992. "Experience." In *Feminists Theorize the Political,* ed. J. Butler and J. W. Scott, 22–40. London: Routledge.

Sennett, Richard.
  1974. *The Fall of Public Man: On the Social Psychology of Capitalism.* New York: Vintage Books.

Shostak, Marjorie.
  1983 [1981]. *Nisa: The Life and Words of a !Kung Woman.* New York: Vintage.

  1989. "'What the Wind Won't Take Away': The Genesis of *Nisa—The Life and Words of a !Kung Woman.*" In *Interpreting Women's Lives: Feminist Theory and Personal Narratives,* ed. Personal Narratives Group, 228–40. Bloomington: Indiana University Press.

Shweder, Richard A., and Edmund J. Bourne.
  1984. "Does the Concept of the Person Vary Cross-Culturally?" In *Culture Theory: Essays on Mind, Self, and Emotion,* ed. R. A. Shweder and R. A. LeVine, 158–99. Cambridge: Cambridge University Press.

Simmons, Leo W.
  1942. *Sun Chief: The Autobiography of a Hopi Indian.* New Haven: Yale University Press.

Smith, Dorothy E.
  1987. "Women's Perspective as a Radical Critique of Sociology." In *Feminism and Methodology: Social Science Issues,* ed. S. Harding, 84–96. Bloomington: Indiana University Press.

Smith, Sidonie.
  1993. "The Universal Subject, Female Embodiment, and the Consolidation of Autobiography." In *Subjectivity, Identity, and the Body: Women's Autobiographical Practices in the Twentieth Century,* 1–23. Bloomington: Indiana University Press.

Spence, Donald P.

    1982. *Narrative Truth and Historical Truth: Meaning and Interpretation in Psychoanalysis.* New York: W. W. Norton.

Spiegelberg, Herbert.

    1976. *The Phenomenological Movement: A Historical Introduction,* vols. 1 and 2. The Hague: Martinus Nijhoff.

    1976. "The Phenomenological Philosophy of Maurice Merleau-Ponty (1908–1961)." In *The Phenomenological Movement: A Historical Introduction,* vol. 2, 516–62. The Hague: Martinus Nijhoff.

Spivak, Gayatri Chakravorty.

    1976. "Translator's Preface." In J. Derrida, *Of Grammatology,* ix–xc. Baltimore: Johns Hopkins University Press.

    1990. *The Post-Colonial Critic: Interviews, Strategies, Dialogues,* ed. S. Harasym. New York: Routledge.

    1995. "Can the Subaltern Speak?" In *The Post-Colonial Studies Reader,* ed. B. Ashcroft, G. Griffiths, and H. Tiffin, 24–35. London: Routledge.

    1996. "Subaltern Studies: Deconstructing Historiography." In *The Spivak Reader,* ed. D. Landry and G. MacLean, 201–35. New York: Routledge.

Stacey, Judith.

    1991. "Can There Be a Feminist Ethnography?" In *Women's Words: The Feminist Practice of Oral History,* ed. S. B. Gluck and D. Patai, 111–19. New York: Routledge.

Stanley, Liz.

    1992. *The Auto/biographical I: Theory and Practice of Feminist Auto/Biography.* Manchester: Manchester University Press.

Stanton, Domna, ed.

    1984. *The Female Autograph: Theory and Practice of Autobiography from the 10th to the 20th Century.* Chicago: University of Chicago Press.

Starr, Paul.

    1978. *The Transformation of American Medicine: The Rise of a Sovereign Profession.* New York: Basic Books.

Stein, Edith.

    1970 [1917]. *On the Problem of Empathy.* Translated by W. Stein. The Hague: Martinus Nijhoff.

    1986. *Life in a Jewish Family, 1891–1916.* Translated by J. Koeppel. Washington, DC: ICS Publications.

Stern, Daniel N.

    1985. *The Interpersonal World of the Infant: A View from Psychoanalysis and Developmental Psychology.* New York: Basic Books.

Stevenson, Roger E., Judith G. Hall, and Richard M. Goodman.
1993. "Limb Deficiencies." In *Human Malformations and Related Anomalies,*
703–20. New York: Oxford University Press.

Stocking, George W., Jr.
1968. "From Physics to Ethnology." In *Race, Culture, and Evolution: Essays in*
the History of Anthropology, 133–60. New York: Free Press.

1974. "Introduction: The Basic Assumptions of Boasian Anthropology." In *A*
Franz Boas Reader: The Shaping of American Anthropology, 1883–1911, ed. G. W.
Stocking Jr., 1–23. Chicago: University of Chicago Press.

1992. "The Ethnographer's Magic: Fieldwork in British Anthropology from
Tylor to Malinowski." In *The Ethnographer's Magic and Other Essays in the His-*
tory of Anthropology, 12–59. Madison: University of Wisconsin Press.

Stoller, Robert.
1988. "Patients' Responses to Their Own Case Reports." *Journal of the Ameri-*
can Psychoanalytic Association 36:371–91.

Stone, Deborah.
1984. *The Disabled State.* Philadelphia: Temple University Press.

Strauss, Anselm L.
1987. *Qualitative Analysis for Social Scientists.* Cambridge: Cambridge University Press.

Sussman, Marvin, ed.
1966. *Sociology and Rehabilitation.* American Sociology Association, in cooperation with Vocational Rehabilitation Administration, U.S. Department of
Health, Education, and Welfare.

Swindells, Julia.
1989. "Liberating the Subject: Autobiography and 'Women's History'—A
Reading of *The Diaries of Hannah Cullwick.*" In *Interpreting Women's Lives:*
Feminist Theory and Personal Narratives, ed. Personal Narratives Group, 24–38.
Bloomington: University of Indiana Press.

Taeuber, Cynthia M.
1996. *Statistical Handbook on Women in America.* 2d ed. Phoenix: Oryx Press.

Talle, Aud.
1995. "A Child is a Child: Disability and Equality among the Kenya Maasai."
In *Disability and Culture,* ed. B. Ingstad and S. R. Whyte, 56–72. Berkeley:
University of California Press.

Tedlock, Barbara.
1992. *The Beautiful and the Dangerous: Dialogues with the Zuni Indians.* New
York: Penguin Books.

Thomson, Rosemarie Garland.

1994. "Redrawing the Boundaries of Feminist Disability Studies." *Feminist Studies* 20:583–95.

1997. *Extraordinary Bodies: Figuring Physical Disability in American Culture and Literature*. New York: Columbia University Press.

Toulmin, Stephen.

1990. *Cosmopolis: The Hidden Agenda of Modernity*. Chicago: University of Chicago Press.

1995. "Occupation, Employment and Human Welfare." *Journal of Occupational Science: Australia* 2:48–58.

Townsend, Dorothy.

1978. "Suicide Spurs Disabled to Ask End to Funds Cutoff." *Los Angeles Times*, March 9, part I, 3.

Townsend, Steven Jack.

1993. "Declaring One's Personhood: Assisted Autobiography as a Therapeutic Tool." M.A. thesis, University of Southern California.

Trillin, Calvin.

1993. *Remembering Denny*. New York: Warner Books.

U.S. Department of Health and Human Services.

1991. *Red Book on Work Incentives: A Summary Guide to Social Security and Supplemental Security Income Work Incentives for People with Disabilities*. Washington, DC: Social Security Administration.

Valentine, C. W.

1929. "The Relative Reliability of Men and Women in Intuitive Judgments of Character." *British Journal of Psychology* 19.

Van Den Berg, J. M.

1954. *The Changing Nature of Man: Introduction to a Historical Psychology*. New York: Dell.

Van Maanen, John.

1988. *Tales of the Field: On Writing Ethnography*. Chicago: University of Chicago Press.

Vincent, Joan.

1990. *Anthropology and Politics: Visions, Traditions, and Trends*. Tucson: University of Arizona Press.

Visweswaran, Kamala.

1994. *Fictions of Feminist Ethnography*. Minneapolis: University of Minnesota Press.

Voget, Fred W.
1996. "History of Anthropology." In *Encyclopedia of Cultural Anthropology,*
vol. 2, ed. D. Levinson and M. Ember, 567–79. New York: Henry Holt.

Wade, Cheryl Marie.
1994. "Disability Culture Rap." In *The Ragged Edge: The Disability Experience
from the Pages of the First Fifteen Years of The Disability Rag,* ed. B. Shaw, 15–18.
Louisville, KY: Advocado Press.

Warkany, Josef.
1971. *Congenital Malformations.* Chicago: Year Book Medical Publishers.

Warner, W. Lloyd, with M. Meeker and K. Eells.
1960 [1949]. *Social Class in America: A Manual of Procedure for the Measurement
of Social Status.* New York: Harper and Row.

Warner, W. Lloyd, and Paul S. Lunt.
1941. *The Social Life of a Modern Community.* New Haven: Yale University Press.

Watson, Lawrence C., and Maria-Barbara Watson-Franke.
1985. *Interpreting Life Histories: An Anthropological Inquiry.* New Brunswick,
NJ: Rutgers University Press.

Waxman, Barbara Faye.
1994. "It's Time to Politicize Our Sexual Oppression." In *The Ragged Edge: The
Disability Experience from the Pages of the First Fifteen Years of The Disability
Rag,* ed. B. Shaw, 82–87. Louisville, KY: Advocado Press.

Weiss, Meira.
1994. *Conditional Love: Parents' Attitudes Toward Handicapped Children.* Westport, CT: Bergin and Garvey.

Wendell, Susan.
1996. *The Rejected Body: Feminist Philosophical Reflections on Disability.* New
York: Routledge.

Werner, Emmy E., and Ruth S. Smith.
1982. *Vulnerable but Invincible: A Longitudinal Study of Resilient Children and
Youth.* New York: McGraw-Hill.

1992. *Overcoming the Odds: High Risk Children from Birth to Adulthood.* Ithaca:
Cornell University Press.

West, Jane.
1991. "Introduction—Implementing the Act: Where We Begin." In *The Americans with Disabilities Act: From Policy to Practice,* ed. J. West. New York: Mil-
bank Memorial Fund.

White, John A.
1998. "Barriers to Employment and the Adaptive Strategies Used to Overcome
Them: An Ethnographic Study of People with Mobility Impairments Using

Title I of the ADA to Fight Employment Discrimination." Ph.D. diss., University of Southern California.

White, Michael, and David Epston.
1990. *Narrative Means to Therapeutic Ends.* New York: W. W. Norton.

Whyte, Susan Reynolds, and Benedicte Ingstad.
1995. "Disability and Culture: An Overview." In *Disability and Culture,* ed. B. Ingstad and S. R. Whyte, 3–32. Berkeley: University of California Press.

Williams, Bernard.
1967. "René Descartes." In *The Encyclopedia of Philosophy,* vol. 1, ed. P. Edwards, 344–54. New York: Macmillan.

Winch, Peter.
1967. "Max Weber." In *The Encyclopedia of Philosophy,* vol. 8, ed. P. Edwards, 282–83. New York: Macmillan.

Wolf, Eric.
1982. *Europe and the People without History.* Berkeley: University of California Press.

Wolff, Geoffrey.
1979. *The Duke of Deception: Memories of My Father.* New York: Vintage Books.

World Health Organization.
1980. *International Classification of Impairments, Disabilities, and Handicaps.* Geneva: World Health Organization.

Wright, Beatrice A.
1983 [1960]. *Physical Disability—A Psychosocial Approach.* 2d ed. New York: Harper and Row.

Young, Michael W.
1983. "'Our Name Is Women: We Are Bought with Limesticks and Limepots': An Analysis of the Autobiographical Narrative of a Kalauna Woman." *Man* 18:478–501.

Zemke, Ruth, and Florence Clark, eds.
1996. *Occupational Science: The Evolving Discipline.* Philadelphia: F. A. Davis.

Zimmerman, Jeffrey L., and Victoria C. Dickerson.
1996. *If Problems Talked: Narrative Therapy in Action.* New York: Guilford Press.

Zola, Irving Kenneth.
1972. "Medicine as an Institution of Social Control." *Sociological Review* 20:487–504.

1982. *Missing Pieces: A Chronicle of Living with a Disability.* Philadelphia: Temple University Press.

Credits

All photographs and texts are from Diane DeVries's family collection, and are used with her permission, except for the following:

Publicity still of Frieda Pushnik: reproduced by permission of Frieda Pushnik.

"Pair of Red Shoes Tiny Girl's Dream" article: *Evening Tribune*, San Diego, California, August 9, 1954, p. A12. Reproduced with permission from the San Diego Union-Tribune.

"Armless, Legless Swimmer" article: *Press-Telegram*, Long Beach, California [date and page number unknown], 1964[?]. Used by permission of Long Beach Press-Telegram.

"Graduating from UCLA the Hard Way" article: *Los Angeles Times*, June 15, 1987, part 1, p. 3. Copyright 1987, Los Angeles Times. Reprinted by permission.

"Disabled Woman Fired, Comes Back Fighting" article: *Press-Telegram*, Long Beach, August 24, 1990, p. E1. Used by permission of Long Beach Press-Telegram.

Index

ablism: practices for challenging, 49, 80–81, 94, 138, 169, 207nn.58,59; severity relative to racism and sexism, 71, 78, 203n.41; similarities to other "isms," 49, 76, 95, 207n.59, 219n.15

Ablon, Joan, *Little People in America*, 168, 185n.7

abortion, based on disability, 189n.27

Abu-Lughod, Lila, 169, 224n.16, 228n.32

activities of daily living, 200n.22

adaptation: concept of, as foundation for occupational science, 181n.41; Diane DeVries's view of life as exemplifying, 114, 169

adaptations (to equipment, environment, or activities): of Diane DeVries, 28, 30–31, 32, 51, 72–73, 132, 141, 142, 144, 148, 151–152; of Charles Jumps, 54

adaptive strategies: associated with dependence and powerlessness, 39, 182n.49; of deinstitutionalized people with low I.Q.,

46, 185n.7; of Diane DeVries, 6, 37–39, 78, 131–132; of litigants under the ADA, 228n.27; of "Sara Lane," 70–71, 201n.28; of Lynn Thompson, 39

adaptive system: in couples, 177n.32; defined, by Frank, 37, 181n.41

adaptive system, in Diane DeVries's life: 1976, in Westwood, 129–136; 1980–87, in Long Beach area, 5, 38, 127; 1988–89, in Redondo Beach and University Park (USC), 5–6, 104; 1993–94, in Hollywood, 7, 136–145; 1996–97, in Long Beach, 7, 37, 42, 78

adjustment to disability, 184n.3, 188nn.18,20

"aesthetic anxiety" (Hahn), 209n.15

Allport, Gordon, 223n.14

ambiguity: defined, by Merleau-Ponty, 123; and narrative strategies for coherence, 123–128, 221n.30; in physical body and material conditions, 127–128; in presence/absence of Diane DeVries's limbs, 124–127, 225n.27

valescent homes, 33; occupations, 34; —,
dancing, 34, 124; —, flirting, 35; —, getting
high, 34; —, making out, 33; —, smoking,
34; —, studying, 154; personal assistance,
34, 152; prostheses, use of, 3, 33–35, 52–54,
151–154; puberty, 53; Rancho Los Amigos
Hospital, 33–35, 153, 154; relationship with
parents, 33–34, 149–156; relationship with
siblings, 51, 62, 124, 151–152; self-care
occupations, 34; —, applying makeup,
34; —, cooking, 34; —, dressing, 34; —,
fixing hair, 34; —, making bed, 34; —, putting on jewelry, 34; —, transferring in/out
of wheelchair, 152; —, using toilet, 34;
socioeconomic class, 200n.23; surgeries,
193n.35; wheelchair, use of, 152–153, 154
DeVries, Diane, adulthood (age 18 on):
activism, 74; adapted van, 137; appeal
to CAPP by, 67–68, 198n.15; appearance,
1–2, 20, 66–67, 93–94, 139, 144, 148–149;
architectural barriers, 6, 73–74, 131–132,
140–141, 142, 148–149, 163; asking for
help in public, 38–39, 142; asthma, 6, 38,
73, 129, 134–135, 211n.30; attitudes toward
body and disability, 27, 34–39, 42, 49,
50–51, 67–68, 74–76, 93–94, 127, 157, 163,
181n.34, 211nn.29,30; "Autobiography"
(manuscript), 3, 18, 38–39, 57–58, 62,
109–113, 116, 152–153, 166–167, 176n.26,
182n.48, 225n.2, 228nn.25,26; baptism, 5;
benefactors, 6, 7, 185n.8; Bible School
attendance, 5, 38; blondness, 1, 20, 67,
198n.13, 226n.7; at Camp Paivika reunion,
20, 180n.22; CAPP, 153–154; character, 146;
child-bearing, 65–67, 147, 225n.28; church
membership, 5, 38; convalescent homes, 5,
38, 73, 78, 128, 139, 154, 163, 165; courts,
use of, 6, 73–75, 133; dating, 67, 93,
141–142; definition of independence, 38;
depression, 6, 103–106, 129, 136, 138–139,
143, 210n.26; and devotees (men attracted
to amputees), 141–142; disability rights
movement, influence of, 5, 42, 68–71,
73–75, 154; discrimination, experiences of,
6, 72–75, 203n.41; docudrama about, 19, 50,
57, 131, 225n.28; drugs, use of, 137; Easter
dinner in hospital, with author, 104–108;
education, graduate (USC, ca. 1988–93),
5–7, 72, 103–106, 137; education, undergraduate (UCLA, ca. 1976–87), 1, 5, 19, 25,
38–39, 71–72, 103, 127, 129–136, 153–154,
203n.41; employment as social worker,
6–7, 37, 42, 72–78, 137–145; Federal/state
entitlements and services used, 37; —, Aid
to the Totally Disabled (ATD), 154; —,

Department of Vocational Rehabilitation,
6, 129, 134, 137, 183n.53; —, In-Home Supportive Services (IHSS), 37, 182nn.44–45,
203n.42; —, Medi-Cal (Medicaid), 37,
153; —, Medicare, 153; —, Supplemental
Security Income (SSI), 37, 75, 130; feminism, influence of, 5, 8, 24–26, 36–37, 154;
financial crises, strategies for dealing
with, 128–136; first meeting with author,
24–25; friendships, 103, 106, 112, 130–131,
137–145; gender and disability identity,
203n.41, 206n.52; graduation ceremonies,
7, 19, 103; grandmother's epithet ("Devil's
daughter"), response to, 50, 59, 93; home,
living arrangements, environment,
129–145; housing crises, 7, 78, 129–136;
housing subsidy, 37, 182n.43; identification
as "a crip," 35–36, 75, 211n.30; image of,
impact on the culture, 23, 36, 122, 155,
162–169, 190n.27; independence vs.
dependence, 37–39, 52–54, 146–149;
informed consent to this study, 18–20,
108–115; life goals, 154–155, 163; media
attention, 7, 19, 103, 169, 176n.27, 203n.43,
208n.31, 209n.16; motivation to narrate
her life story, 18, 57–58, 113–114; Norway
incident, 109–114; observation of others'
reactions to her image, 24–25, 141–144,
166–167, 182n.48; occupations, 129; —,
dining out, 85, 131, 139–142, 148–149; —,
going to films, 137–145; —, going to parties, 42, 130; —, hanging out, 137, 138; —,
hiring personal assistants, 129–136; —,
hospital ministry, 38; —, keeping doctors'
appointments, 6, 135; —, painting crafts,
32; —, participation in this study,
129–136; —, reading, 140, 143, 144; —,
role as godmother, 42; —, shopping,
42; —, travel, 5, 20, 148–149; —, typing,
38, 57; —, using telephone, 72–73; —,
volunteer work, 38, 42; —, watching TV,
143; —, writing, 29, 35, 39, 57, 72–73, 116,
176n.28; pain, 35, 134–135, 148; as "perfect
example" of woman in American culture,
3, 61–69, 205n.45; personal assistance (or
attendant care), 6–7, 34, 37–39, 72, 103–106,
129–136, 140–144, 147–148, 182n.48; physical abuse of, 5, 130–133; physical description, 49, 132; presentation to Barbara
Myerhoff's class, 19, 163; prosthesis use,
129, 153–154; psychotherapy, 88, 210n.26;
publications by author about, 103, 173n.5;
purpose in life, 41–42, 169; reactions by
others to her image, 1–2, 23, 30–36, 48–54,
85, 139–144, 148–149, 157, 162–165,

(traditional societies), 46–47, 55, 185nn.6,9,10, 186n.12, 190n.29, 194n.42
Setoguchi, Yoshio, 153–154
Shostak, Marjorie, 9, 173n.14
Shriners, 227n.12
Simmons, Leo W., *Sun Chief*, 16
60 Minutes program, 39–40, 183nn.53,54
social anthropology, 186n.14, 213n.38
Spence, Donald P., 208n.6
Spence, Jo, 49
Spiegelberg, Herbert, 209n.20, 210n.24, 224n.19
Spivak, Gayatri Chakravorty, 94, 182n.49, 212n.34, 223n.7
Stacey, Judith, 15, 175n.14
Starr, Paul, 173n.14
Stein, Edith: biography of, 210n.27; canonization as Sister Teresa Benedicta of the Cross, 210n.27; destruction of her life in Holocaust, 210n.27; on empathy, 91, 210nn.27–28; experience of sexism and anti-Semitism, 210n.27
Stern, Daniel N., 216n.59
stigma: approaches to, in a non-Western society (rural Botswana), 190n.29; critiques of Goffman's theory, 179n.20, 187n.17; defined, by Goffman, 187n.17; use in ethnography of people with mental retardation, 45–46, 185nn.7–8
Stocking, George W., Jr., 213n.42
Stoller, Robert, 159, 172n.3, 219n.16, 228n.19
Stone, Deborah, 168, 228n.29
structuralism, 187n.14
Swindells, Julia, 173n.15
Switzer, Mary E., 184n.3

"TABs" (temporarily able-bodied people), 80
"tactical humanism" (Abu-Lughod), 169
Tedlock, Barbara, 171n.2
Tedlock, Dennis, 217n.4
temporality: change in popular and scholarly discourses, 49, 50–51, 82–83, 95–97, 158, 167, 189n.26, 208n.5; concept of "the ethnographic present," 8, 173n.12, 222n.3; in ethnography as a process, 146–149, 157, 162–169, 173n.12; in Heidegger's philosophy, 108, 217n.7; in shaping author's understanding of Diane DeVries, 1–8, 101–103, 107, 113–114, 118, 129–145, 146–149, 157, 169
thalidomide, 51, 85–86, 189n.27, 190nn.27–28
"therapeutic emplotment" (Mattingly), 125–126

"thick description" (Geertz), 223n.8
Thomason, Freddie, 156, 191n.30
Thomson, Rosemarie Garland, 178nn.3,4
Thompson, Lynn, 39–41, 182nn.50–51, 183nn.52–53
Toulmin, Stephen, 205n.50, 221n.28
Townsend, Steven, 190n.27
transcendental "I," 115–116, 118–121, 205n.77, 221nn.28–31

Unruh Act (California Law), 74

Van Den Berg, J. M., 208n.5
Venus de Milo, 93–94, 162, 211n.29
Verstehen: defined, by Rickman (after Dilthey), 4, 76, 204n.45; Dilthey's historicism, 4, 76, 96, 159, 204n.45; Dollard's criteria for the life history, 160, 172n.4; ethical and political implications of, in cultural biography, 101–102, 159; and feminist standpoint theories, 205n.45; historicist methods in conventional biography, 21, 157, 160; and the mirror phenomenon, 4, 99–100, 159–161; power, need to add analysis of, 204n.45; problem of typification, 205n.45; "seeing from within," in cultural anthropology, 4, 95–100, 101–102, 204n.45; time and perspective in, producing partial knowledge, 76
Vick, Craig, 193n.40
Vincent, Joan, 213n.38
Visweswaran, Kamala, 207n.61
"vulnerable observer" (Behar), 81

Wade, Cheryl Marie, 24
Waxman, Barbara Faye, 188n.19
"weapons of the weak" (James Scott), 39, 182n.49
Weber, Max, 204n.45
Weiss, Meira, 86
welfare policies, federal and state, 181n.42
Weltfish, Gene, 22–23, 177n.36, 214n.46
Wendell, Susan, 181n.40, 190n.27
West, Jane, 199n.17
Western Law Center for Disability Rights, 74
Westside Center for Independent Living (WCIL), 183nn.54,55
When Billy Broke His Head. . . and Other Tales of Wonder (Golfus and Simpson), 39
Whyte, Susan Reynolds, 47, 185n.10
Williams, Esther, 62, 198n.5
Williams, Raymond, 204n.45, 212n.34
Wilson, Eva Jo, 191n.30

Text: 10/14 Palatino
Display: Bauer Bodoni
Composition: Impressions Book and Journal Services, Inc.
Printing and binding: Edwards Bros.